D1539575

THE PRICE WATERHOUSE GUIDE TO ACTIVITY-BASED COSTING FOR FINANCIAL INSTITUTIONS

THE PRICE WATERHOUSE GUIDE TO ACTIVITY-BASED COSTING FOR FINANCIAL INSTITUTIONS

Julie Mabberley

With a Foreword by Joseph G. Roosevelt,
Price Waterhouse LLP

IRWIN
Professional Publishing®
Chicago • London • Singapore

Irwin Book Team

Executive editor:	Amy Hollands Gaber
Project editor:	Christina Thornton-Villagomez
Production supervisor:	Lara Feinberg
Assistant manager, desktop services:	Jon Christopher
Manager, direct marketing:	Rebecca S. Gordon
Designer:	Matthew Baldwin
Compositor:	Douglas & Gayle Limited
Typeface:	11/13 Times Roman
Printer:	Quebecor

Times Mirror
Higher Education Group

Library of Congress Cataloging-in-Publication Data

Mabberley, Julie
    The Price Waterhouse guide to activity-based costing for financial
institutions / Julie Mabberley ; with a foreword by Joseph G.
Roosevelt.
        p.   cm.
    Originally published: Activity-based costing in financial
institutions. Pitman Pub., 1992.
    Includes index.
    ISBN 0-7863-0143-0
    1. Financial institutions—Accounting.   2. Activity-based costing.
I. Mabberley, Julie. Activity-based costing in financial
institutions.   II. Title
HF5688.F48M3   1996
667'.8333042—dc20   95-19287

Acknowledgments

I must thank the editorial and production teams of both Irwin Professional Publishing and Pitman Publishing, especially David Crosby and Trish Denoon at Pitman and Amy Hollands Gaber at Irwin, for their constructive support.

I must also thank my technical editor, Nick Willmer, for his patience and unstinting assistance, without which I could not have finished this book. Finally, my thanks go to my employer, Price Waterhouse, and its clients for providing much of the experience on which the book is based. Special thanks to Gregory S. Derderian and Henry N. Schweppe III of Price Waterhouse for their technical and accounting assistance.

Foreword

Strictly speaking, financial institutions have no tangible products. Their outputs are services: the clearing of a check, the initiation of a loan. As a consequence, profitability measurement in financial institutions cannot rely on cost accounting techniques developed to determine the value of physical inventory for financial reporting purposes. Those techniques focus on the costs of raw materials and labor. Quite different techniques are required to address the issues of financial institutions, such as common costs, joint costs, and step-wise variable costs.

As early as the 1970s, management in some leading financial institutions recognized the need for profitability measures specifically adapted to their businesses. Because the first perceived requirement was to analyze the performance of managers, efforts initially focused on developing measures of organizational profitability. The approach was effective, since the organizational structure of an institution defined its management structure as well.

Given this foundation, the earliest methods of cost accounting naturally focused on allocating expenses to support organizational profitability. Even those early methods, however, used the fundamentals of activity-based costing, because the basis for allocation was activities. Refinements in accuracy and reliability involved defining progressively more detailed activities and using increasingly sophisticated techniques, such as industrial engineering, to determine the relationship of expenses to activities.

In the late 1970s and early 1980s, management in several large commercial banks pioneered the development and use of other types of profitability information. Typically, product profitability was the next step along the continuum of profitability measurement. But product profitability measurement imposed new cost accounting challenges. Conventional allocations simply could not yield the types of product costs described in Chapter 9 of this book. Yet developing these types of costs was critical to generating useful product profitability information and to performing the analyses described in that chapter.

With real requirements now dictating direction, new methods evolved. The older allocations were replaced by activity costs within units. Once this was achieved, activity costs for all activities related to a product could be summed across all business units of a bank to determine a total product cost. Although this procedure was initially given names such as product costing or unit costing, by whatever name it represented the beginning of true activity-based costing in financial institutions. The techniques were essentially those described in Chapter 3.

Activity-based costing techniques have continued to expand to meet management's ever-increasing demands for different types of profitability information. For example, lines of business have been defined across multistate holding companies in order to identify businesses that merit additional investment and those that should be eliminated. Product management, including many aspects discussed in Chapter 9, is rapidly gaining importance in the competitive world of retail banking. Successfully identifying customer relationships and their associated profitability (Chapter 10) has become more critical to the search for profitable market segments and niches. The principles of activity-based costing have been used to meet these and other specific needs related not just to the operational needs of financial institutions but to achieving informed strategies and targeted growth.

Examples from the experience of Price Waterhouse teams using activity-based costing to help financial institutions improve profitability reinforce the message of the case studies in this book. Our clients have:

- Reduced the cost of services by relaxing the quality of service in instances where it was clear that the existing quality was either not required or not even recognized by the customer.
- Re-engineered expensive processes to simplify them and thereby reduce the cost of delivery.
- Made underperforming customer segments profitable by raising the price of related services until specific customers either became profitable to the institution or sought those services elsewhere.
- Eliminated service offerings on the basis of a measured inability to achieve sufficient economies of scale to reduce activity-based costs to profitable levels.

Unfortunately, not every case study from our files is a success story: it can happen, indeed has happened, that activity-based cost accounting is brought in too late to identify and cure the causes of poor profitability. The pattern of our experience suggests that *without* these techniques, all financial institutions risk being less profitable than they could be, and some financial institutions risk their very survival.

This book thus provides an invaluable service to our industry. As competition increases and the rate of change accelerates, the general diffusion of these techniques in the industry is essential to profitability. It is no longer sufficient for a select few banks to develop and use activity-based information. Most financial institutions can benefit substantively by building these techniques into their management information procedures. But developing the information is only the first step. Financial institutions and their managements must *use* these costs—in the ways described in Chapters 8 through 11.

As this diffusion is accomplished, the industry will undoubtedly face new challenges and require further elaboration of its cost analysis methodologies. The techniques will again be modified and new ones developed to meet these challenges. Just as allocation techniques evolved into activity-based cost methodologies, so pricing and profitability measurement will evolve into sophisticated modeling techniques. Modeling techniques will be needed to address the joint-cost nature of the industry and to analyze in detail the effects of incremental volumes not just upon the business unit under evaluation but upon the entire institution. Better techniques will evolve to plan volumes and thus operating expense budgets, which will let managers evaluate expenses *before* they occur rather than after the fact. More knowledge of the market and the price elasticity of services will provide additional opportunities to coordinate the cost of quality with the value of quality.

Developing these techniques is the challenge for the remainder of the 1990s. This book provides a solid beginning for institutions starting down this road and outstanding guidance for those already on the road.

I want to salute my overseas colleague, Julie Mabberley, of Price Waterhouse in the U.K., for her achievement in this comprehensive and important book. The present edition, adapted for the use of U.S. financial institutions, was ably edited by Gregory S. Derderian and Henry N. Schweppe III.

Joseph G. Roosevelt
Principal
Price Waterhouse LLP

Joseph G. Roosevelt is Price Waterhouse's leading authority in profitability measurement and reporting for financial institutions. He is the principal author of the book *Profitability Measurement for Financial Institutions: A Management Information Approach.*

Contents

Chapter One

An Introduction to Activity-Based Costing

INTRODUCTION

Activity-based costing is a new dimension of cost analysis that has been gaining acceptance in many organizations, mainly in manufacturing industries. It has only recently become integrated into the management process as a useful tool for analyzing costs in the financial sector. The pressure to manage costs more effectively and encourage accountability and cost management has led to the increased use of activity-based costing.

The concept behind activity-based costing is that costing should be much more than a financial system used by accountants; it should be part of the profit-making process of the business. Costs should be planned for and managed before they are incurred, rather than simply monitored after the event.

Activity-based costing gained prominence through studies conducted in 1987 by Professor Robert Kaplan and Robin Cooper of the Harvard Business School. In the same year, Kaplan and H. Thomas Johnson published their much acclaimed book, *Relevance Lost: The Rise and Fall of Management Accounting*. In the book, Johnson and Kaplan traced the development of early management accounting systems in textile mills of the early 1800s and the more fully developed systems of the 1920s. Johnson and Kaplan commented that management accounting concepts and practices did not continue to evolve, while manufacturing technologies and operating environments of American factories underwent a rapid and remarkable transformation:

> Corporate management accounting systems are inadequate for today's environment. In this time of rapid technological change, vigorous global and domestic competition, [and] enormously expanding information processing capabilities, management accounting systems are not providing useful, timely information for the process control, product costing, and performance evaluation activities of managers.

1

Early developments in activity-based costing emanated from the recognition of an inherent flaw in traditional costing systems. Manufacturing enterprises, such as John Deere, Inc., recognized that with the advent of complex, high-speed machines and process automation, the labor content (labor hours and dollars) of manufactured products was steadily declining. In addition, manufacturing overhead and other support-related costs were ballooning out of proportion. However, the traditional cost accounting system continued to allocate overhead to products on the basis of labor hours.

The conventional costing system, still employed at a majority of American corporations, simply provides a means for focusing management attention on the large proportion of costs that are classified as overheads and are effectively outside the control of the individual line manager. Over the past few years, it has become common practice to allocate all overhead costs back to operating functions on a variety of sophisticated bases, such as direct labor/service hours, labor dollars, machine hours, production/service volume, or each of these in combination with other measures.

This practice has a tendency to focus attention on the allocation process, not on the management of the underlying costs. Activity-based costing, however, concentrates on the analysis of activities and reviews overhead costs by means of direct cost management within the overhead function without the need to allocate costs to operations centers.

PROBLEMS WITH CONVENTIONAL PRODUCT COSTING

Conventional cost accounting systems distort the cost of products and services. This is because they fail to recognize that, in today's operating environment, labor hours, labor dollars, and volume are not the only factors that cause cost. The activity-based costing technique recognizes these other factors, called cost drivers, that drive the consumption of resources and cause costs to be incurred.

Conventional product costing systems allocate overhead costs to products using volume-based measures (e.g., hours, dollars, counts). The vast majority of American corporations use some combination of labor hours or labor dollars. Often cost pools are created for the purpose of collecting overhead costs and allocating them to the products that pass through these cost pools. One flaw of existing costing systems that is often overlooked is that it considers only costs incurred within the factory and ignores costs that are incurred during delivery of the product to the customer.

Conventional costing techniques analyze profitability by department or cost center and within each cost center, analyzing costs by category or by type of expense. Many costs are normally allocated on a fixed basis from central or overhead functions using inappropriate allocation bases. This results in incorrect costing data and makes no attempt to establish links between expenditures and their cause.

Another shortcoming of conventional cost systems is the lack of a resource management focus. Companies must recognize that it is resources that ultimately give rise to overhead and support-related costs. The traditional cost system uses standard costs for each product/service, computed by conventional accounting techniques. Variances are computed on a regular basis and a select few of these variances are actually investigated in order to identify and implement corrective action.

Standard costing systems used by American corporations do not attempt to analyze overhead and support-related costs in detail but tend to treat them as given. The huge "blob" of overhead is conveniently allocated to products, resulting in standard costs without identification of the links between overheads and the factors that cause them. In reality, products and services have activities associated with them, and activities are driven by cost drivers. The overhead activities may also be driven by volumes or variations in products and services. Alternatively, they may have little relation to the products and exist purely to sustain the underlying business. Standard costing ignores these differences and assumes overhead can be allocated to products as a blob.

ACTIVITY-BASED COSTING DEFINED

Activity-based costing analyzes the activities of all departments within the organization in order to provide focused information for the purpose of decision making. The goal of activity-based costing is to understand the behavior of all costs within the organization, linking operational and sustaining costs to the value chain in such a way that management can identify the factors that drive expenditure and manage these costs more effectively. The initial objective is to understand the activities that are performed throughout the organization and estimate the costs associated with delivering those activities. Then the costs of the activities can be identified, together with their causes (cost drivers) to produce more relevant information to help fuel the process of decision making more accurately.

Activity-based costing is a tool that can be used to bring about significant changes in the expenditure patterns, operational processes, overhead activities, and organizational structure of a financial institution. It attempts to address the real issues of how and why costs are incurred, so it does not simply record an expenditure and allocate it arbitrarily to cost centers or products. It provides a different dimension to cost information that focuses management attention on the underlying factors that can significantly affect the business.

Financial accounting provides external information to stockholders, regulatory authorities, creditors, and other stockholders, but it is unsuitable for making important internal decisions. Entirely different methods are required to provide managers with the information they need to manage the business and accurately assess the costs of doing business. Managers need rapid feedback on efficiency and performance, which calls for modern computer technology to handle large quantities of data in short periods of time. Some organizations have the data available but do not know how to use it effectively, while other organizations need information that they do not record.

Activity-based costing is not a new technique in essence. It is the application of tried and tested techniques in a focused way that is new. The results can also be understood and interpreted by accountants and nonaccountants alike. It is an approach to cost analysis that helps an organization analyze its cost base in a more meaningful way than with conventional departmental accounting. It analyzes cost behavior by activities, linking actions to the consumption of cost and enabling the identification of factors that cause the expenditure to be incurred. It lets management use cost information for decision making at all levels of the organization, focusing on the factors that drive costs and the effects of changes in those factors on the company's overall profitability.

Many accountants will question how activity-based costing differs from more conventional types of costing. In some ways, it is similar to traditional process or job costing. It attempts to estimate the costs associated with the provision of a product or service. Process costing and job costing are also based on activities, but they do not relate the costs to the factors that inspire the initial expenditure decision (cost drivers). The analysis of cost dynamics can be achieved only through the conventional techniques of variance analysis (rate and volume variances) or activity-based costing. Activity-based costs can be based on standard or actual cost calculations in the same way that process or job costs are.

The results of activity-based costing studies will rarely be precise. The nature of all cost allocation techniques is such that the estimation of costs by activity rarely takes account of capacity utilization. Furthermore, it assumes that the volume of activity remains relatively constant during the period to which the costs relate—which, of course, it rarely does. But this does not detract from the value of the information provided by such a study. The results will be meaningful because they link expenditures to the underlying factors that explain why the expenses are incurred. They may, therefore, be considered with due reference to the volume-related capacity constraints.

In addition to calculating product costs, many manufacturing companies have applied the principles of activity-based analysis to better manage warehousing costs, streamline distribution systems, and evaluate customer profitability. Others have used these principles to analyze costs of service departments and improve their service levels at lower operating costs. While the primary application of activity-based costing has been in product costing, additional uses involve areas such as operational cost management.

ITS APPLICABILITY TO FINANCIAL INSTITUTIONS

In general, there are some major differences between financial institutions and manufacturing industries. Many financial institutions are closer to retail industries or other service industries. Rosander, in the book *Applications of Quality Control in Service Industries* (1985), commented that the major differences are the following:

Direct transactions with masses of people: customers, households, depositors, insureds, taxpayers, borrowers, consumers, shippers, passengers, claimants, patients, clients.

Large volume of paper: sales slips, bills, checks, tickets, credit cards, charges, interest.

Large amount of paperwork movement: receiving, controlling, processing, mailing, filing, accounting.

Relatively small amounts of money per transaction.

An extremely large number of ways of making errors.

Few if any machine and instrumental controls such as exist in a factory.

Often extremely large-scale operations, the largest being the Postal Service and the federal tax system; also large states, cities, banks, insurance companies, public utilities.

No formal specification by the customer of the type, amount, and quality of the service required, and no contract with the supplier of the service. The customer has little or no choice in monopolies such as electricity, gas, telephone, water, and garbage collection, or in banking/insurance where state and federal laws, regulations, and decisions determine the nature of the service received.

Much less competitive than buying products, especially for the household buyer and consumer who constitute the great mass of buyers of the services.

Other financial institutions have fewer customers, larger individual transactions involving huge sums of money, and a high level of competition for the products/services.

In all financial institutions, products and services are created through the complex range of activities of staff within the organization. Departments rarely support only one product or service, and conventional costing finds it difficult to analyze the activities within a department and consider the factors that drive the costs.

Financial institutions will continue to face increased pressures on profitability due to increasing customer awareness, the increased risks of doing business, and the economic environment that is likely to prevail in the foreseeable future.

All financial services organizations operate in an intensely competitive market, with prices for products and services generally being determined by the competition. Margins are continuously being squeezed as competition increases, and it will continue to increase as communications become more global and the financial markets more intermingled.

Bank profits are being reduced by the constraints on margins imposed by the high levels of competition in the lending markets. Insurance companies are also reporting significant losses in their property and casualty business for the first time, as they are subjected to increasing numbers of claims, due mainly to bouts of bad weather throughout the world and increases in both international and domestic crime rates. Even the Lloyds market in London has experienced losses due to worldwide claims for recent catastrophes.

In such a competitive environment, it is vital to know the individual costs of products and services and to determine which of them are profitable, or at least contribute to overhead costs and ultimate profitability. In order to remain competitive, financial institutions are now looking for ways to reduce their cost bases without harming their businesses.

A financial institution can be viewed as a collection of activities that are performed to support the creation and delivery of its products and services. It gains competitive advantage by performing activities at lower cost than competitors or by providing a differentiated product or service for which customers are prepared to pay a higher price.

Financial services organizations are now attempting to make their managers accountable for income, costs, and profitability. Historically, the level of management information in the financial sector has been surprisingly limited. Managers have concentrated on the external information provided to the stockholders and regulators. Internal information has been limited to conventional budgetary control by cost center with full allocation of overhead costs. Measures of performance have focused on sales volumes and maintenance of costs at budgeted levels.

Now that the emphasis has shifted away from volume-based sales targets and toward profit-related objectives, managers are looking for guidance on where to concentrate their limited resources. This greater focus on profitability has resulted in the need to identify controllable costs and the factors that cause them to be incurred (cost drivers), as well as the need to identify profitable product and customer relationships. Managers are concentrating their attention on the costs they can manage and beginning to link the cost/benefit analysis to the value chain. Thus, they are focusing on those activities that add value and differentiate their products and services or delivery capability from the competition's in a way that maximizes the return to the organization as a whole.

STRUCTURE AND CONTENT

This book explains the different uses of activity-based costing within financial institutions, suggests a standard approach to activity-based costing, discusses the problems most frequently encountered, and provides examples in the form of case studies that demonstrate how activity-based costing has been used successfully in financial institutions.

Chapter 2 identifies four principal uses of activity-based costing and relates them to different types of financial institutions. Chapter 3 explains the activity-based costing process in terms of 16 basic steps grouped into six broad phases. Chapters 4 through 7 address four aspects of the process where practical difficulties are most commonly encountered. Chapters 8 through 11 deal, in turn, with the four principal uses of activity-based costing identified in Chapter 2 and provide case studies.

SUMMARY

Activity-based costing, a new dimension of cost analysis that has found rapid acceptance in manufacturing sectors, has enormous potential for improving many dimensions of operational performance for financial institutions. Traditional cost systems routinely distort the costs of products and services because they allocate overhead costs on the basis of labor hours, service hours, or volume, in a manner that is largely arbitrary.

Conventional systems fail to consider both activities, which cause the incurrence of expenditure, and cost drivers, which are the factors that drive activities. This may lead to allocation of costs in inappropriate ways and, subsequently, to the incorrect calculation of product/service costs. This, in turn, may lead to incorrect marketing strategies and erosion of profitability over time.

Activity-based costing is a tool that can be used to focus management attention on the costs within any organization. It links traditional costing techniques to the factors that drive the expenditure in ways that enable managers to analyze the company's value chains.

Activity-based costing can bring about significant changes in management behavior by focusing attention on expenditure patterns, operational processes, supporting activities, and responsibilities throughout the organization.

Chapter Two

Uses of Activity-Based Costing

INTRODUCTION

The objectives of activity-based costing include:

- Providing a way of assessing why costs are incurred, rather than just how much is incurred.
- Providing a basis for aligning costs with activities as a means of focusing attention on cost management.
- Forming a basis for controlling costs by monitoring the underlying causes.

Activity-based costing is an approach to cost analysis that helps an organization analyze its cost base in a more meaningful way than conventional departmental accounting. It analyzes cost behavior by activities, linking actions to the consumption of cost and enabling the identification of factors that cause the expenditure to be incurred. It lets management use cost information for decision making at all levels within the organization, focusing on the factors that drive costs and the effects of changes in those factors on the overall profitability of the institution or a specific section of it.

The results of activity-based costing studies are rarely precise, but this does not detract from the value of the information they provided. The results are meaningful in the context of the decisions being made because they link expenditures to those underlying factors that explain why the expenses are incurred and may, therefore, be considered with due reference to the volume-related capacity constraints.

WHY USE ACTIVITY-BASED COSTING?

Activity-based costing was originally used in manufacturing organizations to:

- Control and manage costs.

• Accurately relate costs to products and types of business.
• Set price and fee levels.
• Manage performance and analyze cost behavior.

It has been applied to the service sectors only since the early 1980s. Key issues that may affect any organization at any time include the need to understand the dynamics of profitability and resource utilization and to be able to answer the questions shown in Figure 2–1.

The pressures on profitability in banking and insurance in the past decade have meant that all financial institutions are focusing on managing and reducing costs to a much greater extent than in the relatively recent past. They are beginning to recognize that this type of costing technique leads to gaining competitive advantage by means of improving

FIGURE 2–1
Profitability questions

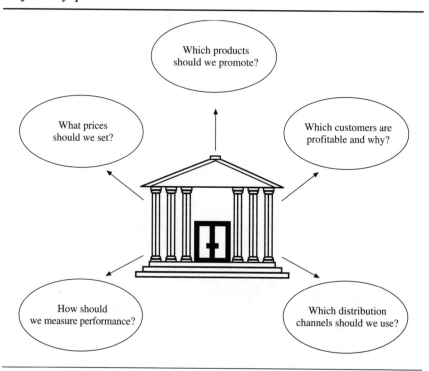

profits and managing costs more than do arbitrary price increases or cuts in the cost base, which can affect the basic structure of the business. It gives them more useful information on which to base key decisions relating to pricing, product promotion, customer profitability, performance management, and use of distribution channels (see Figure 2–2).

The following sections consider, in greater detail, how activity-based costing can be used to gain competitive advantage and how it applies to specific types of financial services, providing an overview of the practical application of this process in the financial sector.

FIGURE 2–2
Key types of decisions

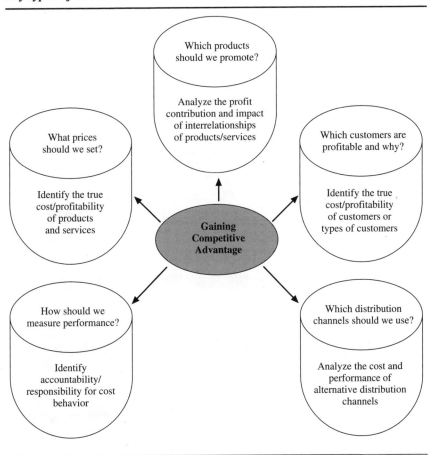

USES OF ACTIVITY-BASED COSTING

Activity-based costing can be used for a variety of purposes, as shown in Figure 2–3. It can form the basis of an ongoing cost and performance management system, which may incorporate activity-based budgeting and use activity analysis to measure and monitor the cost, volume, value, and quality of business processes. It leads to a better understanding of cost/resource management, emphasizing the lag between spending and consumption, by analyzing the factors that cause the initial expenditure and monitoring the consumption of resources and capacity utilization. It does not control the business; it simply provides information that may influence the decision makers by helping to demonstrate cost utilization within the organization.

FIGURE 2–3
Gaining competitive advantage

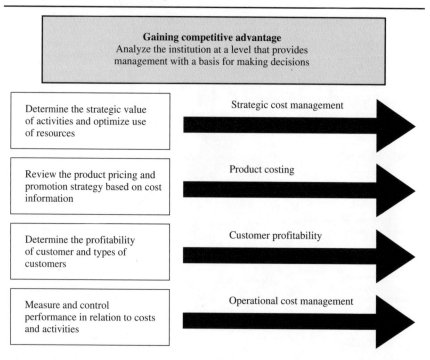

The uses of activity-based costing can be analyzed in different ways. Generally, using activity-based costing for strategic cost management includes some form of "what if" analysis. This is true either in strategic planning or in resource management, when the impact of investment in new or different products, markets, or technical environments requires some form of modeling.

Alternatively, analysis of product and customer cost and profitability is normally based on existing knowledge of costs and behavior and is likely to form the basis of regular reporting. Some modeling may be necessary in new product development in order to estimate the approximate cost of product delivery in advance of the product launch.

In operational cost management, activity-based costing can either be the basis of regular cost analysis through activity-based management, activity-based budgeting, or performance management or be the basis of a one-off cost reduction exercise. Regular cost monitoring by activity may be needed to ensure that identified savings are realized.

Figure 2–4 shows the uses of activity-based costing as discussed in more detail in the following paragraphs.

Strategic Cost Management

In his book *Competitive Advantage*, Michael Porter stated, "While accounting systems do contain useful data for cost analysis, they often get in the way of strategic cost analysis." Activity-based costing has been put forward as one of the most powerful tools yet devised for improving tactical and strategic decisions and enhancing corporate cost control. It enables the managers in any organization to recognize the factors that influence cost dynamics in both the short and longer term.

The need for activity-based costing in strategic cost management in financial institutions has never been greater. Many financial institutions are facing an environment characterized by intense regional and global competition, breakdown of entry barriers for some products (credit cards, for example), shortened response time to competitive forces, rapid product/service obsolescence, the need for innovative product and service introductions, and an absolute commitment to fast, low-cost, high-quality service and the highest levels of customer satisfaction. In such an environment, making the right strategic choices and identifying and making commitments toward strategic groups of businesses, products, and services are of paramount importance.

FIGURE 2–4
Uses of activity-based costing

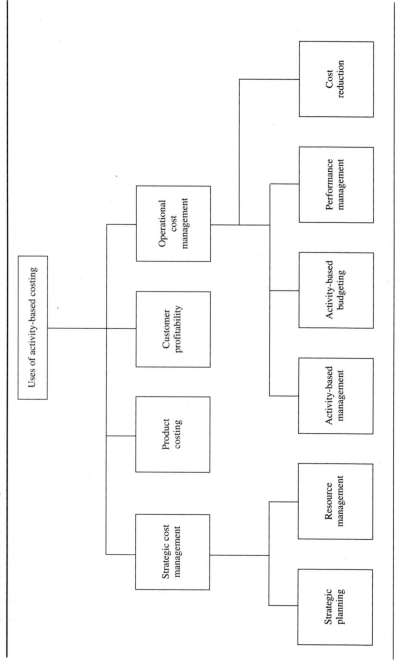

Activity-based costing provides information that emphasizes the areas of high cost on which attention should be focused. It provides a tool for measuring the cost benefit associated with investment in new products, markets, and technology and prioritizing alternative investments in terms of value for money and impact on corporate performance. It also enables management to highlight areas within the institution that use excessive amounts of resource.

Strategic cost management is generally more forward-looking and is likely to be performed less frequently than other types of activity-based costing. It may be used to review the overall direction of the company as the result of a merger, acquisition, or takeover. It may be part of a strategic planning exercise or may simply be necessary as a major investment or divestment decision is to be made. It is unlikely to be performed more than once each year.

The uses of activity-based costing for strategic cost management can be separated into two types: strategic planning and resource management.

Strategic Planning.   Activity-based costing can aid strategic planning by focusing attention on those factors that determine expenditures on, for example, types of products or markets. It can help in prioritizing business activities, because it can provide information relating to the costs/benefits to be derived from the particular businesses, geographic markets, products, or customer groups and the potential benefits to be derived from future investment in a particular strategic direction.

The main strategic focus of activity-based costing is that of influencing business strategy by providing information that identifies flexibility within the cost base. This flexibility relates to the ability to utilize costs already incurred to gain competitive advantage and knowing what expenditure would be necessary to pursue a change in direction.

Financial institutions are recognizing the need to evaluate different groups of products and services on the basis of: core competencies, core businesses, cash cows, low-cost products/services, differentiated costs and services, and special custom services. Activity-based costing can present an accurate evaluation of returns generated by each product and service.

Activity-based costing can also be used in the development of value chain analysis to break down the strategically relevant activities in order to understand the behavior of costs. The value chain involves a consideration of the cost/price relationship and ways value can be added to differentiate products or maximize price.

Resource Management. A resource management focus involves recognizing all activities associated with any expenditure on key projects and identifying the incidence, frequency, and cost of these activities. Focusing on cost drivers and activities provides realistic estimates of project expenditures and facilitates cost/benefit analysis. It also manages resources to maximize the return on investment in line with the strategic direction of the institution.

A financial institution's resources include capital, costs, and people. Management of capital is beyond the scope of this text. Management of costs depends, to a large extent, on the management of staff costs (still more than half of the costs incurred by any financial institution). Management of people depends on motivation, which in turn depends on communication. Communication is assisted by knowledge of the underlying activities and focus of the business.

Activity-based costing can be used to focus attention on those factors that determine the expenditure on key projects or activities, and it can help in the cost/benefit analysis of individual initiatives and, hence, assist the prioritization of alternatives to maximize the return on investment in line with the strategic direction of the company.

Also, because it identifies why costs are incurred and relates these to the activities that take place, it can be used to determine when costs should be incurred, such as whether or when to move to new premises. This enables management to manage costs on the basis of *spending* (the decision to buy/lease a new building), not *consumption* (the occupation of it).

Product Costing

Product costing is the most common use of activity-based costing and often forms the basis for product pricing and product profitability. This is primarily because activity cost analysis is similar to the standard costing technique and encourages organizations to extend existing cost analysis to review the underlying cost drivers in relation to the basic business processes and, therefore, gain a greater understanding of cost dynamics. This is of particular importance in the financial sector, where the increasingly competitive enviroment and the degree of product differentiation necessary to maintain or improve market share require effective information relating to the costs of developing and providing such products and services.

Conventional cost systems in financial institutions tend to use product volume as the basis of cost determinations. They fail to recognize links between products/services, activities, and cost drivers. Product and customer diversity, value, and quality of service provided to the customer all point to the need for more accurate cost analysis.

Activity-based product costs generally include all costs affected by the cost drivers associated with the provision of the product or service. They usually exclude the basic sustaining costs of maintaining the overall organization, although these can be apportioned back to individual products on an arbitrary basis in order to calculate a fully absorbed product cost.

Activity-based costing can be used as the basis of product costing in all types of financial institutions, although a detailed analysis of operational costs by product may be less relevant in organizations where a high percentage of costs is related, not to activities, but to interest or reinsurance cost.

Product costs can be computed using an activity-based costing system that identifies agreed activities associated with each department. Cost drivers are identified for each activity and the activity is costed on the basis of the incidence of cost drivers. For most activities, cost drivers relate to volume of products, activities or transactions, and value or quality of product/service. The activity-based costing reports that show the direct cost of each product can be compared to the income received to identify any products that do not contribute to sustaining costs and any that generate exceptional profits.

Activity-based costing as a basis of product costing applies not only to those products and services offered to the external market but also to those internal services for which some form of transfer cost is required. It can be used as the basis of internal transfer pricing of products and services provided to other parts of the organization and may focus management attention on the opportunity either to provide the service to other organizations or to buy their service from an external supplier at a lower cost. The most common form of internal transfer pricing in the financial sector is the internal charging of fund users and crediting of fund suppliers.

Analyzing the activities performed and attributing them to individual products and services can improve the efficiency and effectiveness of a financial institution. Efficiency can be improved by eliminating duplication and unnecessary activities, improving workflows, and training staff. Effectiveness is dependent on undertaking the right activities, efficiently. By attributing costs to the activities, management can identify areas where effort should be focused to enable working practices to be made both more efficient and effective and where costs could be reduced or performance improved. The review of working practices can result in changes in processes and process management in terms of the automation of existing activities or a more dramatic re-engineering of the service provided.

Customer Profitability

There is great potential for activity-based costing to be used as the basis for customer profitability analysis. Customer demand and differentiated patterns of consumption by customers are very difficult to both anticipate and model. This is probably more complex in financial institutions than in most manufacturing operations. This is because a certain product or service can prove to be unprofitable because of volume, combination, frequency, or even timing of its consumption by a diverse customer base.

Activity-based costing identifies the customer-specific costs that either relate to individual customers or are not attributable to particular products or services. The cost of providing the mix of products and services to a customer or type of customer is usually based on product cost information, but it may be enhanced to reflect those costs that can be attributed directly to individual customers or customer groups. The income associated with the customer is normally available, although there are likely to be some types of fee or commission income that can be identified only by product or service. In those instances, the income per customer is estimated based on the level of activity.

Many financial institutions find it difficult to justify the cost of developing and maintaining customer profitability information for individual customers, since this involves the capture and storage of individual transaction data from all automated and manual systems within the organization, as well as the maintenance of up-to-date customer profiles. The value of this information depends to a large extent on how it will be used, which generally reflects the importance of the individual customer relationship to the company. Some form of customer profitability analysis is important to all financial institutions, although the level of detail will vary.

Operational Cost Management

Operational cost management is a management tool that is performed regularly over time. Cost reduction, however, can be an exception; activity-based costing may form the basis of a single exercise to analyze the costs/benefits associated with discretionary expenditure and the effectiveness of fundamental activities.

Many organizations use activity-based costing for managing operational costs. This can be achieved in a variety of ways, including:

- Activity-based management.
- Activity-based budgeting.
- Performance management.
- Cost reduction initiatives.

These management tools are discussed here and described in more detail in Chapter 11, "Using Activity-Based Costing for Operational Cost Management."

Activity-Based Management. Managing the cost base depends on ongoing planning and control of all aspects of the business. Costs are an integral part of the business infrastructure, and any decision made by management will inevitably involve expenditure in either the long or short term. The objective of activity-based management is to determine the importance and costs of activities within the value chain, giving management the opportunity to focus resources on adding value and on continuous improvement in effective use of costs. Activity-based management uses activity-based costing as the basic component of financial management information that assists the operational control of the business by focusing attention on the key cost drivers and the factors that influence the day-to-day dynamics of the cost base. It can include the analysis of products and customers as described in Chapters 9 and 10 and can also form the basis of ongoing performance management.

It may include the need to set targets for activities or costs but tends to focus on long-term improvements in the delivery of activities through monitoring productivity, capacity utilization, efficiency, and effectiveness.

Activity-Based Budgeting. Activity-based budgeting differs from traditional budgeting in that it concentrates on the factors that drive the costs, not just historical expenditure. Activity-based budgeting is often compared to zero-based budgeting and is based on similar concepts. Zero-based budgeting requires justification of expenditure from a zero base and estimation of costs for differing levels of output and service. Activity-based budgeting, however, assumes an ongoing operation, justifying expenditure on the basis of activities performed in relation to the predetermined drivers. It places responsibility for cost control on the manager responsible for control of the driver. Activity-based budgeting differs from zero-based budgeting in that it assumes that activities exist and are related to the underlying cost drivers. Only if the cost driver can be eliminated can the cost of the activity fall to zero.

Activity-based budgeting separates the analysis of costs/benefits and value of activities from the more mechanistic budgeting exercise. It reduces the complexity of the budgetary process and concentrates attention on the business, not simply the costs incurred. It enables activities to be classified under two main headings: those costs that are incurred to sustain the basic fabric of the organization and those costs that are driven by the levels of underlying business activity in some way. Sustaining costs may be analyzed purely to ensure that the activities are both efficient and effective. Business-related costs, on the other hand, must be reviewed in relation to the factors that drive the costs and managed to ensure that spending remains in line with consumption in terms of both the volume of activity and the quality of service provided.

This information can then become the basis of a regular reporting system, using activity-based budgeting to monitor and control the expenditure, efficiency, and effectiveness of the activities performed in all parts of the organization.

Performance Management. Operational and financial performance can be managed by measuring, monitoring, and controlling the costs, efficiency, and effectiveness of the activities performed within the organization. Activity-based costing can form a key component of this type of reporting, as it facilitates the classification of activities and understanding of the causal relationships between costs and business activity.

Performance management combines objective setting, cost control, and responsibility by setting people-related targets or key performance indicators and monitoring activity against the indicators on a regular basis. Performance can be improved when these key performance indicators are the basis of regular reporting and areas where individual managers can influence behavior toward the achievement of corporate objectives are identified.

The control of cost is a key component of any performance measurement system, and activity-based analysis can focus attention on the areas of cost over which the individual has responsibility.

Cost Reduction Initiatives.   Activity-based costing can be used in a variety of ways to assist in cost reduction initiatives. It can form the basis of an independent one-time review of the cost base. Such a review enables the organization to investigate the activities performed throughout the organization, undertake value analysis, and explore opportunities for improvements in working methods. This may involve the identification of duplicate or extraneous activities across the various functional areas and usually highlights ways efficiency can be improved through the reorganization and rationalization of certain common activities.

Cost reduction initiatives employ the activity-based costing approach to analyze the activities performed throughout the organization and use this analysis to evaluate the costs and benefits of the functions under review. The results of this exercise can then be used to identify areas where the benefits derived do not justify the costs incurred and where activities may be curtailed or eliminated.

The primary benefit of using activity-based costing rather than any other form of costing lies in the essence of the technique itself. Activity-based costing focuses on activities, not responsibilities, so it can be less threatening to the managers of the various functions under review. It depersonalizes the cost review and enables management to value the activities undertaken in relation to the level and/or quality of service provided and factors that cause costs to be incurred.

Activity-based costing is not restricted to an analysis of the direct costs associated with the delivery of a product or service. It also analyzes the support costs that are incurred. This is particularly important in the financial sector, since these costs may be as much as half of the cost base.

Activity-based costing does not manage costs in its own right; it provides the analysis that lets management focus on areas where costs are incurred. It is important, therefore, that management support the activity-based costing initiative and implement the recommendations put forward as a result of the analysis.

SUMMARY

Activity-based costs can be used in a variety of ways, including:

- Strategic cost management.
- Product costing.
- Customer profitability.
- Operational cost management.

Although many uses apply to all types of financial services, product costing and customer profitability may be more or less relevant depending on the services offered and the customer base.

Activity-based costing can form the basis of an ongoing activity management system and may incorporate activity-based budgeting. It leads to a better understanding of cost/resource management, emphasizing the lag between spending and consumption by analyzing the factors that cause the initial expenditure and monitoring the consumption of resources and capacity utilization. It does not control the business; it simply provides information that influences decision makers by providing indicators that demonstrate cost utilization within the organization.

Chapter Three

The Framework for Activity-Based Costing Implementation

INTRODUCTION

Activity-based costing can be used in a variety of ways and costs may be derived differently depending on how the information is used. The process of developing an activity-based costing system comprises six phases with a total of 16 steps. The use of the information will determine the appropriate definitions of products, activities, and cost drivers.

This chapter outlines the process and some of the practical issues. Subsequent chapters expand on the practical problems encountered implementing activity-based costing, using case studies as examples.

THE PROCESS

Figure 3–1 shows the basic steps in the approach that are common to each way of using the information. The process will not change whether the approach is used for a one-time review of activities and cost or a regular reporting system is being developed for either activity-based budgeting or activity-based cost analysis. The need to select appropriate software will be more important, however, when the system is to be used regularly.

Figure 3–2 indicates typical time requirements of the various phases described in the following paragraphs. Obviously the person-days and total elapsed time for the project will depend on the scale of the exercise and the complexity of the requirements. The time required for each phase will also be affected by the type of activity-based costing exercise and the experience of the team performing the analysis.

FIGURE 3–1
The activity-based costing process

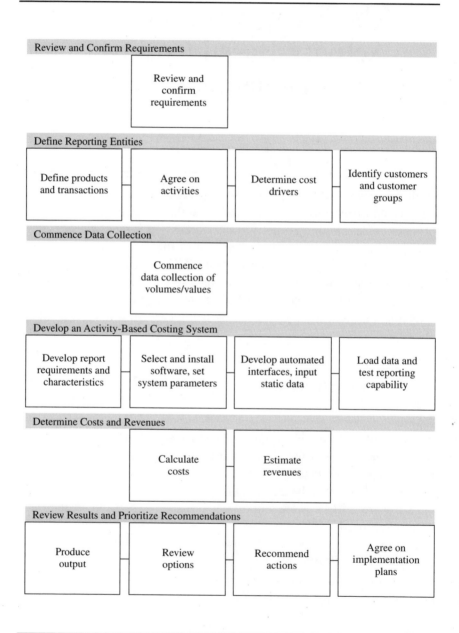

FIGURE 3–2
Indicative elapsed times by phase

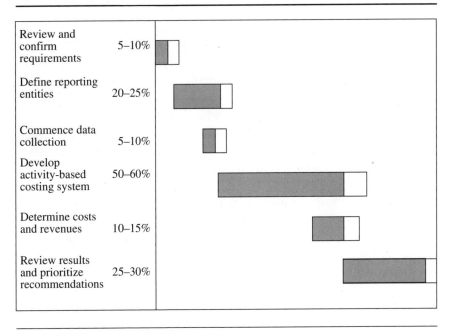

Review and confirm requirements	5–10%
Define reporting entities	20–25%
Commence data collection	5–10%
Develop activity-based costing system	50–60%
Determine costs and revenues	10–15%
Review results and prioritize recommendations	25–30%

Review and Confirm Requirements

The first phase in the development of an activity-based costing system is to ensure that the terms of reference for the project are clearly understood. This should include interviewing key users, identifying information needs, and taking account of best market practice and experience of the management information requirements in the industry. It is important to define the basic terms of reference to define the boundaries of the analysis and the data components that will be used. This normally includes a definition of the areas of activity to be analyzed and the type of cost data (actual, budget, forecast, or the like) to be used.

Define Reporting Entities

The reporting entities for an activity-based costing system will vary with the use of the system. The uses of the system are described in Chapter 2, "Uses of Activity-Based Costing." Products or types of business, activities, cost drivers, and customers may be defined and agreed on.

In strategic cost management, the core definitions will relate to types of business. Cost drivers will be required, focusing on the strategic value chain.

In product and customer cost and profitability management, products and customers must be defined and agreed on and activities identified, analyzed, and classified by type of activity. Cost drivers can be identified relating the volume, value, and quality of the delivery of products and services to external and internal customers.

Operational cost management requires a focus on the principal and subactivities. The activities are classified as fundamental or discretionary and opportunities may then be identified to improve efficiency and effectiveness through business process re-engineering.

Define Products and Transactions.   To ensure consistent data collection and understanding of the information produced by the management information system, it is important to agree on the product and transaction definitions and to see that they are understood throughout the organization.

Agree on Activities.   It is important that common activities are defined and agreed on before any analysis. Otherwise, different definitions will be used in each department and making comparisons will be more difficult. Activities should be defined at a low enough level to allow the operations within a department to be related to the various products and services agreed on. They can then be linked to products and/or customers and classified as fundamental or discretionary and sustaining or operational as discussed in Chapter 4, "Agreeing on Activities."

Determine Cost Drivers.   When the products and activities have been agreed on, then the cost drivers can be identified. Too many costing systems assume that responsibility for costs coincides with the organization structure. Cost drivers, however, recognize that this is not the case and focus instead on the decisions that give rise to costs being incurred. Cost drivers generally relate to volume, quality, time, and level of service.

Identify Customers and Customer Groups.   If activity-based costing is being used as the basis of customer profitability, then common definitions of customers and customer groups must exist throughout the organization. Customers can be classified into types or analyzed individually. They may also be grouped for summary analysis, but the classifications and groupings must be agreed on before any data collection.

Commence Data Collection

It is important to begin data collection as soon as the data requirements have been defined. The data requirements will be derived from the definition of reporting entities agreed on and must be translated into detailed data components for which sources can be identified. Although most data should be available from financial accounts, transaction processing systems, accounting systems, and customer information files, some must be gathered manually. Procedures and data collection forms will, therefore, be required.

When the means of data gathering have been identified and agreed on, the data can be accumulated and stored until required for analysis and reporting. Any data that is not readily available can be identified and a means of collection determined. Missing data can cause serious delays to the project, as all other activities may be held up while it is located.

Develop an Activity-Based Costing System

Even when activity-based costing analysis is used as an ad hoc exercise, some form of system will be required to evaluate the data. The system can be limited to a simple spreadsheet, but the discipline of identifying reporting requirements, identifying static and variable data, and system and report testing should still be required.

Develop Reporting Requirements and System Characteristics.
It is rare to find users who know exactly what format of reporting they wish to use before they are presented with alternatives. It may be necessary to develop a range of reports that can act as a catalyst to focus the users on their own reporting requirements. When the requirements (level of detail, degree of comparative data, frequency and style of reporting, and so on) have been agreed on in outline, then the appropriate system's characteristics can be defined.

Characteristics that need to be defined normally include:

• The hardware platform to be used.

- The degree of integration to other systems.
- Types of reporting.
- Types of activity analysis required.
- Types of apportionment for support and sustaining costs.
- System capacity.
- Complexity of maintenance.
- Timing requirements of reporting.

Select and Install Appropriate Software and Set System Parameters. There are several software packages on the market that can produce multidimensional profitability analysis on either mainframe or personal computers. The packages differ significantly in terms of the features and facilities they offer. Before selecting a package, therefore, make sure its features will provide the analysis required.

When the appropriate package has been identified, it can be installed and the system parameters can be set. These base parameters will determine how the system will store and report the data. Any changes later in the project may involve a significant amount of effort reworking reporting and data analysis, so decisions should be made at this point rather than later if at all possible.

Develop Automated Interfaces and Input Static Data. Most systems have standard input formats that must be used to load data into the system, by means of either automated downloads or manual input. The volume and complexity of the data collection will determine the mode of input used. Any automated downloads will inevitably involve development of a bridge between existing applications (such as the transaction processing or administration system) and the management information system.

When the basic parameters have been set up on the system, the static data can be loaded. Static data comprises the standard definitions of products, transactions, and cost drivers and the interrelationships between them. The system should relate the regular variable data to this base data to ensure consistent reporting and summarizing. It will also define report layouts and reporting hierarchies.

Load Data and Test Reporting Capability. Once the static data has been loaded and verified, the first variable data can be input and the first test reports produced. Normally, in a systems implementation, test data is used for input and report testing, but in practice users will review the reports and comment on data accuracy only when real data is used. It is therefore more practical to use for the basic system tests a subset of actual data that can be verified against expected results and presented to the users as test results.

The project team must be fully satisfied with the results of the systems tests before any reports are shown to users. This is because the credibility of the whole project depends on the reporting capability, and the users must have confidence in the reports produced. They usually identify errors in the accuracy of data used but should not be able to question the way the reports are produced

When the users have accepted the reports from the system, the remaining data can be loaded. Most systems require data to be loaded and processed by period, so input may take some time if the data relates to several periods. Clearly, if the system is to be used on an ongoing basis, it is necessary to document operator and user procedures.

As the project team loads the year-to-date data, it should develop user procedures. These procedures should refer to (not duplicate) the system user manuals but should also provide step-by-step instructions for operating the system. Without this type of documentation, the organization is dependent on the project team members to operate the system in perpetuity.

Determine Costs and Revenues

When the first activity and driver data has been analyzed, the associated costs and revenues can be estimated and the validity of the product definitions and cost drivers confirmed. This is important; the users will focus on the definitions and sample reports only when real costs and revenues are used and, hence, when they can review and agree on them in detail.

Calculate Costs. Costs can be calculated as the system is developed, by confirming the definitions of activities and the relative time or cost spent on each activity. Costs can be standard or actual costs and may be based on historical or current costs, budgets, forecasts, or long-term expenditure projections. They should, however, be reconcilable to existing reports to ensure data consistency and integrity.

Estimate Revenues.   When activity-based costing is used as the basis of profitability analysis, it is also necessary to estimate the revenue generated by products or types of business, or by customers or types of customers. It is rare to be able to identify revenue by individual activity. In general, activities must be summarized to products for which interest, fees, or commissions are paid or received. Customer profitability analysis should also include analysis of actual revenues received, as it is common in the financial sector for fees and commissions to be discounted or waived for particular customers or types of customers.

Review Results and Prioritize Recommendations

It is important not to stop the analysis of activity-based costs with the production of the reports. Reports are of little use unless actions are identified and implemented.

Produce Output.   Reports should be produced and presented to the users. Managers cannot be expected to understand reports in isolation and should have the content explained and the information put into context.

Review Options.   When the output has been produced and explained to the users, the information can be put to use and the options for improving cost control and profitability can be identified.

When the system is designed to be used for cost reduction or resource allocation, it is necessary to identify the benefits associated with the delivery of each activity or group of activities. The cost/benefit of any activity should enable it to be ranked in relation to other activities in terms of its value to the organization. This involves obtaining consensus as to the value placed on each activity in relation to the strategic goals of the organization as a whole (for example, whether it values customer marketing more than new product development). When the value of the individual activities has been calculated, a cost/benefit matrix can be completed and a review of the activities undertaken in a more focused way. (See Chapter 11, "Using Activity-Based Costing for Operational Cost Management.")

Recommend Actions.   Any activity-based costing exercise is likely to identify opportunities for improvements in the way activities are performed. These must be evaluated, agreed on, and prioritized to ensure that they are accepted and the necessary action can be recommended.

Although it is important to involve the management and staff in any activity-based costing exercise, it is essential that they be involved in any analysis of opportunities for cost reduction or efficiency improvement. They should be involved in the identification of opportunities to eliminate, curtail, or improve the efficiency or effectiveness of activities undertaken. This is usually done by means of interviews with those involved in the activities, as well as discussions between the managers responsible for the activities and their peers or users.

Agree on Implementation Plans.   The final task in any activity-based costing exercise, regardless of whether it is an ad hoc exercise or the development of an ongoing system, is the agreement on priorities and the implementation plan. Even when a regular reporting system has been developed for product costing, customer profitability, activity-based management, activity-based budgeting, and/or performance management, it is necessary to ensure that the reports are used and actions taken as a result of the analysis. Without this, the exercise loses all meaning. Users of reports should be trained in interpreting the information to ensure that it is not used out of context and to maximize the benefit obtained from the exercise.

PRACTICAL ISSUES

Many practical issues may be encountered in the development of activity-based costing systems. The most complex are discussed in detail in succeeding chapters and are:

- Agreeing on activities.
- Determining cost drivers.
- Calculating costs.
- Implementing change.

Others issues are addressed below:
- Confirming requirements.
- Defining products and services.
- Identifying benefits.
- Seeking out opportunities for improvement.

Let us look at these in turn.

Confirming Requirements

Activity-based costing is, fundamentally, an analytical approach to the study of activities undertaken within an organization and their associated costs/benefits. Its relevance to the management of the business depends, to a large extent, on the presentation and understanding of the use of the information. It is important that management use the information in context and understand the approach on which the analysis has been based. Presentation of the results is therefore considered in the context of how they will be used and is discussed in Chapters 8 through 11, where the use of the activity-based costing technique and the resulting information is explained with worked examples.

Activity-based costing reports differ from more conventional financial reporting as they relate cost consumption to expenditure decisions and enable management to focus on improvements in profitability in the long and short term. The calculation of activity-based costs provides the information necessary to provide strategic cost evaluation and product costing. Product and customer profitability reporting requires not only activity-based cost analysis but also revenue data. (The capture and analysis of revenue data are considered further in Chapter 6, "Calculating Costs.")

Cost reduction and efficiency improvement require the activity-based cost information to form the base data for evaluation of the cost/benefit associated with the current level of expenditure on the activities identified. Management can then search for opportunities and identify the areas where costs can be curtailed or eliminated, where activities can be made more efficient or effective, or where further investment should be made to maximize the benefits received.

Defining Products and Services

The initial tasks in any activity-based costing exercise include achieving agreement on the definitions of products, activities, and cost drivers that will be used in the analysis. These definitions must be carefully worded and documented to minimize confusion within the organization and to ensure common understanding of the results of the analysis.

The importance of these tasks cannot be overstated. Unless the appropriate definitions are used, the analysis may not provide sufficient information to identify the true cost issues or, alternatively, it may provide too much detail and cloud the real issues that should be addressed.

The definition and classification of activities are discussed in Chapter 4. The determination of cost drivers is addressed in Chapter 5.

The first definitions that need to be agreed on are those of the products or services for which activity-based costs are required. One unfortunate feature of the financial sector is that many of the products and services offered are difficult to define. A service may be defined as any activity one party can offer to another that is essentially intangible and does not result in the ownership of anything. Definitions of products and services depend on the assistance provided to various types of client and on the quality of service provided. The definitions of products and/or services may differ depending on how the information is used. If, say, the resulting reports are to be used for strategic purposes, the products defined will generally be at a higher level than those defined for product and customer profitability analysis.

For strategic cost management, the products and services are likely to be generic product groups, such as lending, deposit taking, remittance services, trade finance, foreign exchange, corporate finance, and credit life insurance. They may be differentiated by customer type (corporate, retail, etc.) or by geographic area (state, region, etc.).

For product costing and customer profitability, the products and services defined are normally those to which revenue can be attributed or which customers identify as being different from each other. (For detailed examples, see Chapter 9, "Using Activity-Based Costing for Product Costing," and Chapter 10, "Using Activity-Based Costing for Customer Profitability.")

For cost reduction and efficiency improvement, products and services are less important. The emphasis of activity-based costing normally shifts to concentrate on the analysis of activities and opportunities to reduce, eliminate, or improve the individual activities performed. Products and services are necessary only as a means of differentiating between similar activities from which disparate benefits are derived.

Identifying Benefits

When the activity-based costs have been derived, it is time to evaluate the benefits obtained from performing the activity. The evaluation should consider the level of service or benefit provided and the incremental costs associated with provision of a different level of service. This may be either a higher quality of service with an increase in cost, or a reduction in quality and cost. The benefits identified may be qualitative rather than quantifiable. For instance, the objective of customer service training is to train staff to provide improved customer service; although this does not provide an immediately quantifiable benefit, it should be measurable in a reduction in customer complaints in the future.

Seeking out Opportunities for Improvement

Cost reduction, resource management, and efficiency improvement depend on the activity-based cost and benefit information that forms the base data for the identification of areas where costs can be curtailed or eliminated, activities can be made more efficient or effective, or further investments should be made to maximize the benefits received.

This opportunity search can be performed by either interviews with those involved in performing the activities or discussions between groups of senior or middle management within the organization. The manager responsible for the delivery of the activity or group of activities should discuss with his or her peers the value of the activity and the benefits derived. The group may decide that the level of service provided is too high and should be reduced to reduce costs. Or it may be decided that the activity can be undertaken more efficiently in another manner. Don't underestimate the value of asking the individuals undertaking the activities to suggest ways in which efficiency or effectiveness could be improved. These individuals are closer to the tasks and often have good ideas that have never been voiced.

When all opportunities have been identified, they should be classified by cost/benefit and priority to enable an implementation plan to be produced. It is easy to develop the opportunities in theory, but it is important that the exercise be completed and the benefits achieved in practice. The plan must, therefore, be agreed on and its implementation monitored on a regular basis.

SUMMARY

The process by which activity-based costs are derived can vary according to how the information is used. The use of the information will determine how products, activities, and cost drivers are defined, and the additional steps that need to be added to the basic approach.

The process of developing and implementing an activity-based costing system comprises six phases with a total of 16 steps. These are:

- *Review and confirm requirements.*
- *Define reporting entities.*
  Define products and transactions.
  Agree on activities.
  Determine cost drivers.
  Identify customers and customer groups.
- *Commence data collection of volumes and values.*
- *Develop an activity-based costing system.*
  Develop reporting requirements and system characteristics.
  Select and install appropriate software and set
  system parameters.
  Develop automated interfaces and input static data.
  Load data and test reporting capability.
- *Determine costs and revenues.*
  Calculate costs.
  Estimate revenues.
- *Review results and prioritize recommendations.*
  Produce output.
  Review options.
  Recommend action.
  Agree on implementation plans.

There are many practical problems that may be encountered in the process. These include:

- Confirming requirements.
- Defining products and services.
- Identifying benefits.
- Seeking out opportunities for improvement.

The most complicated are agreeing on activities, determining cost drivers, calculating costs, and implementing changes. Subsequent chapters analyze these problems and provide examples that relate the problems to how the information is used.

Chapter Four

Agreeing on Activities

INTRODUCTION

As we saw in the last chapter, the first phase in any activity-based costing exercise is to review and confirm requirements. This ensures that the terms of the project are clearly understood by both the sponsors and the project team. The detailed scope and extent of the project are further confirmed in the second phase, define reporting entities, in Figure 4–1. The reporting entities for an activity-based costing system will vary with the use of the system, but they require an agreement on common definitions of products, activities, and cost drivers that will be used in the analysis. These important definitions must be carefully worded and documented to avoid confusion and make the results of the analysis accessible to everyone.

A financial institution can be viewed as a collection of activities that are performed to support the creation and delivery of its product and services. It gains competitive advantage by performing activities at lower cost than competitors or by providing a differentiated product or service for which a customer is prepared to pay a higher price.

Activities are generally performed for a purpose. They result in an output. If the output can be assessed in terms of benefit, then a cost/benefit relationship can be derived and used to value the activity. Activities are often undertaken on behalf of another part of the organization. They may, therefore, confer benefits to one part of the organization by incurring cost in another part of it. This creates interorganizational conflict when activities are evaluated within part of the company. Activity-based costs can best be applied across the whole company or at least within a stand-alone entity that is not heavily reliant on services provided by other parts of the organization.

FIGURE 4–1
The activity-based process, phase two: define reporting entities

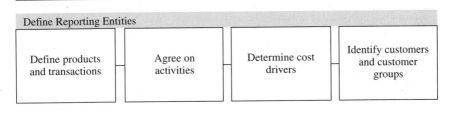

When the principal activities across the organization have been defined, the detailed activities performed within each department can then be identified and agreed on. All activities identified by the departments must then be categorized as fundamental or discretionary and sustaining or operational and be capable of linkage to measure cost drivers that may be product- or service-related. This chapter details this process and gives examples.

DEFINING ACTIVITIES

It is important that common activities are agreed on before any analysis is undertaken. Otherwise different definitions will be used in each department and comparisons will be difficult.

Definitions of activities will vary depending on how the information will be used. In all instances, however, detailed activities should be defined at a low enough level to allow the operations within a department to be related to the level of decision making for which the analysis is focused.

The definition process should be undertaken at two levels: first, for the principal activities performed in the department (normally no more than 12 in each department) and second, for the detailed components of the principal activities that relate to different products or are affected by different cost drivers. Depending on how the information is to be used, this may require only one or two activities to be defined within operating departments for strategic cost management purposes. Alternatively, it may require approximately 10 principal activities and several detailed activities below each principal activity to be defined in order to cost the product or improve efficiency. Table 4–1 shows some sample activities defined at the lowest levels and identifies the levels that are appropriate for the various uses described.

TABLE 4–1
Sample activities and their usage

Activities	Strategic cost management	Product costing	Customer profitability	Cost management
Customer makes loan request	Secured Lending	Loan application	Request	Complete application {f}
Complete loan application form			Loan application	
Enter application into system				
Check credit rating			Obtain authorization	Authorize credit facility {f}
Authorize facility (account manager)		*		
Authorize facility (branch manager)		*		
Authorize facility (regional manager)		*		
Authorize facility (general manager)		*		
Authorize facility (credit committee)		*		
Notify customer of acceptance		Notification	Accept loan facility	Open loan account {f}
Review security provided				
Open loan account		Open loan account		
Set up repayment standing order				
Credit checking account		Drawdown		
Monitor repayments		*		{f}
Close loan account on maturity		*		{f}
Supervise lending staff		+	+	{f}
Maintain on-line system	+	+		{f}
Management reporting	+	+		{d}
Loan service training	+	+		{d}
Maintenance of customer information	+	+		{d}

Key

*Separate activity +Allocated over related activities {f}Fundamental activity
{d}Discretionary activity

For strategic cost management, the activities defined are likely to be high level and may relate to the operation of a whole department, for example, credit authorization or loan administration. Activities typically identified within financial institutions for the purpose of strategic cost management are:

- Life insurance.
- Investment management.
- Lending.
- Deposit taking.
- Trade finance.
- Foreign exchange.
- Cash management.
- Correspondent banking.
- Corporate banking.
- Retail banking.
- Card services.
- Private banking.
- Asset management.
- Corporate finance.
- Discount brokerage.
- Capital markets.
- Treasury.

For product costing and customer profitability, the activities defined are normally those to which costs or volumes can be attributed and, hence, to which different cost drivers will be attributed. As the products and services are agreed on at a lower level, then the definitions of the activities will also be more detailed. For example, in bank lending, each type of loan product may require a variety of operations for which the frequency of occurrence will differ: loan set-up, credit authorization (within branch limit), credit authorization (within area limit), loan repayment, loan renewal, loan maturity, and so on. The activities defined should allow the costs of the individual operations to be calculated and the different product costs to be analyzed. Table 4–2 provides a sample list of the activities that can be identified within corporate and personal banking for the purposes of product costing and customer profitability analysis.

These typical activities may be applied to individual products, types of business, customers, or groups of customers. They may be specific to a particular product or customer. Or they may apply to a range of products, although the frequency of occurrence may vary. In a letter of credit, for example, the number of amendments and the complexity of the amendments may vary by customer, so the time and cost of processing will be different. The number of payments made may also differ, but the process of making a payment is likely to be the same.

TABLE 4–2
Typical activities included in product costing and customer profitability analysis

Foreign exchange department Travelers' checks purchased Travelers' checks sold Wire transfer Inward remittance Mail transfer Journal entries (intercurrency account transfer) Journal entries (single-currency account transfer Issue of bankers' payments/checks Set up forward deal Set up spot deal	Negotiation repayments Currency loan against bill Outward documentary/clean collection Collection proceeds paid away Confirmation of letter of credit Advising letter of credit without confirmation Amendment to inward letter of credit Pay/check documentation presented under letter of credit Payment of bills at maturity drawn on opening bank Credit bills negotiated (advances under acceptances) Clean reimbursements Opening/issuing letter of credit Amendment to outward letter of credit Check documentation presented under letter of credit Dispatch documentation presented under letter of credit Accept draft in respect of documents presented Payment against documents presented under letter of credit
Payment services department Effect payment by bankers' payment/check Effect payment by SWIFT Receive payment by SWIFT In-house funds transfer Receipt of payments over $10,000 Effect cover payment, etc., by bankers' payment Wire transfer Mail transfer Issue of draft Effect payment by CHIPS	
Teller services Deposits Checks cashed Cashier's checks Loan payments Withdrawals	**Loan services department** Open account Set up direct debit Input loan application Obtain credit authorization Obtain/verify security Review facility Monitor repayments Debit account for loan fees Close account Issue of special corporate checkbooks Deposit of safe keeping items Withdrawal of safe keeping items Temporary withdrawal of safe keeping items
Documentary services department Documentary/clean collections Payment of collections Discount of bills Advance against bill/check purchased Advance repaid Negotiations of exchange	

(continued)

TABLE 4–2
(concluded)

Provision of lists of securities held	**Management**
Provision of valuations of holdings	General management
	Strategic planning
Human resources	Contingency planning
Recruitment	Marketing
Training	Public relations
Appraisals/counseling	Product development
Payroll	Legal
Employee relations	Security
	Organization and methods
Finance	
Accounts payable	**Systems**
Bank reconciliations	Systems planning
Financial accounting	General management
Statutory and regulatory reporting	Contingency planning
Consolidations	Capacity planning
Tax management	Computer operations
Management reporting	Systems maintenance
Budgeting and forecasting	Systems development
Capital budgeting	Communications management
Internal audit	Storage management
Float management	PC support
Asset and liability management	Network support

For cost reduction, the definition of activities is key to the analysis. Here, activity-based costing normally concentrates on the analysis of common activities throughout the organization and opportunities to reduce, eliminate, or improve the individual activities undertaken. The activities identified tend to provide more detailed analysis of common activities, such as training, secretarial support, or management reporting, and to place less emphasis on the operational activities.

Alternatively, activity definitions for improving efficiency must be at a level that enables the improvements to be identified. This is likely to require a lower level of detail than any other use of activity-based costing.

Table 4–3 lists the activities typically identified within financial institutions for the purpose of operational cost management. The activities are grouped together for easier analysis, but this may not necessarily reflect their location within the organization.

This level of detail is likely to be required for any type of operational cost management, whether the information is used for activity-based

TABLE 4–3
Activities typically identified for operational cost management

General management	Claims (insurance)
General management	Claims inquiries
Project management	Claims recording
	Claims reserving
Planning	Claims investigating
Strategic planning	Claims case management
Contingency/disaster recover planning	Claims settlement
	Claims recoveries
Sales/marketing	Litigation
Market research	
Public relations	
Product development	**Premium accounting (insurance)**
Competitor analysis	Billing
Advertising/promotion	Collections
Distribution network management	Credit control
(insurance)	Agency remuneration
Direct sales (insurance)	
Underwriting (insurance)	**Treasury management**
Risk assessment and quotation	Accounts payable
Policy issue	Asset and liability management
Policy renewal	
Policy administration	
Reinsurance	**Dealing**
	Money market dealing
Actuarial (insurance)	Foreign exchange dealing
Rating	Futures and options trading
Fund valuation (reserve calculation)	Equity trading
Bonus calculation	Bonds/securities trading
Surrender/maturity calculation	Commodities trading
	Position management
Lending	
Loan application	**Investment management**
Credit review	Research and analysis
Loan opening	Property management (insurance)
Loan administration	Fixed asset management (insurance)
Loan closure	Portfolio management
Credit management	
Deposit taking	**Management information**
Deposit taking	Budgeting/forecasting
Deposit administration	Regular management reporting
Withdrawal	Ad hoc management reporting

(continued)

TABLE 4–3
(concluded)

Human resources	**Financial accounting**
Recruitment	Statutory and regulatory reporting
Training (general)	Consolidation of accounts
Training (technical)	Bank reconciliations
Career development/appraisals/	
counseling	**Information technology**
Remuneration/benefits	Systems planning
Outplacement	Capacity planning
	Computer operations
Trade finance	Systems maintenance
Letters of credit	Systems development
Collections	Communications management
Guarantees	
Acceptances	**Compliance**
	Audit
Corporate finance	Tax management
Mergers and acquisitions	
	Office services
Payments	Secretarial support
Incoming payments	Office supply management
Outgoing payments	Legal
Queries	Cafeteria
	Transportation
Card services	Security
Card issuance	Internal communication
Merchant processing	Risk management
Transaction processing	

management, activity-based budgeting, performance management, or cost reduction, although the emphasis on particular types of activities may differ.

Using activity-based costing for cost reduction initiatives tends to provide details about such common activities as training, secretarial support, and management reporting, and moves the focus away from the operational activities. Alternatively, definitions of activities for performance management and improving efficiency may initially be at the level shown in Table 4–3, but they may have to go down a level so improvements in efficiency can be identified.

AGREEING ON ACTIVITIES

When the common definitions have been agreed on, it is necessary to identify and agree on which of the principal and detailed activities are undertaken in each department and what the unit of measure is for the activity. Some activities will be specific to individual departments (for example, review loan application, complete credit check, approve borrowing limit, authorize payment, set up standing order for repayments). Others will be common at either the principal or detailed level and may occur in a number of departments (such as strategic planning, management reporting, recruitment, training, staff appraisals and counseling, secretarial support, customer liaison).

After the activities undertaken have been identified, the staff cost or time spent within each department can be apportioned to the activities. This can be done in a number of ways, including self-logging, historical averaging, relative values, activity sampling, stopwatch, and predetermined time standards.

Activity analysis or work measurement techniques have formed the basis of standard costing and productivity measurement in manufacturing for many years and have also been used for clerical work measurement in some financial institutions. Which technique is chosen depends on:

- The complexity of the activities.
- The level of detail required.
- How the data collected is to be used.
- The cost/benefit perceived from the study.
- The culture of the organization.
- The type of costing system required.

It would be unusual for one technique to be applied to all the areas (within a department or group) to be measured. There are often instances when particular departments or activities require different approaches. However, the main considerations are likely to be the level of detail required and the usefulness of the data produced.

Opinions diverge within financial institutions as to just how much detail is required. The administration of work measurement can be costly. Automation and the use of relative values allow financial institutions to approximate standards without incurring major costs. Conversely, increased competitive pressure has led to many organizations feeling the need for a daily detailed breakdown of each cost component. Each situation is unique, however, and should be approached as such, because the degree of detail in the activity analysis phase dictates the type and nature of information used in activity-based costing exercises.

The following sections give a brief overview of the main work measurement techniques, together with an indication of their limitations and possible applications. Remember that while work measurement enables the labor costs to be identified, the costs of other resources (equipment, materials, computer time, etc.) may not be allocated to activities on the same basis, so separate analysis is often required to attribute them.

Self-Logging (Time Ladders)

Self-logging, also called time ladders, relies on workers to account for the time they have spent on activities in segments, such as 5 to 15 minutes each. At the end of each time period, they make a note of what they have just been doing on a prepared reporting sheet, which usually has the working day broken down into the select segments on a vertical axis. A horizontal axis often contains the department's major work categories.

There are several variants of this method, including predefined codes for the different activities, which facilitates the use of computers in analyzing the data. A further variation is a special clock with a random prompting alarm; workers log what they are doing when the alarm sounds.

Any self-logging study needs to be carried out for a representative period of time—which may be several weeks—and the usefulness of the data depends on all the sheets being fully and accurately completed. It is very difficult to collate the results without a computer.

Self-logging can be useful where no previous work measurement has been carried out or where a wide variety of products and/or services, many of them low in volume, are being handled. Its main practical advantage is that it does not require the valuable resources of senior staff, specialists, or consultants to carry out the actual data collection, although these resources will usually establish the parameters for completing the self log.

The main disadvantage is that it is tempting to interpret what has been done in the most favorable light. Even in the best cases, there are always problems caused by inconsistency in interpretation of what activities are actually being performed. It can also increase the inaccuracy of product times inherent in all methods that measure what *is* happening as opposed to what *should* be happening, by failing to identify slack time or the underutilization of capacity.

Historical Averaging

Historical averaging involves comparing relationships of previously recorded data in order to develop time estimates. This method is the least complicated of all and usually only applies to situations where the area being costed involves few activities.

The net staff hours worked are divided by the output volume to arrive at a time standard. Net staff hours can be taken as the total paid hours, but if the information is to be used for detailed productivity measurement, vacations, absences, and training should be deducted. The figure is only an estimate, since one cannot ascertain idle time and other such factors. There may, therefore, be distortions in the time standard. Other limitations are that the time values derived may be obsolete and workers' performance cannot be rated as it can in other methods. Due to these limitations, this method is usually applied on an interim basis, and followed by a more comprehensive method.

The only advantage of historical averaging is that the work can usually be done quite rapidly. The disadvantages are that, as it is volume sensitive and takes no account of other activities in the service center, its outcome is likely to be little better than an approximation. Also, it really applies only to areas that have just one product.

Relative Values

The relative values method works on the principle of weighting tasks or activities relative to each other based on their consumption of resources.

For the purpose of the following examples, assume that the service center consists of direct people costs and overheads that are to be absorbed equally over the whole spectrum of activities of the center. It may be necessary to assign a second set of figures to these activities that reflects their use of these resources.

Usually, the activity that takes the least time (or is performed most frequently) is given the lowest value (base value) and assigned a weight of 1.0. All other weights are constructed from their resource usage relative to this value. Under normal circumstances the relative weighting is based on the activity. For example, it takes three times as long to perform one task X as one task Y. However, in some instances, the information provided may be on terms of total time. That is, we need three people to perform task Y. So two activities with the same weighting will have the same unit cost.

The major advantage of this method is that it takes much less time to arrive at cost indicators than most other methods. In addition, it is easy to use and does not disrupt the work of the service centers.

The big disadvantage is that its accuracy relies almost totally on the relative value selected. These estimates are sometimes quite inaccurate. This is often caused by attributing the weighting of staff positions within the service center, but not taking account of any over- or undercapacity in these positions, nor of the fact that some of the staff spend part of their time on administrative or housekeeping activities.

Activity Sampling

Activity sampling is a direct observation method of work measurement that uses random sampling to identify the proportion of time spent on the various products, services, or activities in an organization. From these random samples, statistically significant results can be obtained that show how the time was used in the group being studied, allocating this time to the activities and functions performed. When these proportions of time are related to the people costs of the group, costs per activity can be calculated.

Activity sampling can be used to collect as much (or as little) detail about the work being performed as required, but in order to ensure the accuracy of the results, it must be carried out over a representative period of time, perhaps a month. It can be used to obtain base information for unit costing (products and services), cost allocations, and capacity planning for cost reductions.

Activity sampling is usually carried out by the supervisors of the sections being studied. They make a predetermined number of observations each day at randomly selected times. The observer walks around and notes, in coded form, exactly what each employee is doing. This process is repeated every day until the end of the sampling period. When all the observations have been completed, analysts calculate the time spent on each activity by working out the number of observations of each activity as a percentage of the total number of valid observations.

Activity sampling has some major advantages. It can provide a lot of detailed information, including the identification of direct and indirect activities for various costing purposes and it is easy to learn and to apply without disrupting the work of an organization.

The disadvantages are that it identifies only how time and costs are used, rather than how they should be used. There is the potential, therefore, for bad work practices to be compounded (although this is the case with all methods that do not have predetermined time standards). In addition, it may have to be repeated if organizational or environmental factors change dramatically. The total time required for one comprehensive study is about 8 to 10 weeks.

Stopwatch

Sample observations of activities are measured with a stopwatch to determine standard times. This methodology should be used only to derive standard cost, calculate times for commonly performed functions, or capture times for low-volume activities, even though the actual time spent on them may be quite short.

Stopwatch observations should be undertaken after thorough preparation. This includes defining in detail the activity to be measured, listing the steps or functions involved, and then measuring the time taken to perform each activity several times. The average time taken can then be calculated.

The biggest difficulty with using a stopwatch is that it can be culturally unacceptable and may actually lead to a distorting of the performance being observed because of the artificial climate it creates. It is also very time-consuming if it is the only technique being used.

The advantage of this method is that it enables measurement of activities that are difficult to capture using many of the other methods, either because they do not occur very often or because they are fragmented. Its most appropriate application is for key activities where several functions that are spread out across an organization need to be measured to produce a total time and cost for a product or project.

Predetermined Time Standards

Predetermined time standards methods classify body movements into time values. They save the analyst from having to actually measure tasks afresh each time, as in the stopwatch method.

Three techniques in common use are methods time measurement (MTM), modular arrangement of predetermined time standards (MODAPTS), and integrated business control (IBC). These three methods require special training and are time consuming and costly to maintain. The standards also need to be carefully aligned for costing purposes and sometimes this linkage is difficult to achieve. This kind of measurement applies only to highly repetitive and routine work.

Methods time measurement expresses values as time measurement units (TMUs). Body movements are classified into major categories and TMU values are assigned to each. Some body movements are specific to particular activities and may or may not be included in standard measurements. One TMU is 0.00001 hour.

MODAPTS classifies specific anatomical body movements. It relies on predetermined standards for "gets" and "puts." Basic movements are called MODS and one MOD is 0.129 second. MOD values are assigned to 21 types of body movements, such as by the hands, arms, feet, and eyes. This may be more applicable to physical activities than the more clerical and intellectual activities carried out in the financial sector.

The major steps to follow when using predetermined standards include:

• Observing work activity and recording a sequence of motions.

• Classifying the motions to conform to predetermined standards.

• Assigning predetermined time values.

• Applying frequency factors where needed.

• Adjusting and/or leveling values where necessary (this includes adjustments for personal needs, fatigue, and delays).

The amount of detail these techniques can go into is so great and the amount of training required to use them is so extensive that they are almost certainly inappropriate for costing purposes in financial institutions. They could be used as a basis for standard costs, but only for very repetitive work, and there are other methods available for this area. There are also problems in applying them to computer-related work, where the number and types of keystrokes may be less relevant than the computer's response time to verify and accept data.

The basic concept of the integrated business control system of clerical work measurement is that every procedure (activity) can be broken down into a series of events, or data blocks, for which predetermined time standards exist, together with appropriate allowances for environmental factors. Examples of data blocks include Read, Write, File, Fasten (and their equivalents in machine operations), each of which can be further categorized.

The simplicity of the vocabulary means that it is easy to train staff how to use this method themselves, so the system does not require too much input from a specialist after the early stages.

The major steps involved in IBC are:

- Reviewing each procedure step by step.
- Translating these steps into IBC terminology.
- Importing this data, plus allowances, into the software.
- Analyzing output in the context of volumes and percentage of available time.
- Setting targets for phased reductions in terms of method, system, and environmental improvement.

The advantages of IBC are that it can be undertaken fairly by internal staff and does not have to be done all at one time. It is probably the most culturally acceptable predetermined time standard methodology and the most appropriate for developing standard times. An added benefit is that it identifies areas appropriate for cost reduction and productivity improvement and makes proposals for how to get costs down to the standard level.

The disadvantages are that it does not reflect how costs are currently being generated nor provide sufficient detail for cost studies or cost allocations.

The emphasis of IBC is in cost reduction. It can be applied as part of an overall cost management review and for target setting in conjunction with budgetary techniques.

ANALYZING ACTIVITIES

All principal activities identified by any department should be identifiable as fundamental or discretionary. Within these basic boundaries, they are further classified as sustaining or operational. Table 4–4 shows how such analysis is done.

This analysis is needed only when activity-based costing is being used to reduce costs or improve efficiency. Fundamental activities must be performed at some level and management must decide what level of effort and associated expenditure is necessary.

Discretionary activities, however, can be eliminated without affecting the basic fabric of the organization. Table 4–4 gives examples of these kinds of activities that can help to reduce costs and highlights the fundamental, discretionary, sustaining, and operational classifications. The classification is subjective and is used only as an aid in seeking opportunities for cost reduction or efficiency improvement. Classification of an activity is an art, not a science, so it may vary in different companies. For example, managing client relations may be viewed as absolutely fundamental in one organization but be discretionary in another.

Finding Fundamental Activities

A fundamental activity is one that must be done, either because it is a legal requirement (such as filing statutory accounts) or because the business will cease to function if the activity is not performed (for example, checking account processing in a retail bank). This generally includes all operations directly related to the provision of products and services and those activities that are necessary to maintain the basic infrastructure of the business.

It is easy to classify all activities as fundamental, but the object of the exercise is to identify those nonessential activities that are discretionary and should therefore be justifiable in terms of value added. Fundamental activities will still be reviewed in any cost reduction of efficiency improvement exercise, but the focus will be on making operations more effective through some form of business process re-engineering.

TABLE 4–4
Classifying activities

Example activities	Sustaining activities	Operational activities
Fundamental activities	Statutory reporting Remuneration/benefits Health and safety General management Compliance	Lending services Deposit services FX trading Facilities management Investment management
Discretionary activities	Strategic planning Market research Public relations Management accounting Treasury management	Systems development Customer marketing Sales New product development Product costing

Determining Discretionary Activities

Discretionary activities are those that are not fundamental and may not vary with the level of business undertaken. Principal activities defined by any department are likely to include at least one or two discretionary activities. The administration functions may be able to identify only one or two fundamental activities, and the rest will be discretionary.

One way of identifying whether an activity is discretionary is to assess whether products and services could still be supplied for the forthcoming year if the activity was curtailed. Activities that may fall into this category include strategic planning, management accounting, training, new systems development, new product development, and office refurbishment.

Selecting Sustaining Activities

Sustaining activities are those nonproduct-related activities that are performed in order to stay in business (such as regulatory reporting). These activities are generally fundamental in nature but can include such discretionary activities as corporate advertising, which is not related to a product or product group but is undertaken to maintain the corporate image in the marketplace. Any discretionary sustaining activities should be discussed critically to see whether they are justified in terms of their costs/benefits.

Indicating Operational Activities

As shown in Table 4–4, operational activities can be classified as either fundamental or discretionary. That decision will determine, to some extent, the effects of the analysis. Where activity-based costing is used for reducing costs or improving efficiency, how the activities are classified will facilitate the search for ways in which these improvements can be made. (See Chapter 11, "Using Activity-Based Costing for Operational Cost Management.")

PRACTICAL PROBLEMS

Defining activities and agreeing on which are to be undertaken where in the company is fraught with practical problems. Several of the most common problems may be overcome by carefully designing and operating an effective activity-based costing system, including:

• Clarity of activity definition.

- Level of detail.
- Maintenance of the data.

Clarity of Activity Definition

It is important that the definitions of the activities used are clear and unambiguous. Departmental managers need to be able to recognize and apply the definitions to their own organizational unit and feel comfortable that all activities performed there have been included. Definitions must be general enough to apply across organizational boundaries when necessary, but still specific enough to ensure that the managers can recognize the activity within their own operation.

Facilities management is one activity that should be carefully defined. It may relate to two very different activities—one is the management of a property portfolio in an insurance company for investment purposes—including the purchase, leasing, development, and sale of properties, maintenance of existing properties within the portfolio, selection of tenants, and collection of rents. Or it may mean the management of the properties occupied by the company, including the acquisition and disposal of appropriate accommodation and management of the infrastructure necessary to relocate departments and divisions within properties to optimize the use of space within the organization. The former definition indicates an activity that should be considered within a strategic cost review as a product that is offered in the investment management portfolio and for which a product cost may be required. The latter may be defined as a sustaining activity that is part of the basic infrastructure of the organization.

Level of Detail

The level of detail required in the activity analysis depends, to a large extent, on how the information is to be used (see "Defining Activities" at the beginning of this chapter). It may be tempting to perform the analysis at a lower level of detail than is required for the current purpose. This data may serve a variety of uses, but it can create discontent among the staff responsible for data collection. This is a greater problem where activity-based costing forms part of a regular reporting system than where it forms the basis of an isolated exercise. An isolated exercise may, however, be a good way of developing a prototype for a system that will be used regularly in the longer term.

When activity-based costing forms the basis of a regular product costing or customer profitability system, the level of detail in the definitions of activities forms the essence of the system. Judging the level correctly is important because as shown in Chapter 10, "Using Activity-Based Costing for Customer Profitability," the analysis is framed on activity-based costs within the departments that can be related to cost drivers. The cost drivers, in turn, determine the allocation of costs to each product or customer and must therefore be measured on a regular basis. (This data may be available from automated sources, but generally the systems will need to be modified.) Consequently, the detailed data requirements must be agreed on at the correct level of detail when the systems enhancements are specified to ensure that the data is made available as required.

The number of activities identified will also determine the size of the database required to perform the analysis. (This is discussed in more detail in Chapter 7, "Implementation Issues.")

Maintenance of the Data

Maintenance of the data will be a problem only in a regular reporting system. Where activity-based costing is used for an ad hoc analysis, maintenance will not be necessary. The complexity of maintenance depends, to some extent, on how frequently reports are required. A system that produces information monthly or quarterly will require more frequent updating but will generate a greater interest in the accuracy of data by the users. When a system produces reports semi-annually or annually, the users tend to be less motivated to maintain the data because its importance has been diluted in their memories.

The accuracy of data in any management information system tends to increase when users begin to use the information. As they start to depend on the reports, they are motivated to focus on the accuracy of the base data and to instigate improvements in data quality.

SUMMARY

The second phase of an activity-based costing exercise is to define reporting entities. The reporting entities for an activity-based costing system will vary with the use to which the system is put, but will require agreement on common definitions of products, activities, and cost drivers. These definitions must be carefully documented to minimize confusion within the organization and to ensure common understanding of the results of the analysis.

Defining, identifying, and agreeing on the activities throughout the organization can be a time-consuming exercise. Activity-based costs can best be applied across the whole institution or at least within a stand-alone entity that is not heavily reliant on services provided by other parts of the organization.

Definitions of activities will differ depending on how the information is to be used. It is important to match the use of information to the level of detail of activity analysis required and then to agree on common definitions for at least the principal activities before analyzing the departmental activities in detail. Otherwise, different definitions will be used in other departments and comparisons will be difficult. Also, strategic cost management may require only one or two activities to be defined within operating departments, but approximately 10 principal activities and several detailed activities below each principal activity may be required for product costing or improvements in efficiency.

After the activities have been identified, the staff cost or time spent within each department can be apportioned among the activities. This can be done in a number of ways: self-logging, historical averaging, relative values, activity sampling, stopwatch, and predetermined time standards. Which technique is chosen depends on:

- The complexity of the activities.
- The level of detail required.
- The use of the data collected.
- The cost/benefit perceived from the study.
- The culture of the organization.
- The type of costing system required.

However, the main considerations are likely to be the level of detail required and the usefulness of the data. The administration of work measurement can be time-consuming and costly, so automation and relative values can be used to allow financial institutions to approximate standards without incurring major costs. Conversely, increased competitive pressure has led many organizations to want a fairly detailed breakdown of each cost component. Each situation is unique; the degree of detail worked in the activity analysis phase dictates the type and nature of information used in future activity-based costing exercises.

All activities may also be classified as being fundamental or discretionary and sustaining or operational. The process of identifying which activities are fundamental (those that must be performed) may unearth opportunities for improving efficiency or effectiveness. All other activities must be discretionary and therefore could be eliminated without affecting the basic fabric of the business. Operational activities, both fundamental and discretionary, can normally be linked to measurable cost drivers, which relate to the products and services offered by the institution. Sustaining activities generally involve overall business management and may be linked to measurable cost drivers that are more strategic in nature and relate to the business policy of the organization.

Chapter Five

Determining Cost Drivers

INTRODUCTION

As we saw in the previous chapter, the second phase of activity-based costing is to define reporting entities (see Figure 4–1). The reporting entities vary depending on how the system is to be used but require agreement on common definitions of several of the basic components of activity-based costing: products, transactions, activities, cost drivers, customers, and customer groups. The definitions that will be used in the analysis must be carefully agreed on and documented to minimize confusion within the organization and to ensure common understanding of the results of the analysis.

The use of cost drivers is the nucleus of activity-based costing. This is the key difference between traditional approaches of standard costing or average costing and activity-based costing. All three approaches analyze activities and calculate costs by activity and product. Traditional costing methodologies use allocation criteria that are based on unit-level characteristics of the products, such as product volume, staff time, square footage, and number of staff. An activity-based costing system, however, uses cost drivers, which assists the decision-making process by concentrating on the factors that give rise to the cost without clouding the issue with irrelevant or arbitrary allocations.

Costs can be controlled in various ways, at diverse levels, and over differing time frames. Cost drivers enable management to link expenditure to the factors that affect the value and frequency of the expense and hence to control it in a more focused way.

Assigning cost drivers to activities and other cost types as an integral part of the process provides a means of linking cost behavior to decision making as well as handling joint costs. The emphasis given to the type of cost driver will depend on the objectives of the analysis. Activity-based costing systems tend to be more complicated than traditional unit-based cost accounting systems. Since costs are rarely driven by a single factor, the identification of appropriate cost drivers is not always easy. It is important to involve the line managers in the identification process in order to understand the key driver that is most instrumental in a particular activity or cost type. Cost drivers generally relate to volume, value, quality, time, and level of service. In general, short-term variable costs can be traced to products using volume-related cost drivers, but these are inappropriate for most long-term costs because they are driven by complexity and diversity, not volume.

In practice, the identification of cost drivers in an activity-based costing system calls for both judgment and analytical skills. The first principle is to identify those activities with large time or cost values and consider the relationship between the diversity of products, services, and customers supported by the activity and the degree of variation in the performance of the activity for each product, service, or customer. This will determine the level of accuracy needed to maximize the value of the exercise. (A larger variation in the activity between products, services, or customers will suggest that greater accuracy is necessary and that activities must be defined at a lower level.) Second, identify the balance-related costs and ascertain the drivers to be attributed to interest income and expense to take account of the rates and risks associated with products and counterparties. Finally, consider the nonactivity-related costs and the drivers necessary to analyze how and why the costs arise.

The minimum number of cost drivers an activity-based costing system uses will depend on the desired accuracy of the information produced and the complexity of the institution's products and services. As the number of cost drivers increases, the accuracy of the resulting information should also increase. In general, the higher the relative cost of an activity, the greater the distortion caused by using an imperfectly correlated cost driver to trace the cost to products or customers. This must, however, be balanced by the availability of the information and the cost of obtaining and processing it. This latter cost of activity-based costing systems development and operation must be justified by the usefulness of the information obtained.

Cost information is required for two types of decisions: first, for the strategic or tactical product or market decision and second, for cost control. The following sections consider the types of drivers relevant to the decisions discussed here and then examine the drivers that are most appropriate to the activity types in financial services.

PRODUCT OR MARKET DECISIONS

Cost analysis for product or market decisions tends to relate to strategic costing, product costing, or customer profitability. This requires identification of cost drivers that allow for all appropriate costs to be linked to the product or market and exclusion of the costs that remain unaffected by this type of decision, such as central administrative costs. Cost drivers for central costs tend to separate the basic sustaining costs of the business (general management, regulatory reporting, etc.), which may be affected by the size and complexity of the financial institution, from the administrative costs of running the day-to-day business (human resources, facilities management, etc.), which may be driven by the number of employees, staff turnover, geographic location, or age and condition of properties.

For product- or market-related decisions, it is necessary to identify all costs that are driven by factors that are linked to products or services, or at least to groups of products or services by market or geographic area. The contribution to sustaining costs and profitability can be estimated by analysis of the direct product- or customer-related revenues and costs. This involves identifying all direct or operational activities (see Chapter 4, "Agreeing on Activities") and defining associated cost drivers, as well as determining drivers relating to nonactivity costs, such as premises, marketing, and information technology. This highlights the need for drivers that may not be related to the volume of products or customers. Cost drivers generally relate to volume, value, quality, time, and level of service.

For the support or overhead functions, the goal of activity-based costing is to understand what activities are being performed and why. All activities must in some way support the delivery of products and services, but the actual link between the support activities and the customer may be difficult to identify. There are fundamental activities for which the cost drivers relate to the need to meet regulatory or statutory requirements, but these requirements exist because of the types of products and services offered and the environment in which they are provided.

Indirect or sustaining costs must not be ignored, but they have different behavior patterns and are unaffected by the product- or market-related activity. They may be apportioned to products or services to provide a fully absorbed product cost that may form the basis of strategic or tactical decision making (see Chapter 6, "Calculating Costs").

COST CONTROL

For cost control, costs (and hence activities) must be traced back to the point of *expenditure* rather than the point of *consumption,* which is usually shown in the financial accounts. This is because costs can be managed only at the point of initiation. Cooper and Kaplan developed an activity-based costing approach that relates overhead costs to the forces behind them. Too many costing systems make the assumption that expenditure coincides with organization, but this is not generally true. Costs can be controlled only by the management responsible for the factors that affect expenditure, which are the cost drivers.

Managers need feedback on both the cost incurred and the underlying factors that caused it. They need to understand the reasons for the cost. This can be achieved only by measuring and monitoring the factors that drive the cost.

For most operating or administrative departments, cost drivers tend to relate to the volume and variety of products and services offered. Such factors are readily measurable and such information may already be reported regularly. Activity-based costing simply relates the expense analysis to the business behavior that influences the expenditure.

For overhead or support functions, cost drivers relevant for cost control generally relate to the level of service provided and the efficiency and effectiveness of its delivery.

DETERMINING COST DRIVERS

When the products and activities have been agreed on, then the cost drivers can be identified. As noted earlier, too many costing systems assume that responsibility for costs coincides with the organization structure. The process of identifying cost drivers, however, recognizes that this is not the case and focuses instead on the decisions that give rise to costs being incurred.

The key decision at this stage of the exercise is how many and what types of cost drivers should be used? The complexity of the activities performed in any financial institution is virtually endless, but experience proves that the major drivers are such factors as:

- The number and diversity of products or services offered.
- The rate of new product launches.

- The number or variety of distribution channels used.
- The quality of service.
- The number and diversity of customers serviced.
- The value and risk associated with the product offered.
- The number of transactions performed.

Typically, the number of major drivers used in a division/business line is fewer than 15. These are the generic drivers, such as volumes (transactions, products, number of accounts, number of staff, etc.), values, quality of service, and variety (products, instruments, customers, currencies, time, etc.). This is then complicated by the number of products and activities to be included in the analysis. Let us look at an example.

Before a loan can be granted, an application must be completed, reviewed, and authorized, securities reviewed and accepted, accounts opened, facilities agreed on, repayment schedules agreed on, and payments paid. Despite this complexity, the drivers associated with the approval of a loan in a well-designed activity-based costing system might be limited to the number of applications made, size of facility, and term of the loan.

Short-term variable costs can be traced to products using volume-related cost drivers, but these are inappropriate for most long-term costs because they are driven by complexity and diversity instead of volume. Consider, for example, the cost of an insurance operation. The number of systems and employees required will be driven by a combination of the number of new and renewed policies and the variety of policies offered. A system may be maintained for many years to service a policy that has been withdrawn from the market but for which policies have not yet matured.

The minimum number of cost drivers an activity-based costing system uses depends on how accurate the information produced needs to be and the complexity of the products and services the institution offers. As the number of cost drivers increases, the accuracy of the resulting information should also increase.

All financial institutions have a large number of joint costs (costs and activities that support more than one product or service). Where activity-based costing is used to support product or customer cost and profitability analysis, the joint costs must be assigned to products, customers, or product groups. This may require additional cost drivers. Account relationship management, for example, may relate to a range of products and services offered to particular customers or customer groups. It may be possible to use a single cost driver such as "relationship management hours" that can then be attributed to individual products, services, and/or customers in different proportions without introducing unacceptable levels of distortion. Several factors determine if a single driver is acceptable. These include the diversity of weighting to products and services and the relative costs of the activities included in the principal activity to which the driver is applied. If, for example, the costs of account relationship management comprise 20 percent of the cost base, then more detailed analysis of the activities within it and the identification of individual drivers relating to relationship maintenance, new account development, new product development, and sales of products and services may be necessary. In general, the higher the relative cost of an activity, the greater the distortion caused by using an imperfectly correlated cost driver to trace the cost to products or customers. This must, however, be balanced by the availability of the information and the cost of obtaining and processing it. This cost of activity-based costing systems development and operation must be justified by the usefulness of the information.

Drivers can be assigned to all cost types, not just those costs that are incurred due to the execution of operational or sustaining activities. There are many cost types in financial institutions that are not related to activities. The key cost types that must be considered when determining cost drivers are operational activities, interest costs, claims, facilities costs, marketing costs, information technology (IT), and support or overhead activities. Many organizations use arbitrary allocation bases such as staff time to allocate facilities, marketing, IT, and support activities to products and/or customers, but this may be misleading. The drivers that are appropriate to each cost type are considered in more detail in the following sections.

Operational Activities

Activities that can be directly identified with products and services are generally the easiest to assign cost drivers. Table 5–1 shows the activities and drivers applicable to a securities trading operation. The drivers

TABLE 5–1
Activities and cost drivers in securities trading

Activities	Cost drivers
Securities trading:	
Trading	Number of trades/type of instrument
Confirmation	Number of trades/type of instrument
Domestic settlement	Number of domestic trades/type of instrument
Foreign settlement	Number of foreign trades/type of instrument
Stock lending	Number of trades/type of instrument
Dividend collection	Number/variety of holdings
Corporate advisory	Number/variety of holdings
Research:	
Research and analysis	Variety of instruments traded
Relationship management:	
Customer liaison	Number of accounts/level of service
Customer reporting	Number of accounts/level of service
Balance sheet management:	
Postion management	Variety of instruments traded
Regulatory reporting:	
Regulatory reporting	Variety of instruments traded
Management reporting:	
Regular management reporting	Level of detail required
Staff management:	
Supervision	Number of securities staff
Recruitment	Securities staff turnover
Career development/appraisals/counseling	Number of securities staff
Internal communication	Number of securities staff
Training:	
General training	Number of securities staff
Technical training	Experience of securities staff
Administration:	
Secretarial support	Number of accounts/level of service
Filing	Number of accounts/trades

relate, not only to the number of trades performed, but also to the diversity of trades, the number of customer accounts, the value and diversity of stocks held, and the need to meet regulatory requirements.

Transaction volume or direct labor is not an appropriate cost driver for many types of activity, yet it remains the most common cost driver in any financial institution.

Interest Costs

The primary business of banking and insurance revolves around obtaining funds from policy holders, depositors, the money markets, and other sources and investing these funds in loans, securities, and investment funds. The sources of funds equal the uses of funds for the total organization. However, when the organization is subdivided into units, products, or customer relationships, the sources and uses will frequently not be in balance. Some units, products, or customers are net providers of funds (liabilities exceed assets) and some are net users of funds (assets exceed liabilities).

When a financial institution measures costs and profitability performance of its organizational units, products, or customer relationships, a mechanism is required to ensure that the interest cost associated with being a net provider or user is taken into account. This mechanism is referred to as funds transfer pricing (see Chapter 6, "Calculating Costs").

Funds transfer pricing involves placing a value on the institution's funds by paying or crediting providers (an imputed interest income) and charging users of funds (an imputed interest expense). The drivers associated with the imputed interest income or expense relate to the type of product (floating-rate loan, fixed-rate deposit, ten-year life policy), the average balance of the asset or liability, and the risk associated with the product and counterparty. Drivers may not be necessary for each product, balance, and risk mix; products can be pooled by profile, which takes account of the rate, maturity, and risk character of the product being offered and relates driver to the product pool. The analysis of funding cost for interest-related products can be complicated and so is a separate exercise.

Premises

Premises costs relate to acquisition and maintenance of the premises occupied by the financial institution. The factors that give rise to the expenditure relate to the need to purchase or sell premises or maintain existing buildings. This tends to be driven by organizational decisions at a strategic or tactical level, such as mergers, acquisitions, or reorganizations, as well as the need to repair ordinary wear and tear. Allocating premises costs to products and services as a means of cost control is counterproductive, unless the expenditure is needed as a result of changes to the product or service offered.

Premises should, therefore, be treated as a sustaining cost unless they form part of the decision-making process. For example, if the financial institution is extending its range of products or services and will require new or renovated premises, such as a new trading room, this should be identified as the cost driver associated with the premises expenditure and this activity will then form part of the investment appraisal.

Marketing

Marketing costs may be allocated to products or customers on the basis of product volumes or value, which generally bear little relationship to the actual factors that drive the expenditure. Marketing costs tend to be driven by three key factors: first, the need to maintain the corporate image; second, the need to reinforce market perception of the range of products and services offered by the institution; and finally, the need to notify customers of a new product or service.

The drivers associated with each type of expenditure may be different. The need to maintain the corporate image may be considered a sustaining cost, driven by the importance of a universal corporate image to the marketing policy of the institution. The need to reinforce market perception of the range of products and services offered may be driven partly by the degree of competition for the products and services in the marketplace, partly by the buying patterns of the consumers, and partly by the amount of differentiation between competing products. Finally, the need to notify customers of a new product or service is driven by the number of new products and services launched by the institution and the need to create demand for them against those offered by the competition.

The focus on marketing policy and market position created by the cost driver approach allows management to make decisions based on the true factors that drive the expenditure. Allocating new product launch costs to the appropriate product ensures that the incremental costs of the development and launch are included in the decision-making process, which is a big improvement.

Overhead/Support Activities

As with facilities, overhead or support activities should be related to product- or customer-related drivers only where they affect the investment decision. Determining the cause of many types of overhead or supporting activities in financial institutions (that is, the cost drivers) is not easy. It involves talking to each department and finding out what creates work for that department. This is particularly difficult in support functions, where at the detailed level each week will be different, but at the higher level staff should be able to identify the activities (as described in the previous chapter) and determine their causes.

For example, on a day-to-day basis, the finance department may find it difficult to determine its core activities, but looking at it from a slightly different angle reveals that certain activities must be undertaken each month, quarter, or year. These include the principal and detailed activities shown in Table 5–2.

A cost driver can be identified for each of these activities, as shown in Table 5–3. Those activities identified as sustaining tend to be more difficult to associate with a cost driver. It is difficult, for example, to determine the driver associated with the annual audit or review of the tax position. However, it is possible to determine the costs associated with doing these activities to the current quality or service level.

SUMMARY

The cost driver approach looks for the factors that give rise to the cost. Major drivers are:

- The number and diversity of products or services offered.
- The rate of new product launches.
- The number or variety of distribution channels used.
- The quality of service.
- The number and diversity of customers serviced.
- The value and risk associated with the product offered.
- The number of transactions performed.

Too many costing systems assume that responsibility for costs coincides with the organization structure, but in the process of locating cost drivers, the focus is on the decisions that give rise to costs being

TABLE 5–2
The principal and detailed activities in a finance department

Management reporting
Tactical planning/budgeting/forecasting
Regular management reporting
Ad hoc management reporting

Financial accounting
Statutory and regulatory reporting
Financial accounting
Fixed asset accounting
Payroll (remuneration/benefits)

Staff management
Supervision
Career development/appraisals/counseling
Recruitment
Internal communication

Training
General training
Technical training

Audit
Audit liaison

Taxation
Tax management

Administration
Secretarial support
Filing

incurred. These decisions may take place in other parts of the organization and may simply be implemented within a particular department or division.

Cost drivers generally relate to volume, value, quality, time, and level of service. Short-term variable costs can be traced to products using volume-related cost drivers, but these are inappropriate for most long-term costs because they are driven by complexity and diversity, not volume.

In practice, identification of cost drivers in an activity-based costing system calls for both judgment and careful analysis. The first principle is to identify those activity costs with large values and consider the relationship between the diversity of products, services, and customers

TABLE 5–3
Activities and cost drivers in a finance department

Activities	Cost drivers
Management reporting	
Tactical planning/budgeting/forecasting	Level of detail required
Regular management reporting	Level of detail required
Ad hoc management reporting	Number/variety of requests for reports
Financial accounting	
Statutory and regulatory reporting	Regulatory requirement
Financial accounting	Number of items to be accounted for
Fixed asset accounting	Number of items to be accounted for
Payroll (remuneration/benefits)	Number of staff
Staff management	
Supervision	Number of finance staff
Career development/appraisals/ counseling	Number of finance staff
Recruitment	Finance staff turnover
Internal communication	Number of finance staff
Training	
General training	Number of finance staff
Technical training	Experience of finance staff
Audit	
Audit liaison	Quality of audit team
Taxation	
Tax management	Complexity of tax environment
Administration	
Secretarial support	Degree of automation/computer literacy of finance staff
Filing	Number of reports produced

supported by the activity and the variety within the activity for each product, service, or customer. This will determine the level of accuracy needed to maximize the value of the exercise. Second, identify the balance-related costs and ascertain the drivers to be attributed to interest income and expense to take account of the rates and risks associated with the products and counterparties. Finally, consider the nonactivity-related costs and the drivers necessary to analyze how the costs arose.

The minimum number of cost drivers an activity-based costing system requires to operate effectively depends on how accurate the information produced needs to be and the complexity of the products and services offered. As the number of cost drivers increases, the accuracy of the resulting information should also increase. In general, the higher the relative cost of an activity, the greater the distortion caused by using an imperfectly correlated cost driver to trace the cost to products or customers. This must, however, be balanced by the availability of the information and the cost of obtaining and processing it.

Chapter Six

Calculating Costs

INTRODUCTION

There are three basic components of activity-based costing: activities, cost drivers, and costs. Activities and the associated cost drivers were discussed in the two preceding chapters; this chapter concentrates on the costs themselves and the associated revenues.

The fifth phase of the activity-based costing process is to determine costs and revenues (see Figure 6–1). Although the basic concepts behind activity-based costing relate purely to cost analysis, it is important not to forget revenues. Without being able to relate costs and revenues for reporting entities, the analysis can only monitor and control costs in isolation. Revenues provide the input necessary to monitor and control return on investment and profitability.

Costing is the process of identifying, measuring, assigning, and analyzing the expenses associated with items that are to be costed. The items may vary from activities to lines of business, individual products, customers, organizational units, or any definable output.

Cost accounting concepts have primarily been developed for and applied to manufacturing companies. Indeed, the development of the cost of goods in process and finished goods inventories required for financial accounting in manufacturing is accomplished by means of cost accounting. The obvious difference between costing in manufacturing and in financial institutions is that manufacturing companies require raw materials to produce tangible finished goods for sale. In financial services, however, the raw materials are the funds offered or borrowed by customers.

Both financial services and manufacturing operations use labor, equipment, and facilities, but financial institutions do not produce a tangible product. Products and services offered by financial institutions to their customers may be the provision of insurance, financial management,

FIGURE 6–1
The activity-based costing process, phase five: determine costs and revenues

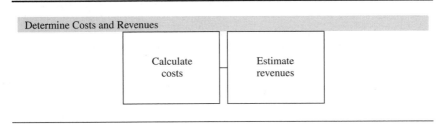

lending or deposit facilities, and financial advice. Other characteristics of financial institutions also make costing within these environments different from that within manufacturing companies. For example, the speed at which services or products are provided has an impact on cost and profitability due to the time value of money and to the customer service component of a service or product. Since interest expense is a principal component of the cost of funds, operating more efficiently reduces only a portion of the unit cost of providing a service. Interest costs cannot be managed and controlled by traditional cost management techniques.

The raw materials a financial institution handles are the funds obtained from deposits, premiums, or borrowings. Even if the cost of obtaining these funds can be worked out, it is difficult to identify the specific depository balance and associated interest rate that was the resource for a specific product, such as a loan. Most financial institutions have high volumes of transactions that fluctuate widely, due both to peak or slack business times and to economic conditions. They tend to have high fixed costs, due to unavoidably idle or underutilized capacity, partially due to the high and fluctuating volume of transactions.

Table 6–1 summarizes the characteristics of management accounting, including cost and profitability measurement and reporting, as it applies to manufacturing and financial institutions.

COST TYPES

Costs within a financial institution can be classified into several basic types:

TABLE 6–1
Characteristics of management accounting

Costs/revenue	Financial institutions	Manufacturing companies
Products	Loans Fee-based financial services	Tangible finished goods
Raw materials	Deposit Premiums Borrowings Labor	Tangible-raw materials Labor
Cost components	Funds Labor Equipment Facilities	Raw materials Labor Equipment Facilities
Revenue components	Interest margin Fee-based income Trading income Investment income	Sale of goods
Identification of cost and revenue streams by organizational unit, product, and customer	Interest cost, interest revenue, and noninterest revenue are accounted for by product, unit, and customer, while noninterest costs are accounted for only by unit. Complex adjustments are required to associate all cost and revenues to all three dimensions.	Costs and revenues are accounted for on a product basis, which can generally be associated with units and customers.
Traditional cost accounting for:		
— organizational unit	Yes, if any cost accounting at all	Yes, almost always
—product	Limited cost analysis	Yes, always
— customer	Rarely costed	Limited, generally through product analysis
Traditional profit measurement for:		
— total operation	Yes, always	Yes, always
— organizational unit	Yes, if any internal analysis	Yes, almost always
— product	Yes, possibly	Yes, always
— customer	Unlikely	Limited

- Interest costs.
- Claims.
- Commissions paid.
- Operating costs.
- Overhead or support costs.

For activity-based costing, it is also useful to separate the fixed and variable elements within each classification, as these generally relate to different cost drivers.

Interest Costs

Interest costs, for example, are usually variable costs within financial institutions that can be attributed directly to an account and hence to a product. Interest costs can be analyzed as net or gross. Net interest is defined as interest income net of funding cost. This requires some means of estimating the cost of funds to be attributed to the product.

Claims

Claims costs are also variable costs that can be attributed to a particular policy or type of policy.

The principal elements of cost within an insurance company are the claims paid to policy holders for losses they have suffered. Claims are usually recorded as gross and net (of reinsurance recoveries). At any point in time, a claim may be either paid/payable, outstanding, or incurred but not reported; these are described in more detail below.

The claims reserves of a property and casualty insurance corporation principally comprise the total of notified outstanding claims (as adjusted) and a provision for claims incurred but not reported. Insurance companies prepare various statistics to monitor their performance on claims, which generally falls into two categories:

- Contract profitability.
- Settlement performance.

Each insurance company has its own method of monitoring the performance of its claims department. The prompt settlement of claims can be a key factor in customer service and, accordingly, may be an area of focus in the settlement statistics.

Claims Paid/Payable. Claims paid/payable are claims the insurance company has judged valid and passed for payment. They represent a cost to the insurance company and can therefore be aligned with the relevant policy type for activity-based costing. The claim may relate to a policy that was issued in previous accounting periods, for which provisions have been made. It is important that double counting is avoided and that the cost of claims is reported as accurately as possible by policy type.

Notified Outstanding Claims. Notified outstanding claims are those claims that have been reported to the insurance company as losses but for which payment has not yet been agreed by the insurance company. The total of the notified outstanding claims at any point in time represents a reasonable estimate of the liability to the insurance company of notified claims, and the movement on the total of notified outstanding claims is an adjustment to cost.

Claims Incurred but Not Yet Reported. Claims incurred but not reported are losses covered by insurance contracts that have not yet been reported to the insurance company. The insurance company usually establishes a provision for claims incurred but not reported, and movement in this provision will affect the cost of claims. Calculation of the provision for claims incurred but not reported is a subjective process and generally calls for actuarial techniques. The insurance company usually performs a detailed exercise at year-end to calculate this provision, but it is sometimes updated more frequently for management accounting purposes.

Commissions Paid

Commissions paid are variable costs that relate to services purchased by the company. Services purchased are generally advisory or brokerage and can be linked directly to types of business if not to individual products.

Commissions are paid by financial institutions to other organizations for services they provide. These may include insurance commissions paid to agents and brokers, trading commissions paid to securities or foreign exchange traders or brokers, payments or commissions paid to members of the clearing organizations, commissions paid to credit agencies and commissions, or fees paid to research organizations that specialize in economic or industrial research.

The two main types of expense, apart from claims, for an insurance company are commissions and administration expenses. Commissions are paid to individuals or companies by the insurance company, principally for services rendered in acquiring business for the insurance company. They form the major part of acquisition costs, for example. Commissions are generally paid up front for new business; the insurance company may match these costs against the respective policy term, not as an expense for the full amount of these costs in the period in which they are incurred. An amount is therefore carried forward as deferred costs.

Trading, payments, and credit commissions tend to relate to individual transactions, although there may be a basic annual charge associated with maintenance of the relationship with the supplier. These costs can be assigned accurately to their activities, products, and services. Research costs, however, rarely relate to individual activities and may be incurred to support the general activity of trading in a particular market. In this instance, the cost is assigned to the product group, not to individual products or activities.

Operating Costs

Operating costs and overhead or support costs include both fixed and variable elements. Staff costs, for example, are semivariable and relate directly to the activities identified. They can therefore be classified by activity as direct or indirect. The truly variable staff costs (for example, overtime) are usually related to the volume of particular activities and can be accurately attributed. Facilities costs are generally fixed costs that may be apportioned to products or services on the basis of utilization (the trading room is attributed directly to the foreign exchange products, say), but there may be a significant proportion of administrative areas that must be treated separately. Information technology and communications costs are mainly fixed costs, although some variable components relate to the volume of activity. Other expenses include marketing and advertising, travel and entertainment, stationery, public relations, cafeteria, and distribution. These cost classifications are generally variable costs that may be directly attributable to products and services. But they may also be indirect costs that form part of the general overhead, which must be analyzed in more detail.

Operating costs within a financial institution normally include all direct costs relating to the provision of products and services to customers or other parts of the organization. These costs may be identifiable by organizational unit as direct costs before the allocation of overheads. Activities are identifiable in each cost center at the detailed level and are normally reported by expense type.

Types of expense shown in management reporting vary by organization. They generally include, as a minimum, staff, premises, equipment, and other direct costs. They may detail individual expense lines, as shown in the financial accounting system. Or they may ignore conventional accounting and analyze costs by business line, product, or service.

Overhead or Support Costs

Overhead or support costs may include all costs that are not directly attributable to products or services and that traditional cost accounting would apportion to products and services according to some standard allocation basis. The use of activity analysis and cost drivers allows for the factors that cause the expenditure to be identified and, hence, for the costs to be aligned, which is very helpful to the decision-making process. In the same way that activities are identifiable in each operational unit, activities should be agreed on for each overhead or support function. Each cost center normally receives a cost analysis reported by expense type.

For activity-based costing, it is necessary to separate the controllable costs from those costs allocated to the cost center. The controllable costs in a support function may include the same expense types that are controllable by the operating areas. They may also include other costs that are controllable at the more tactical or strategic level, such as premises/facilities, systems development, capital expenditure, and marketing, which form part of the core responsibility of that particular support center. All costs are ultimately controllable by someone within the organization, although it is not always easy to identify the relevant manager.

TIME FRAMES

Costs can be calculated on a variety of time frames. Historical costs generally relate to the actual costs for the previous period, which is usually the previous year. Actual costs are generally the costs of the current period and may need to be annualized for comparison. Budgeted costs are the cost plans that are normally agreed on before the period to which they relate. Forecast costs are the replanned figures, which are revised estimates of the projected expenditure. Long-term expenditure projections are estimates of future expenditure beyond the period covered by the budget or forecast.

Activity-based costing can be based on any of these cost types. Long-term expenditure projections are most useful, though, in strategic cost analysis and capital appraisals. Actual, budget, or forecast costs are more normally used for product costing, customer profitability, and operational cost management. Whatever basis is used, it is important that the volume of activities identified relate to the same time frame and are based on the same assumptions.

Costs are usually available within the organization at a cost center level and may include allocated costs from central support or service areas. Costs must be returned to the point of origin. This enables the analysis to be performed on direct costs, which can be more accurately attributed to cost drivers.

When the activity analysis and cost drivers have been analyzed, the associated costs and revenues can be estimated and the validity of the product definitions and cost drivers confirmed. Only when real costs and revenues are utilized will the users be able to focus on the definitions and review and agree on them in detail.

It is important to agree on the type of cost information to be used before beginning the analysis. Where budgets and/or forecasts are available at sufficient level of detail and can be associated with defined levels of activity and transaction volume, these may be the most appropriate costs on which to base the analysis. If the budgets have not been approved or verified by the individual line managers, then it may be more appropriate to use actual costs for a defined period over which the levels of activity and transaction volumes can be collected.

TOTALS AND SUBTOTALS

Any cost analysis should include all the costs of doing business in order to maintain integrity of the cost base. It is important, however, not to cloud the analysis by arbitrary allocation of costs just to ensure reconciliation to the financial accounts. The balance between the need to include all costs and the requirements of the decision-making process can be achieved by using reconciling statements and subtotals that highlight the key results.

For management decision making, activity-based costs can be reported as marginal costs, direct costs, or fully absorbed costs. How a financial institution defines costs in relation to strategic cost management or product costing is essentially a function of its management philosophy. Some managers prefer costs to be reported as fully absorbed—that is, with all fixed and variable costs included in the reporting. Others prefer costs to be reported with only those items that relate directly to the product or product group being analyzed.

Marginal costs are defined as those costs incurred by the production of an additional unit of an activity, product, or service that are also variable. Due to the relatively fixed nature of operating costs in most financial institutions, marginal costs are rarely relevant; generally, they include only interest, claims, commissions paid, and sundry direct expenses (stationery, for example). Marginal costs do not normally include the activity costs, as staff costs tend to be fixed costs, at least in the short term. There are, however, always exceptions to the norm. Some financial institutions employ operational staff on a piecework basis, and payment is related directly to the availability of work. This is particularly relevant in retail financial services in high-volume activities, such as check or credit card processing, where volumes fluctuate with customer demand.

Direct costs are defined as those prime costs incurred by the operating functions and exclude all indirect or overhead costs. Direct costs form the nucleus of activity-based costing. They generally include all costs that can be legitimately assigned to the activity, product, or customer. This includes interest, claims, commission paid, and all direct operating costs, as well as those support costs that can be assigned to an individual activity, product, or customer. These costs therefore exclude those items that can be assigned only to product groups or are classified as sustaining costs. Care must be taken to ensure that managers understand the definition of direct costs and the proportions of overhead or support costs that are excluded. Otherwise, they may assume that *all* costs have been apportioned and therefore that any income level that exceeds direct costs creates profit.

Fully absorbed costs are defined as a total of all fixed and variable costs that can be allotted to cost units. They are the basis of most traditional cost accounting systems and are easily reconcilable to the financial accounts since all costs are allocated to activities, products, or customers. They cloud the analysis performed in an activity-based costing exercise, however, in that they ignore the analysis of cost behavior and assume that all costs can be aligned with products and customers.

The most appropriate cost will vary depending on how the information is to be used. In strategic cost management, for example, where activity-based costing is used to identify the costs associated with a particular business activity or market, it is important to include all costs that can be attributed to the activity or market. The costs will, therefore, include all product-related expenditure and any sustaining costs that would change as a result of the strategic decision.

In product costing and customer profitability analysis, only the direct costs that relate to the provision of the product or service should be included. Although it is important to highlight the sustaining costs, to ensure that pricing decisions cover the full costs of the organization, these costs can be shown as a percentage increase in direct cost.

In operational cost management, all activity-related costs are analyzed, including all sustaining costs. Costs are classified as fundamental or discretionary, and attention may focus on the discretionary activities, but no costs should be excluded from the analysis and costs need not be allocated.

ASSIGNING COSTS TO ACTIVITIES

Assigning interest, claims, commissions and staff costs to the activities identified above should be relatively easy, but assigning information technology and communication systems costs can be much more difficult. Other costs will either be directly attributable to products, services, or customers (marketing costs, travel and entertainment, stationery, etc.) or be analyzed according to the use that will be made of the information. For example, premises/facilities costs can be attributed to products on the basis of staff utilization, but if they are to be reduced, then any apportionment may be counterproductive.

In some organizations, cost centers may be organized according to the support of particular products and services and may be easy to analyze. Branches, however, generally support a range of products and services and so must be analyzed in more detail. The following sections consider alternative techniques for assigning the various cost types to activities or cost drivers.

Assigning Staff Costs

Staff costs are normally assigned to the activities performed within the department or cost center on the basis of the time they take to perform.

As discussed in Chapter 4, "Agreeing on Activities," the activity analysis techniques of self-logging, historical averaging, relative values, activity sampling, stopwatch, and predetermined time standards have different characteristics. A choice has to be made.

All the activity analysis techniques will facilitate breaking down the staff-related costs of the department's activities. The process should also serve as a check that all activities have been identified by verifying that the total of all time allocated equals the available total hours.

Most financial institutions use at least two techniques to analyze the use of staff time by activity. They may also wish to use some statistical measurement to estimate the time associated with operational activities where there is a larger volume of the more repetitive tasks. They may also use some form of relative value analysis to estimate the time required for support or overhead activities, which could be more difficult to analyze using statistical techniques.

The results of relative value analysis can be used to calculate unit costs based on departmental staff costs. Relative value analysis can express activity times as proportions of a person-year. The annualized departmental staff cost can be divided by the total number of person-years available within the department to calculate the cost per person. This type of costing assumes that all person-years within the department have the same value and that staffing remains constant throughout the period to which the costs relate. It does, however, provide a quick and simple means of assigning costs to activities at a departmental level.

The costs of the activities for which minute values have been identified can be calculated in two ways. First, you can estimate the value of a minute in the relevant department by dividing the cost of the department by the total available staff time to calculate the value of the time taken to perform the activity. Or you can take the normal volume of activity within the department and calculate the number of productive minutes within the department before estimating the value of a minute on which to base the cost of each activity.

Using total available staff time to calculate the cost per minute does not include any idle time allowance. If the time taken to perform the total volume of activities does not equal the total available staff time, there will be unallocated staff costs that relate to the unutilized capacity in the department. Alternatively, using the normal volume of activity as the basis for estimating the number of productive minutes assumes that the department is working at full capacity and will allocate all departmental costs to the activities identified.

Assigning Systems Costs

Many IT and communication systems costs vary with the diversity of products offered, not with the volume of transactions. The system must have sufficient capacity, however, to cope with the maximum number of transactions that could be performed. It is not sufficient to apportion the activities within the systems department to the products, because many of the costs incurred are related, not to activities, but to other types of cost. In these circumstances, costs will be assigned to cost drivers, not to activities.

Typical cost drivers associated with IT and communications include the number of transactions processed, the level of service provided, the number and complexity of communication channels, the amount of storage required, the number of terminals supported, and the size and complexity of the network. The use of activity-based costing will determine the level of detail required for analysis of the systems-related costs. In most organizations, costs can be assigned to a business area or product group but are unlikely to be assigned to individual products or services unless a particular system or machine is used only by that product or service. Most costs, therefore, must be analyzed in a matrix, as shown in Table 6–2.

There are still costs within the systems department that may be classified as sustaining. These include the maintenance of supporting systems, such as the financial control systems and the operational control programs. The estimation of costs of duplicate facilities, system backup, and spare capacity remains an issue in activity-based costing, as in any other form of cost analysis.

TABLE 6–2
Analysis of checking account–related systems costs

Checking account services	Payment system	Account maintenance	Card management	ATM	Interbank clearing
Cash withdrawals		▓		▓	
Cash deposits		▓			▓
Check deposits		▓		▓	
Balance requests		▓			
Statement requests		▓			
Credit card issuance			▓		
Debit card issuance			▓		
Check card issuance			▓		▓
Credit card usage	▓		▓		▓
Debit card usage	▓	▓		▓	
Check usage	▓	▓			
Standing order payment	▓	▓			
Set up standing order	▓	▓			
Set up direct debit	▓	▓			
Direct deposit payment	▓	▓			▓
Account transfer	▓	▓			

Assigning Other Direct Costs

Other direct costs include marketing and advertising, travel and entertainment, stationery, public relations, cafeteria, and distribution costs. For product and customer analysis, some of these costs may be assigned directly to individual products, customers, or product groups.

Marketing, advertising, and public relations expenditures, for example, may relate to campaigns that support particular products or product groups. There may, however, be some marketing and advertising costs that cannot be assigned to specific products or business areas and are classified as sustaining costs.

Travel and entertainment expenses can, if necessary, be assigned to products or customer relationships. This level of detailed analysis can be undertaken for individual product and customer profitability but, unless the costs are material, they are normally included in staff costs and assigned to activities on the basis of time utilization.

Stationery costs can also be assigned to particular products or services, but again, unless the costs are material, they are normally included in staff costs and assigned on the basis of time utilization. Distribution costs could also be product-related—the distribution of checks, drafts, letters of credit, and securities, for example. Cafeteria costs, however, are rarely product-specific and may be treated as overhead costs, as discussed below.

Overhead and Support Costs

In the same way that activity-related costs are identifiable in each operational unit, they should be agreed on for each overhead or support function. Overhead and support functions could include premises/facilities, cafeteria, security, systems development, financial control, human resources, strategic planning, executive management, public relations, and marketing.

In a traditional cost accounting system, premises and security costs are normally calculated centrally and allocated to individual cost centers on the basis of floor utilization. In activity-based costing, these costs are monitored and controlled in relation to property management activities. They may be apportioned to product groups or business areas where this is relevant to the use of the information. The cost of a retail branch network, for example, may be included in an analysis of the retail banking activity within a financial institution.

Financial control, human resources, strategic planning, executive management, public relations, and corporate marketing are all part of the overall management of the business. Costs may be monitored and controlled by activity within the individual departments, but they should be assigned to products, customers, or business areas only where they are relevant to the business decisions.

SUMMARY

Costing is the process of identifying, measuring, assigning, and analyzing the expenses associated with items that are to be costed. These items may vary from activities to lines of business, individual products, customers, organizational units, or any definable output.

Costs within a financial institution can be classified into several basic types, including interest costs, claims, commissions paid, operating costs, and overhead or support costs. Interest costs, for example, are usually costs within financial institutions that can be attributed directly to a product. Claims costs are also costs that can be attributed to a particular policy type. Commissions may include insurance commissions paid to agents and brokers, trading commissions to securities or foreign exchange traders or brokers, payments commissions to members of the clearing organizations, commissions to credit agencies, and commissions or fees to research organizations that specialize in economic or industrial research. Most commissions paid can be assigned to products or product groups.

Operating costs within a financial institution normally include all direct costs relating to the provision of products and services to customers or other parts of the organization. These costs may be identifiable by organizational unit and can then be assigned to the activities performed within the operational area. Overhead or support costs may include all costs that are not directly attributable to products or services and that traditional cost accounting would apportion to products and services by some standard criterion. Activity analysis and cost drivers allow the factors that cause the expenditure to be identified and the costs to be aligned for the purpose of decision making. In the same way that activities are identifiable in each operational unit, activities should be agreed on for each overhead or support function and costs assigned in the same way.

Costs and revenues can be based on a variety of time frames. Historical, actual, budgeted, and forecast costs and long-term expenditure projections are all cost bases that may be used in activity-based costing.

Any cost analysis should include all the costs of doing business in order to maintain the integrity of the cost base. It is important, however, not to cloud the analysis by arbitrarily allocating costs just to reconcile the financial accounts. The balance between the need to include all costs and the requirements of the decision-making process can be achieved by reconciling statements and subtotals that highlight the key results.

Assigning interest, claims, commissions, and staff costs to activities should be relatively easy, but assigning IT and communication systems costs can be difficult. Other costs will either be directly attributable to products, services, or customers (marketing, travel and entertainment, stationery, etc.) or be analyzed by cost driver and included in the reporting according to the use that will be made of the information.

Chapter Seven

Implementation Issues

INTRODUCTION

Although there are many complicated issues associated with the definition and calculation of activity-based costs in any financial institution, the key to any successful system lies in its effective design and implementation. Previous chapters have concentrated on the definition of activities and cost drivers and the estimation of costs and revenues linking issues to the tasks included in phase two, "define reporting entities," and phase five, "determine costs and revenues." This chapter concentrates on the practical issues relating to phase three, "commence data collection," and phase four, "develop an activity-based costing system" (see Figure 7–1). It considers the types, sources and availability of data, systems solutions, likely modules, and operational considerations.

The key requirement for all data in activity-based costing is that it be available at the lowest level at which reporting is to occur. Whether activity-based costing is to be used for strategic cost management, product or customer cost and profitability analysis, or operational cost management, the cost and usage data must either be originally captured or be allocated to the lowest level of analysis required (that is, activity).

The primary sources of data are likely to include the general ledger system, the cost accounting system, and the budgeting and forecasting systems. The transaction processing systems, accounting applications (payroll, fixed assets, and the like), customer information file, and to a lesser extent, the administration systems, risk management systems, and trading systems may also provide information that enables more detailed analysis of usage and direct operating income and balances by product and customer. In addition, the accounting systems in different organizations carry varying degrees of information. Data that one institution receives from its general ledger, another institution must obtain from

FIGURE 7–1

The activity-based costing process, phases three and four

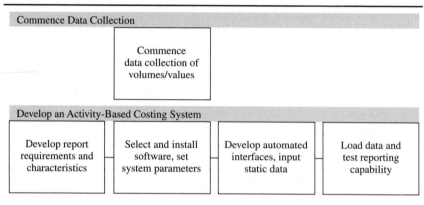

the application systems. Although it is preferable to avoid manual capture and entry of data into an activity-based costing system, some data requirements may not be met in any other way. Care must be taken to ensure that all data sources used are compatible and that the data can eventually be reconciled to the financial results.

In addition to the specific data required for profitability reporting to take place at the lowest level, a reporting system needs various calculation, accumulation, and history retention capabilities. The contents of a specific report often require calculations of subtotals, differences, ratios, averages, and so on from the data. A basic requirement of the system involves making sure all reporting characteristics and needs have been considered.

Just as there is no one correct approach to using activity-based costing information, there is no one system that will provide that information. This is not because software vendors are uninterested in developing such packages, but because of the complexity and individuality of a good activity-based costing system and the need to obtain data from transaction processing applications, customer databases, and financial systems.

Any package or custom activity-based costing system should include features that fall into two essential categories: cost accounting features (relating to the activity-based costing requirements) and profitability measurement and reporting features (which add the income, balance, and usage information to the activity-based cost analysis). While the requirements for a particular company will obviously be specific to it, the basic functional modules of cost and profitability reporting systems can be considered. The features may be modules of a separate cost and profitability system or other systems accessed to pull together the data required for cost and profitability reporting.

In implementing an activity-based costing system, some operations and maintenance factors also need to be considered. On a generic level, it is not possible to estimate the cost of these various factors, but in a specific situation the cost involved in operating and maintaining a system should be weighed against the value of the information to the institution. Human resources, data processing, and maintenance costs of the system may or may not be material to the decision to begin operating a system, but there will be an upper limit on the value of activity-based cost and profitability information.

DATA REQUIREMENTS

Cost and usage data can be originally captured or allocated to the lowest level of analysis required more easily when activity-based costing is used for cost control than for product or customer reporting. This is because most organizations utilize a responsibility accounting and reporting system subdivided into segments, often called cost centers or profit centers.

In general, the data required for product and customer reporting is more difficult to obtain by activity than is the data for cost control. Although the basic data is the same, it must be available with the desired product and/or customer identification. Cost data must, therefore, be analyzed below responsibility centers into individual activities performed to support defined products and services. Interest income, interest expense, and most other forms of revenue may be identifiable by product within the general ledger, but volumes and customer usage information will probably come from the transaction processing systems.

The data required for comprehensive customer reporting is the most difficult to obtain. Customer reporting usually depends on a customer information system that links all pieces of a customer's relationship with the institution together or, at least, on some common customer identification number. The normal financial accounting system plays virtually no role in customer reporting, as virtually no data within it can be associated with an individual customer because it is normally accumulated at a summary level prior to capture by the accounting system.

The characteristics of the data required for activity-based costing do not simply relate to the basic components of cost, income, balance, and usage data necessary to calculate the activity-based costs; they also include how information is summarized and reported. These characteristics include:

- The definitions of profitability used (controllable profits, marginal profits, fully absorbed profits).
- The components of income included.
- The components of cost and definitions to be used.
- The comparative data used (historical data, budgets, forecasts, other units, competitors).
- The definitions of ratios used.
- The specification of items included in subtotals and totals.

Types of Data

Data may be financial or statistical. Financial data includes interest income, premium income, fees and commissions, trading income, investment income, claims, operating expenses, and asset and liability balances. Statistical information may include volume and qualitative data by cost driver and usage data by product and customer. It may also include staff numbers, occupancy details, and other operational statistics to assist in the basic activity-based costing calculation. Whether data is financial or statistical, it may be reported as historical actual data or as projected data. Projected data is sometimes classified as budget, forecast, outlook, or plan data. Budget data is generally set at a point in time for a fixed future period. Forecast or outlook data tends to be dynamic and may be constantly revised to reflect what has taken place as well as the latest predictions for the future. Plan data, in the current year, should remain fixed.

Financial Data.   As defined above, financial data forms the core of most reports. Interest income is earned primarily from loans and deposits to and from customers. Premium income is earned from the amounts received for the policies written by the company. Fees and commissions are earned from a variety of sources, including loan arrangement, service charges, documentary services, foreign exchange, and advisory services. Trading and investment income is earned from investment and trading securities.

Expenses within a financial institution fall into several basic groups: interest costs, claims, commissions paid, operating costs, and overhead or support costs. Interest costs, for example, are usually costs within a financial institution that can be attributed directly to a product. Claims costs can be attributed to a particular policy type. Commissions may include insurance commissions paid to agents and brokers, trading commissions to securities or foreign exchange traders or brokers, payment commissions to members of the clearing organizations, commissions to credit agencies, and commissions or fees to research organizations that specialize in economic or industrial research. In general, all commissions paid can be assigned to products or product groups. Operating costs within a financial institution normally include all direct costs relating to the provision of products and services to customers or other parts of the institution. These costs may be identifiable by organizational unit and can be assigned to the activities performed within the operational area. Overhead or support costs may include all costs that are not directly attributable to products or services and that traditional cost accounting would apportion to products and services according to some standard. Activity analysis and cost drivers identify the factors that cause the expenditure to be incurred and, hence, provide the alignment of costs for decision making. In the same way that activities are identifiable in each operational unit, activities may be agreed on and costs assigned for each overhead or support function.

Assets and liabilities are reported either as average balances over a period of time or balances at a particular point in time. Due to the calculation of interest rates and yields, average balances are preferred. Asset balances may be categorized as earning (such as loans) or non-earning (such as fixed assets). Further distinctions are often made according to product type (e.g., commercial loans, real estate loans) and other subcategories.

Liability balances are usually reported by type and/or sensitivity. Several balance sheet accounts are frequently not captured at the lowest organizational product or customer level and may or may not be allocated. They include statutory reserves, equity, and loss reserves.

Statistical Data.   Statistical data is a key component of most activity-based costing reports. The statistical information may represent data at a point in time (number of accounts at month end) or accumulated data (number of activities performed per day). Some reports require that statistical information be expressed in financial terms but not be part of the financial results of the organization, such as waived fees or uncollected premiums.

SOURCES OF DATA

The primary sources of data required for activity-based costing and profitability reporting are the general ledger, cost accounting, budgeting and forecasting, and numerous product and special application systems. These application systems include transaction processing, accounting systems, management information (if present), and many others.

The general ledger in different companies carries varying degrees of information. Data that one company obtains from its general ledger, another must obtain from the application systems. Although it is preferable to avoid manual capture and entry of data into an activity-based costing system, some data requirements may not be met by any other means.

Systems That Must Be Accessed

Several main types of systems must be accessed to provide the basic components of data for any activity-based costing system, as Figure 7–3 will show later in this chapter.

Financial Accounting.   The capturing of income, expense, and balances data is the basic function of all general ledgers. This same data is the primary component of all cost and profitability measurement and reporting, but additional components are necessary to allow the analysis to be performed.

Transaction Processing.   These systems include the deposit, loan, trading, investment management, claim (life, disability, health, property), benefit payment (annuities, pensions), collection, investment trading, and policy management systems, as well as numerous transaction processing systems. Financial data generally interfaces from the systems with the general ledger, so when the level of data carried in the general ledger is not sufficient for cost and profitability reporting, transaction processing systems must be accessed. The types of data normally extracted from these systems include rates, average balances, income, waived and discounted fees and commissions, product volumes, and customer activity levels.

Some organizations use work measurement techniques to provide detailed costing, which may then be extended to produce activity-based costs for each product. However, this degree of detail is useless if revenues cannot be allocated as accurately, and revenue data is usually available in most detail from the transaction processing systems. Reports are only as accurate as the least accurate data within them.

Accounting Applications. These systems include the payroll and fixed assets systems, accounts payable, accounts receivable, and risk management. They represent the initial capture and processing point for various internal transactions not normally related to financial services activity. Financial data generally interfaces from these systems with the general ledger, so when the level of data carried in the general ledger is not sufficient for cost and profitability reporting, accounting application systems must be accessed. The types of data normally extracted from these systems include payroll expenses by responsibility center, staff numbers and availability, allocation of fixed assets, and direct expenditures relating to products and customers.

Although the fundamental data reported for activity-based costing by product is the same as in the institution as a whole, generally the level of detail required for product reporting precludes use of the general ledger, cost accounting, budgeting, and forecasting systems as the primary sources of data. Much of the information required for product costs and profitability reporting can be obtained from a comprehensive financial database that holds items with some form of product indicator. This type of system is becoming much more common. Where this is not the case, however, data must be analyzed outside the normal accounting framework, either manually or using other systems.

In general, transaction processing systems are the primary source for statistical information. The sources of income, balances, and cost data for product reporting could include the general ledger, cost accounting, budgeting and forecasting systems, but statistical and balance data are required to enable the activity-based costs to be calculated. All data sources used must be compatible and must eventually reconcile with the financial results.

Without such a system, income by product can be identified only by capturing income from the operational systems and feeding it directly into the activity-based costing system. When this cannot be achieved, data can be obtained by statistical sampling techniques, usually on a less regular basis. These techniques are likely to concentrate on the major products and services.

Customer Information Files.   Although customer identification is generally available in transaction processing systems, it is rarely if ever carried over to general ledgers. In addition, as transaction processing systems are rarely required to interface with each other, customer data is not related between the systems unless a customer information file system is in place. A customer information file is a key component in regular customer profitability reporting of any substantial magnitude. Some customer information file systems also have profitability reporting features.

Because the data required for customer reporting is the most difficult to manage—primarily due to the level of detail—the main sources of data required for customer reporting tend to be the customer information or operational application systems. Few, if any, cost accounting, budgeting, and forecasting or general ledger systems maintain customer-level detail. Some subsystems (direct billing systems) may contain customer-level information, but it will be limited to those products and services for which direct billing takes place. Although it is always preferable to avoid manual data capture, some data may require it.

Customer profitability reporting normally relies on accurate product information and the availability of additional information by customer. This information is rarely available in any accounting system. The most accurate approach is normally to use product costs that have been amended by adding in those cost elements that can be directly attributed to individual customers. Reliable customer reporting may be achieved only if product costs have been calculated and customer-specific income information can be incorporated with product costs based on usage statistics.

DATA AVAILABILITY

When any activity-based costing system is initiated, rarely will all requested data be available exactly as the user wants. Compromises, assumptions, and allocations may have to be made to attain the desired form of reporting. Sometimes these will be permanent if it is deemed too expensive to obtain the desired level of accuracy. Often, even if the budget does allow for the necessary changes in the long term, temporary solutions must be found while system changes or other procedures are put in place that will capture the necessary data.

One common issue arising in connection with activity-based costing is that data within the general ledger does not contain adequate detail. For example, general ledger accounts are generally established to reflect some categorization of the institution's assets and liabilities. It is unlikely that the accounts will also reflect every other way in which it might be meaningful to report. More often than not, a particular application system must be interrogated for information at a more detailed level.

Another common data availability problem occurs when, within the application system, the data is not accumulated in a form that makes it easy to retrieve. For example, although information may be available in the particular application system with a certain value, the information is generally not passed to the general ledger in the level of detail required. The data may not even be accumulated in the appropriate manner. To overcome this limitation permanently would require system modifications that might not be cost effective.

If data is to be reported for both actual and budget purposes, it is generally useful to have information at the same level of detail. Generally, budget figures are recorded at a higher level than is needed for reporting of actual costs. The budget may be prepared for key cost and income items within each cost center and so may not incorporate sufficient detail to allow analysis by activity or cost driver. There are two solutions. First, budgeting can be carried out at the activity level. Second, the budgeted costs and income can be apportioned to the lower level of detail required according to some criterion, such as last period's actual data.

Two more substantial data limitations occur when an institution does not have a responsibility accounting and reporting system and when balance sheet items are reported with balances only as of a point in time instead of averages over a time period. The lack of a responsibility reporting system can be overcome if allocations are based on samples, statistics, or the like, but this will be satisfactory for a one-time or special analysis, but not for ongoing reporting. In practice, most financial institutions now have some form of financial accounting or management information system by responsibility or cost center. Some banks still control all performance using the banking system, which will produce trial balance reports of operating income, costs, and balances. Administrative costs in these circumstances are normally controlled by a separate purchase ledger, which may be operated by a finance or purchasing department. The lack of average balances in such a system substantially limits the reasonableness of rate and yield calculations. To obtain average balances in these organizations, major system changes would be necessary, but they might not be justified.

The most common problem with regard to customer analysis is that all parts of the customer's relationship with the financial institutions are not identified and linked together in a way that facilitates reporting. This is not only a problem when reporting is initiated; it is an ongoing maintenance problem as the customer establishes new facilities and uses other products or services. Sometimes organizations have a customer information system, but it may not hold data on all the relationships that the customer has with every part of the organization.

Although customer identification exists within most application systems, the information may be difficult to retrieve. And certain identifying factors, such as customer segment, may not be readily available or may require conversion routines to be meaningful. As substantial systems changes are often called for in order to report needed information from the applications systems, the solution frequently involves development of a customer information file or other form of customer database.

REPORTING REQUIREMENTS

In addition to the specific data required for profitability reporting at the lowest level, a reporting system needs various calculation, accumulation, and history retention capabilities. The contents of a specific report often require calculations of subtotals, differences, ratios, averages, and the like from the data. In addition to the lowest level of activity, product or customer reports usually require the accumulation of several tiers within one or more hierarchies, at either the detail or summary level. Reports may present data from any of the following: current period, prior period, year-to-date, same period last year, or rolling month or period (3-month moving, 12-month moving) basis. The basic design of the system should ensure that all reporting characteristics have been considered. These include the following:

- The level of reporting provided.
- Definitions of reporting units used.
- The level of detail used for reporting.
- The degree to which sustaining or indirect costs are allocated to direct activity costs for reporting purposes.
- Users of the reports.
- Frequency of reporting.
- The acceptable lead time to produce the reports after close of business for data collection.
- The activity and cost driver definitions.
- The need for summary reports.
- Any foreign currency reporting requirements.
- Integrity of actual data.
- Report formats (amount of information per page, the narrative, graphic, and numeric presentation style).
- The maximum number of columns of numerical information shown on a report.
- The reporting media used (paper, on-line reporting, floppy disks, or microfiche).

In practice, users of the activity-based costing data should perceive the integrity of the reports as acceptable and should be able to reconcile the figures to the financial results. The reports should balance the need to be produced accurately with the need to have timely information, early enough after close of business. Indeed, it may be preferable to produce less accurate but adequate information in a more timely manner than completely accurate information too late to be useful.

It is important that the revenues, costs, and balances reported reflect the same level of activity, in terms of the timing of cost and income flows. Income may, for example, be received on a quarterly or semi-annual basis, while costs are incurred on a regular basis. If data is reported quarterly, any fees or commissions charged less frequently may be included as accrued or notional figures in the reports.

SYSTEMS SOLUTIONS

Just as there is no one correct approach to using activity-based costing information, there is no one system that will provide that information. The main advantage of custom software systems is that they can be constructed to closely match business requirements, both now and in the future. This usually implies a strong knowledge of costing techniques and systems analysis and is likely to require an extensive development period.

Software packages do exist but must be implemented and used in the most appropriate way to meet the specific needs of the institution. Currently, only a handful of suppliers actively market activity-based costing systems that are not aimed exclusively at manufacturing companies, although this is changing. Packages are available that can operate on mainframes and personal computers with varying levels of complexity and diversity of functions. Most packages are produced for personal computer usage and offer fairly basic ranges of functions. Also available are large embedded, advanced costing systems that form modules within complex manufacturing and accounting systems. Package solutions are likely to mean compromises in terms of the functions you want and the functions available or costly modifications to the standard system, but shorter development and implementation timetables can be achieved.

SYSTEMS MODULES

Any package or custom activity-based costing system should include features of two basic types: cost accounting features relating to the activity-based costing requirements and profitability measurement and reporting features that add the income, balance, and usage information to the activity-based cost analysis. While the requirements for a particular company are obviously specific to it, it is possible to consider the basic functional modules of cost and profitability reporting systems.

Cost measurement and reporting generally require some form of systems solution, as shown in Figure 7–2.

The features in Figure 7–2 may be modules of a separate cost and profitability system or may represent features of other systems that are accessed to pull together the data required for cost and profitability reporting. A general ledger system may be the key component of an activity-based costing system, but it will be unlikely to contain all data required for products and be even less likely to contain the data required for customer reporting. Further, with the increasing need for more sophisticated features, the possibility that all the capabilities will be found in a general ledger system decreases. There are two options at that point: First, develop separate modules to accomplish the special processing for products and customers not possible within the general ledger, while continuing to use the general ledger for basic profitability reporting. Second, develop a separate profitability reporting system that not only performs some of the special processing but is the primary reporting tool relegating the general ledger to the role of one of the principal data sources.

The modules required to enhance or amend a general ledger system will increase the complexity of the required reporting. Each module identified in Figure 7–3 is discussed here. Those modules that perform processing activities are discussed in sufficient detail to establish their input, process, and output operations.

Cost Accounting Module

The cost accounting module may have two separate functions: cost development and cost transfer. A cost development module is used to analyze the support and overhead costs to identify the unit costs. These unit costs or values are then input to the cost transfer module. Inputs to this module could include support and overhead costs, activity levels, definitions of activities, and cost components to be included in activity-based costs. Processes to be completed within this module may comprise calculation of activity-based costs and identification of sustaining costs that may be allocated. Outputs from the module may include activity-based costs accumulated as necessary to meet reporting needs. A cost transfer module assigns costs from one entity to one or many entities (organizations, products, or customers) utilizing specific rules. The rules may be activity-based or higher level allocation bases.

FIGURE 7–2
Systems solutions

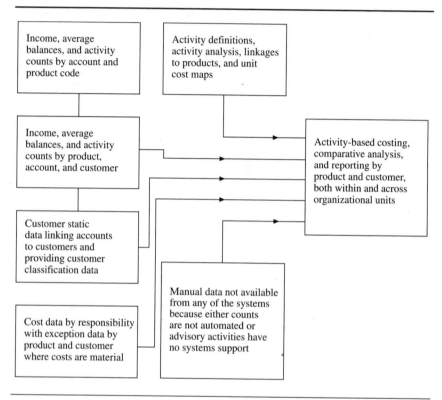

Funds Transfer Pricing Module

The transfer of the costs associated with the use of funds and the credits associated with providing funds is one type of transfer that can become very complicated and require a special system.

Inputs to this module normally include interest rates used in transaction processing systems; balances by pool, activity, responsibility center, product, or customer to which the rates should be applied; and internal transfer rates to be used for each pool. The module may calculate the cost of funds and earnings credits, which should be applied to each balance.

FIGURE 7–3
Modules to enhance general ledgers

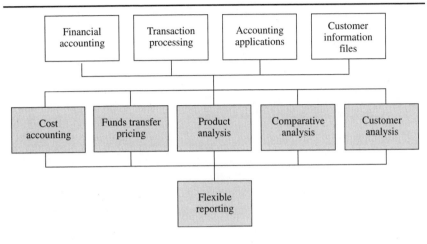

Outputs from this module normally are the cost of funds and earnings credits that have been transferred and the activities, products, or customers to which the debits and credits relate.

Product Analysis Module

Product data is normally available either from the general ledger or directly from the transaction processing systems. The raw data must be analyzed by product using the activity-based indicators that link the core costs and activities to products and services by using cost drivers. This analysis must be performed and stored to enable further analysis of data relating to differing time periods.

All data modules discussed here will provide data by activity within responsibility center or product that must be consolidated or stored. The information should ideally be stored separately so that the direct activity costs of fundamental and discretionary activities and the sustaining costs can be itemized on reports for the individual managers responsible for the cost or profitability. Depending on the number of components required, this may require a large storage capacity.

Inputs to the product analysis module normally include income, expenses, balances, volumes, and interrelationships by product or activity. The process that takes place within the module is the quantification and calculation of costs and income by product or type of business. Outputs from the module are the standard or actual costs and revenues by product or type of business.

Comparative Analysis Module

The most common comparative data used in cost and profitability reporting is budget data. Budgeting systems may be part of the general ledger or a separate system. Budget information is most frequently developed along the lines of organization or responsibility centers and based on historical information. Budgeting systems for product and customer data are less common.

Inputs to a budgeting module normally include historical income, expenses, balances, volumes, assumptions, and projections. The process that takes place within the module is the quantification and calculation of plans and budgets by activity within organizational unit or product. Outputs from the module are the budgets by activity within responsibility center and/or product.

Another common form of comparative data is historical information, which may be retained in the general ledger (if originally captured there) or maintained in separate historical data files. Like other data not in the general ledger, historical data may be maintained in the transaction processing or application systems.

Customer Analysis Module

Where customer profitability reporting is required, the data by product must be further analyzed by customer or customer group and then consolidated and stored. As with other activity-based information by product and responsibility center, it should ideally be stored separately so the direct activity costs of fundamental and discretionary activities and the sustaining costs can be itemized on reports for the individual managers responsible for the customers concerned. Depending on the number of customers or customer groups reported, this may require a large storage capacity.

Flexible Reporting Module

Any system needs the ability to report the results of cost and profitability measurement with desired flexibility and frequency and through the desired media. The degree of flexibility available will depend on the amount of information accumulated and stored in the modules discussed above and on the information's accessibility.

OPERATIONAL CONSIDERATIONS

Generally, it is not possible to estimate the cost of the operations and maintenance factors that should be considered in developing or evaluating a system for cost and profitability reporting in financial institutions. But in a specific situation, the cost of operating and maintaining a system should be considered, together with the value of the information to the company. Human resources costs, data processing costs, and the cost of maintaining a system may or may not be material to the decision to begin its operation. But whatever its cost, there will be a limit to the value of the cost and profitability information it produces. Operational considerations include cost implications, time constraints, and maintenance of information.

Operational Cost Implications

Whether a cost and profitability measurement and reporting system is mainframe-based, PC-based, manual, or any combination of these, data must be input into the system, processed, and output produced, analyzed, and distributed.

For data to be input, it must be accumulated either within automated systems or manually. If it is accumulated within an automated system, such as an operational processing system or the general ledger, there is the expense within the computer of accumulating, storing, and in some manner reporting or interfacing the data. If accumulated manually, the costs of staff, including salaries and benefits, must be considered.

Data may be automatically interfaced or manually entered. Both cost and control factors associated with data entry must be considered. Costs include those of computer terminals, telecommunications, computer storage and run time, and people costs. As the level of manual data collection and input into a system increases, the risk of errors also increases. Balancing procedures and controls must be established to ensure the continued accuracy and integrity of both manual and automated data capture.

Unless a system is entirely manual, most processing costs are computer related. Depending on the amount of data to be processed, the efficiency of the system, and the frequency with which data is processed, the costs associated with the system will vary extensively. If a system is mainframe-based, there may be times when access is limited or the ability to process the system is controlled by other priorities. One advantage of smaller computer systems is that they are often under the full control of the user.

Output from a system may take several forms. Traditionally, the most common form has been printed paper reports, with the associated costs of printers, paper, and report distribution. The trend is toward more on-line access to the output or results of cost and profitability reporting systems. This access may be provided in many different ways with different costs, access, and control implications.

There are generally employees responsible for the maintenance and analysis of any cost and profitability reporting system. Immediately after output is generated, these employees will review the output and perhaps further analyze the results. To be integrated into the decision-making process of the company, the results must be available for review by appropriate managers throughout the institution. All of these steps require time and therefore generate expense.

Time Constraints

Other concerns that affect the operation of a system are the frequency with which the system is run and the time constraints under which results must be produced. If results are required within two days of period end instead of, for instance, 10 days, operation of the system may be more expensive and there may be a greater risk of errors. Regardless of the time constraints or frequency, the logistics of operating a system that relies on data from numerous sources must be thoroughly documented, including what data is needed, where that data comes from, where it goes, who is responsible for it, and the steps in the system's operation.

Maintenance of Information

Corporations and the systems that support decision making do not remain constant. Not only has the financial industry been changing over the past few years, but technology advances so fast that systems of just a few years ago are obsolete.

Recurring causes of maintenance of cost and profitability reporting systems include changes to the definitions of activities, revisions to activity-based costing assumptions, changes within the organizational structure, new systems and products, and growth within the organization.

Regardless of the uses for or level of detail within the activity-based costing system, the data must be updated periodically. Maintenance of cost accounting data will depend on the level of detail required, the frequency of updates, and the availability of data needed for updates. After cost accounting data is revised, entry into the system and confirmation of the data will require resources.

Changes within the organization can take many forms. They may affect the staff time required to generate cost and profitability reporting and may also require system maintenance. Often sufficient time is not available to make the needed changes to the system before the change, so temporary solutions must be found. The most common change is that a company will reorganize itself and so require its cost and profitability reporting to reflect the new organization. A system must be flexible enough to accept organizational changes. Sometimes historical data may be requested but must take into account the new organizational reporting structure. In other instances, the historical data may need to retain the former reporting structure. Organizational changes are often effected with a new budget cycle, so the system must maintain two structures— one for actual and another for budget accounts.

When new application systems are installed, the impact on the existing cost and profitability reporting system must be considered. The continued availability of current data, the possibility of obtaining new, previously unavailable data, and the maintenance or expansion of interfaces, downloading and uploading capabilities, and so on must be examined.

In addition to new systems, new products and services will be offered by the institution. The system should be flexible enough that the new products can be integrated into the system. As most cost and profitability systems interface closely with the general ledger system, the ability to recognize and handle new general ledger systems, new general ledger account numbers, and new responsibility centers should be available. The inability of the system to adapt to any of these changes will require substantial human intervention and, potentially, expensive maintenance.

Growth within the institution can mean that the system requires maintenance from several directions. First, size constraints may appear—number of units, products, activities, customers; levels and hierarchies for pyramiding of reporting; absolute size of data fields for both statistical and financial information. Second, as the company grows and as time passes, the retention of historical data may become impossible or very expensive. Growth of the company because of mergers and acquisitions can put pressure on a system and require considerable maintenance. Indeed, this may result in the integration of multiple charts of accounts and application systems.

There are other operations and maintenance considerations, but each situation will have unique characteristics that deserve careful evaluation at the outset. The important thing to remember is that the development and installation of a cost and profitability measurement and reporting system are not the only factors to consider. The ongoing operation of that system and its future maintenance also affect its design and success.

SUMMARY

The key requirement for all data in activity-based costing is that it be available at the lowest level at which reporting is to occur. The primary sources of data are the general ledger, cost accounting, and budgeting and forecasting systems. The transaction processing, administration, risk management, and trading systems may also provide information that will yield a more detailed analysis of usage and direct operating income and balances by product and customer. All data sources used must be compatible and the data must eventually reconcile to the financial results.

In addition to the specific data required for activity-based cost analysis, a reporting system requires various calculation, accumulation, and history retention capabilities. The contents of a specific report often require calculations of the subtotals, differences, ratios, averages, and so on from the data.

Just as there is no one correct approach to using activity-based cost-ing information, there is no one system that will provide that informa-tion. While the requirements of a particular company are obviously specific to it, the basic functional modules of cost and profitability reporting systems apply almost universally. The features may be modules of a separate cost and profitability system or may represent features of other systems that are accessed to pull together the data required for cost and profitability reporting.

When implementing an activity-based costing system, you should consider operations and maintenance factors. In a specific situation, the cost of operating and maintaining a system should be weighed against the value of the information it produces to the company. Human resources, data processing, and maintenance costs of the system may or may not be material to the decision to begin operation of the system, but there is a limit to the value of activity-based cost and profitability informa-tion. That is, there comes a point at which you are putting in more than you are getting out.

Chapter Eight

Using Activity-Based Costing for Strategic Cost Management

INTRODUCTION

Strategic cost management is an activity that is just becoming popular in the financial sector. Under the present competitive and economic environment, the potential for mergers and takeovers among banks and insurance companies is growing. This leads to board-level attention to the vulnerability of the institution's profitability.

The executive team must understand the dynamics of the strategic cost and income profiles within the organization and ensure that the strategic goals concentrate on improving shareholder value in both the short and longer term. This can be achieved only by also understanding the factors that affect the profitability of the various aspects of the business and the impact of changes on the market's perception of the value of the organization.

The following sections discuss the determination of strategic direction and definitions of strategic cost drivers. A demonstration of the use of activity-based costing in strategic cost management in the case of a bank follows.

DETERMINING STRATEGIC DIRECTION

The fundamental objective of any organization is to maximize its value to shareholders, yet, according to a survey in the United States, the great majority of banks lack the tools to achieve this objective. The value of a company to its shareholders can be defined as expected future worth as estimated by those with an equity stake in the organization. A typical financial institution includes a variety of business activities, some of which may be unprofitable. Management needs to know the impact of each part of its business on the institution and how it is likely to change over time.

Strategic Planning

Activity-based costing can be used in strategic planning to focus attention on those factors that determine the expenditure on business activities. It can assist in the prioritization of alternative business activities, providing information relating to the cost/benefit to be derived from the particular businesses, geographic markets, products, or customer groups and the potential benefit to be derived from future investment in particular strategic directions.

The main use of activity-based costing in strategic planning is in identifying flexibility within the cost base. This flexibility relates to the ability to utilize costs already incurred to gain competitive advantage and the knowledge of the incremental expenditure necessary to pursue a change in direction. Activity-based costing can also be used in the development of value chain analysis to break down the strategically relevant activities in order to understand the behavior of costs. The value chain considers the cost/price relationship and ways value can be added to differentiate the products or maximize the price that can be realized.

Activities are defined as the types of business executed by the institution, normally analyzed by market, either geographic (state or region) or type of customer (retail, high net worth, corporate, or international). Cost drivers relate primarily to volumes of activity, service, quality, and technology.

As discussed in Chapter 1, another powerful application of activity-based costing is in analyzing performance of groups of products/services within and across strategic groups. Products/services may be categorized into two or more strategic groups. Activity information can then be used to generate performance reports in each category. This helps senior management evaluate how each strategic group is performing and base strategic plans on that evaluation.

Resource Management

Activity-based costing can be used to focus attention on those factors that determine the expenditure on key projects or activities. It can help in the cost/benefit analysis of individual projects and hence assist the prioritization of alternative projects, managing resources to maximize the return on investment in line with the strategic direction of the institution.

It identifies the reasons why costs are incurred and relates these to the activities that take place. It can, therefore, be used to determine when costs should be incurred (such as when to diversify and move into a new business area). This will enable management to manage costs on the basis of spending (the investment in a new market or business activity), not consumption (the operation of the business). Such a focus ensures that organizations evaluate the costs associated with each strategic decision well in advance.

STRATEGIC COST DRIVERS

The rate of return to shareholders is based on the key factors that drive both cost and revenue for the organization as a whole. These are generally of four types:

- The competitive position of the organization.
- The volume dynamics within the various business activities.
- The cost/quality balance.
- The degree to which technology is used to support the effective and efficient operation of the company and to help it respond to changes in the market.

Competitive Position

The competitive position of the institution is a function of its market share, product differentiation, market volatility, economic environment, and the internal cost/income profiles of the various aspects of the business.

Market share can be measured at a variety of levels. A bank may, for example, have a large share of the retail market but specialize in secured lending to certain customer types and have a much smaller market share of depository and unsecured lending business. Some markets are heavily dominated by a few participants. This may be a result of the presence of entry barriers to certain businesses which require heavy investment in order to even enter the market (life insurance, for

example, where administrative expenses and claims arise before sufficient premium income has been accumulated). Or it may be caused by
the degree of control exercised by the regulators.

Market shares are measured and monitored regularly by financial
analysts, and the position of the organization in relation to the competition
at corporate, business, and product level can be easily identified.

All financial institutions have at least an implicit strategy relating to
product development and product differentiation. They can adopt one
of the following strategies:

- Market makers.
- Reactors.
- Conservatives.

Market makers are normally the first organizations to initiate a particular new product or line of business. For example, a market maker
may be the first to market a phone banking service. Reactors watch the
market makers carefully and decide whether or not to follow with a
competitive offering. Conservative organizations watch the market makers
and reactors carefully but are unlikely to follow until the product or
market has reached the maturity stage of its life cycle and all development risks have been eliminated.

Product differentiation may be as simple as repackaging or repricing existing products. The breakdown of entry barriers in the credit
card business, for example, has seen the emergence of a number of
new entrants. Automakers like GM and Ford have introduced credit
cards with bonuses that are applied to the purchase of their cars. Airlines
followed, with bonuses applied to their frequent flyer programs. Financial institutions today are responding by waiving annual fees and drop-
ping interest rates.

Market volatility also affects a company's competitive position;
a dynamic market will be more changeable and the strengths and
weaknesses of the organization in the marketplace will influence its
competitive balance. Corporate finance activity and the Lloyds insurance market are two examples of volatile markets where the position of the organization is influenced by the level and diversity of
customer demand. The degree of specialization within the organization means that its position in the market is governed, to a large
extent, by the degree of customer demand for the special services
provided.

Competitive position is affected by economic conditions to the extent that some organizations may be less influenced by the changes in interest rates, exchange rates, inflation, political factors, and other economic effects. Also, those organizations that successfully predict and benefit from changes in economic conditions are likely to provide the highest value to their shareholders (at least in the short term).

The internal cost/income profiles of the various aspects of a business may influence the competitive position of the organization, at least indirectly. The impact of several of the environmental conditions mentioned above will be a function of the cost/income profiles within the organization. The inherent profitability and risk/reward relationships of the various aspects of a business should influence its corporate strategy and, hence, its competitive position. It would be an unusual strategy for a company to aim to be the market leader in a business in which it was losing money in the longer term, but it could form part of an overall corporate plan to buy into a market, recognizing that this involves incurring losses in the short term.

Volume Dynamics

The volume dynamics within the various business activities must be understood by those individuals with responsibility for enhancing a company's value to its shareholders. Factors that should be considered include the key step costs, the impact of excess capacity, the impact of changes in product mix, and the volatility of the underlying cost base.

Strategic changes in business volumes can have a significant impact on the dynamics of the cost base. The step cost principle assumes that the consequences of increases in volume are known and reflected in strategic decision making. One of the complications encountered in step costs in the financial sector is that incremental costs can be triggered by a range of volume changes and so are rarely linked to one isolated factor. A new computer, for example, will be required to handle increases in volumes across a range of business activities, and any increase may have only an incremental impact.

Alternatively, where excess capacity exists, costs are incurred and volumes can be increased at little incremental cost. Many costs in the financial sector are fixed in nature and so bear little relationship to business volumes in other sectors. Excess capacity is an opportunity to provide an additional contribution to fixed costs and profitability, but it must be managed to ensure that it does not cross the boundary and create additional fixed costs when the excess capacity has been used.

The product mix may have a significant impact on a company's value to its shareholders in that the balance of profitable and unprofitable products needed to maintain the competitive position must be monitored carefully to ensure that profitability is maximized within the levels of capacity and cost profiles are attainable within the equity base.

Given the emphasis on fixed costs in the financial sector, cost volatility should not be a problem. Unfortunately, although a large proportion of operating and overhead costs may be fixed (at least in the short term), interest and claims-related costs can be very volatile and therefore require careful management to minimize exposure. There are many sophisticated techniques, such as simulation and duration analysis, that can provide detailed evaluation of the risk and volatility profiles of the interest-rate costs, but these are usually the domain of the finance function and so are outside the scope of this book.

Cost/Quality Balance

The cost/quality balance is important in any strategic review, and the drivers associated with the provision of all components of financial services can be considered in six segments of the value chain, as shown in Figure 8–1.

Product Development. Cost/quality factors in product development relate to the balance among innovation, complexity, and the need to maintain profitability in the short and longer term. Innovation in products tends to involve new systems and procedures to enable staff and customers to understand the product or service and the associated benefits. Alternatively, product tailoring or product differentiation may be achievable quickly and easily in response to competitive action but may be perceived by the customer as less innovative. Innovation is expected in some parts of the industry—capital markets, corporate finance, and, to a lesser extent, investment management are all areas where customers may be attracted by innovative developments within the institution. There may also be a delicate balance between product complexity and understandability. An example is a bank that simplified its range of checking accounts to three types of accounts with

FIGURE 8–1
Segments of the value chain

Product development	Processing	Distribution	Risk management	Customer service	Marketing and sales
Innovation	Accuracy	Proximity	Quality of analysis	Accuracy	Speed of response
Product tailoring	Speed of response	Speed of delivery	Completeness	Speed	Brand names
Complexity	Speed of processing	Convenience		Service level	

differing and complicated fee schedules. Although market research suggested that the three types most closely matched customer requirements, neither the customers nor, to some extent, the staff understood the accounts in detail. They preferred to stay with the traditional product types.

Processing. The key factors that affect the cost and revenue flows of transaction processing relate to the need to balance accuracy of processing with the speed and cost of the operations. The strategic goals of the organization should include the factors that drive the operational efficiency of the processing of products and services offered and may differentiate the levels of accuracy, response, and speed needed for different types of customers or levels of service.

Accuracy of processing should be an important factor in the management of any financial institution. Accuracy can continually be improved by the introduction of additional checks and controls, but these will affect both the speed of the operation and the costs associated with processing transactions. Technology can improve the efficiency and accuracy of processing, but there may be costs connected with the automation of the operations, and the training of staff (and possibly customers) in new techniques and procedures.

Speed of response and speed of processing are separate factors that will affect the cost and quality of operational processing and may be defined differently for different types of customers and products. Speed of response may involve no more than confirming to the customer that his or her instructions have been received and are understood. This may be more important in private banking than in other retail financial services, but it could differentiate the product in the competitive marketplace.

Speed of processing includes completion of the operations necessary to ensure that the instructions received can be carried out effectively. Corporate financial services must generally be processed quickly, since the value of large sums of money depends on interest rates and exchange rates, which vary over time. Penalty interest may be payable if the needed amounts are not made available on a timely basis. There may be an opportunity to differentiate services by providing a cheaper service at a slower rate or simply balancing response and operational efficiency. However, in today's competitive environment, financial institutions are finding that they simply have to provide fast and efficient services at low cost. Many are implementing quality programs that improve efficiency *and* reduce cost. Activity-based costing projects can help this process by providing activity cost intelligence and identifying activities that do not add value.

Distribution.   One key factor that can affect the cost and revenue of any financial institution is the distribution of the products and services offered. This may be analyzed by type of customer, geographic location, or type of distribution channel. Any analysis must, however, consider the proximity of provision of the service (both relationship management and operational support), the speed of delivery, and the convenience to the customer.

In general, proximity to the customer is less of an issue in commercial financial services than in retail financial services, because most corporations handle much of their financial business by telephone and fax. Only when original documentation is required (trade finance and final signed contracts) or when an account officer visits a customer does physical location become important.

Proximity and convenience of retail outlets may be important to retail customers, because of both the need to obtain cash from branches of the bank or automated teller machines (ATMs) and the need to obtain application forms or signatures for insurance or loans. When a bank or insurance company reviews its physical locations, it must consider the impact of any closure or relocation on the retention of its customers, both the actual customers with accounts or policies at that office and those who use the office as a convenient point of access to the organization, even though their accounts or policies may be based at other offices.

Convenience of business hours must also be considered and the emergence of telephone banking and insurance sales have reduced customers' dependence on retail counter services. This does, however, have the negative effect of reducing opportunities to cross-sell other financial services. This factor has forced financial institutions to use mailings and telephone solicitations to market other services. In the insurance industry, agents are encouraged to market additional services, and there is extensive direct mail marketing. However, branches continue to be useful sales outlets, enabling financial institutions to promote their services to a target market at minimal incremental cost.

The location of processing centers may also be an issue to the organization. Economies of scale may be obtained by concentrating or grouping processing operations in regional or centralized centers. Any physical documents (checks, debit and credit card vouchers, shipping documents, contracts, and the like) must then be transported to the centers for processing. The cost of distribution and the time lost in their physical transportation must be evaluated as part of the strategic review.

Speed of delivery may be an issue in commercial financial services when documents must be made available at particular times. However, this is more likely to be an operational issue, as discussed above.

Risk Management.   Risk management may also form a key component of any strategic review of cost and revenue in terms of both the quality of the analysis available to enable management to manage all types of risk and the completeness of the information.

Risks vary by type of business and type of customer, and the strategy of each business activity should include a statement on the level of risk acceptable to the institution.

The cost of products and services will be affected by the risk premium that must be applied to counter the types of risk and their likelihood. Risk is therefore a key strategic cost driver for any financial institution and is affected by external factors and the corporate strategy.

Customer Service.   Factors that affect the level of service provided to customers must be considered in the cost/quality balance. Some have already been touched on, but they should be related directly to the quality of customer service as a key to maintaining and improving the value of a company's stock to the shareholders, both in the tangible sense of maximizing returns and the intangible value of quality customer care.

Accuracy remains a key factor in customer service in any financial institution. It is important that the organization is seen to take sufficient care with individual transactions to ensure that values, rates, accounts, and value dates are accurate.

Speed of customer service relates to both response times and processing times. Speed of response may often be more important than speed of processing. Service levels can be a key factor in differentiating products and services both within the organization and from those of competitors.

Marketing and Sales. Speed of response to new offerings in the marketplace is normally a strategic decision. All financial institutions have at least an implicit strategy relating to their responses to competitive activity (either new products or changes in prices or rates). They may be market makers, reactors, or conservatives, as discussed earlier.

Brand names are becoming more important in the retail financial sector as the degree of competition increases. Many institutions have differentiated their products and services by using different distribution channels and different service levels. Effective product differentiation may be as simple as repackaging, renaming, or repricing existing products.

Technology

The degree to which technology is used to support the effective and efficient operation of any financial institution and the extent to which technological solutions assist the organization in responding to change in the market can have a significant effect on shareholder value. The factors that drive the costs associated with the use of technology are generally strategic in nature. Investment in technology has a material impact on the overall cost structure of any organization.

The strategic cost drivers associated with technology include the extent and suitability of automation, the degree of innovation, capacity utilization, and the level of integration.

Automation.   The extent to which the delivery of products and services can be automated and how suitable existing systems are to deliver the products and services demanded by customers will have a significant impact on the cost base. The need to replace existing systems (which may have been built on old technology, using out-of-date design and delivering services that are no longer required) can have a material impact on short-term profitability. In the longer term, providing more up-to-date systems that are geared to meeting the needs of the current customer base should improve profitability. Technology will, however, continue to date and will eventually need replacing again.

Innovation.   All financial institutions must innovate to some extent. Retail organizations must maintain or improve their market share by offering distinctive products and services. Capital markets, merchant banking, and corporate finance operations must continually create products that meet customer needs. This need for innovative products and services must be reflected in the flexibility of the underlying technology to deliver, or at least record, the resulting transactions. This is not easy to achieve in practice. The need for technology capable of delivering new products efficiently will therefore be a key cost driver.

Capacity.   Systems must be capable of handling the peak transaction throughput within predefined time frames. Maximum utilization may occur either during working hours (in dealing rooms, for example) or in the overnight processing runs (when accounting systems are maintained and daily transactions consolidated). Inevitably, systems will operate below full capacity for some period of time during the day or week.

Most financial institutions also require duplicate machines to ensure that business can be maintained if one computer develops a fault or loses power. These parallel machines are normally maintained at separate locations with at least partial duplication of facilities. This inevitably results in significant excess capacity, which can be utilized for any systems that are not time critical and halted if the facilities are required for the main banking systems.

Capacity utilization is a strategic cost driver in that the step cost principle applies. Any increase in transaction volume will have an impact on capacity utilization and may, therefore, result in the need to enlarge the systems environment. This may result in significant additional cost.

Integration.   Integration of systems can result in more error-free, efficient processing because it reduces the need for rekeying data when transferring it from one system to another. Unfortunately, many financial institutions have a variety of systems that have been developed over time and may be difficult to integrate. The organization that has integrated systems may have a strategic advantage. It is important that the institution has a coherent systems strategy that does not change too frequently, ensuring that any developments can be integrated into existing systems.

Case Study I

ABC Bank

ABC Bank is an international bank with a variety of financial services that it offers to both retail and corporate customers throughout the world. It is about to undertake a strategic review of its operations with a view to planning its long-term growth and wishes to analyze the profitability of the various activities it undertakes. This should enable senior management to review the key factors that affect the strategic emphasis on the business activities and the components of the value chain and identify areas of strength or weakness. Other studies will be undertaken in parallel to review its market position and vulnerability to competition in the markets in which it operates.

BACKGROUND

ABC Bank has operations in retail, corporate, and international financial services. Its activities are shown in Table 8–1.

ABC Bank operates in 10 countries: the United States, Europe (England, Scotland, Switzerland, Spain, Germany, and the Netherlands), Australia, Japan, and Hong Kong. It is organized into three geographic profit centers: the U. S. head office, Europe, and the rest of the world. The annual financial summary is shown as Table 8–2. There is currently no regular analysis business or customer type. The types of business by country are shown in Table 8–3.

TABLE 8–1
ABC Bank—analysis of business activities

Branch networks and retail delivery	Banking operations and IT	Management structures/ central functions	Corporate and institutional banking	Private banking and investment management
Branch networks ATMs Card services Insurance Leasing	Banking operations IT	Senior management Finance Human resources Other central functions	Treasury and capital markets Corporate banking Correspondent banking International banking services Developing countries Corporate finance	Private banking Investment management Global custody Offshore trust business

The income is easily analyzed by business type from the chart of accounts and can therefore by obtained from the trial balance, as shown in Table 8–4. Cost analysis is more difficult but is necessary in order to analyze the profitability of the various activities undertaken and identify the key cost drivers that affect the strategic emphasis on the business activities and the components of the value chain.

APPROACH

The approach to be undertaken is discussed in Chapter 3, "The Framework for Activity-Based Costing Implementation." Its practical application to ABC Bank follows.

Review and Confirm Requirements

The first step in the development of any activity-based cost analysis is to interview key users and identify information requirements, taking account of best market practice and experience. The ABC Bank wants strategic cost information that will let it analyze the profitability of the

TABLE 8–2
ABC Bank—profit statement 199x ($000s)

	United States	Europe	Rest of world	Total
Net interest income before provisions	$ 2,520	$ 720	$ 0	$ 3,240
Provisions	(2,141)	(337)	(83)	(2,561)
Net interest income after provisions	379	383	(83)	679
FX income	$ 628	$ 428	$ 245	$ 1,301
Fees and commissions	1,246	1,424	30	2,700
Other income	66	18	45	129
Total revenues	$ 2,319	$ 2,253	$ 237	$ 4,809
Human resource costs	$(1,686)	$ (630)	$(118)	$(2,434)
Premises cost	(270)	(102)	(71)	(443)
Systems costs	(218)	(24)	(8)	(250)
Other costs	(432)	(54)	(11)	(497)
Total costs	$(2,606)	$ (810)	$(208)	$(3,624)
Income before taxes	$ (287)	$(1,443)	$ (29)	$(1,185)
Taxes				(285)
Net income				$ (900)

various activities undertaken and identify the key cost drivers that affect the strategic emphasis on the areas of business and the components of the value chain.

Define Reporting Entities

ABC Bank has identified its business activities as shown in Table 8–1. It is now necessary to define in more detail the products and services offered to the customers in each country.

Define Products and Transactions. Table 8–3 shows the areas of business by country, and the income can be taken from the trial balance, shown in Table 8–4. The individual account lines in the chart of accounts may define the products or areas of business in sufficient detail to be used as the basis of cost analysis. Further analysis at transaction level

TABLE 8–3
ABC Bank—country analysis

Areas of business	U.S.	England	Scotland	Switzerland	Spain	Germany	Netherlands	Australia	Japan	Hong Kong
Branch network	■	■								
ATMs	■		■							
Cards	■		■							
Insurance	■				■					
Leasing	■				■					
Treasury and capital markets		■		■		■		■		
Corporate banking	■			■		■	■		■	■
Correspondent banking	■	■								■
International banking		■				■		■	■	■
Developing countries	■									
Corporate finance	■									
Private banking				■	■					
Investment management	■									
Global custody	■			■						
Offshore trust										■

TABLE 8–4
ABC Bank—excerpt from trial balance, year ended 199x

Business activity	Country	Income
Branch network	U.S.	$2,520
Branch network	Scotland	720
Cards	U.S.	233
Cards	Scotland	68
Insurance	U.S.	291
Insurance	Scotland	231
Insurance	Spain	231
Leasing	U.S.	180
Leasing	Scotland	108
Leasing	Spain	162
Treasury and capital markets	U.S.	29
Treasury and capital markets	Switzerland	11
Treasury and capital markets	Germany	18
Treasury and capital markets	England	69
Treasury and capital markets	Australia	29
Treasury and capital markets	Hong Kong	48
Corporate banking	U.S.	179
Corporate banking	Scotland	36
Corporate banking	Switzerland	102
Corporate banking	Spain	60
Corporate banking	Germany	84
Corporate banking	Netherlands	48
Corporate banking	Hong Kong	168
Correspondent banking	U.S.	66
Correspondent banking	England	18
Correspondent banking	Australia	18
Correspondent banking	Hong Kong	27
International banking	U.S.	17
International banking	Switzerland	24
International banking	Spain	6
International banking	Germany	14
International banking	England	8
International banking	Australia	3
International banking	Japan	5
Developing countries	U.S.	420
Corporate finance	U.S.	416
Private banking	Switzerland	357
		(continued)

TABLE 8–4
(*concluded*)

Business activity	Country	Income
Private banking	Spain	$ 195
Investment management	U.S.	68
Global custody	U.S.	41
Global custody	Switzerland	20
Offshore trust	Hong Kong	22
		$7,370

will not be required. The definitions of the income accounts are shown in Table 8–5. These are the summary accounts used throughout the ABC Bank Group. Individual accounts used in each country may differ in line with local practice but must be capable of summarization to these levels.

Agree on Activities. Activities should be defined at a low enough level to allow the operations within a country to be related to the types of business agreed on above and to enable significant differences in cost to be identified. Activities must also be defined for the support functions within the organization as discussed in Chapter 4, "Agreeing on Activities." The strategic activities to be used within ABC Bank are shown in Table 8–6. As the summary income account definitions relate mainly to customer types, they have been used to define the key business activities to be analyzed. In addition to the areas of business, the supporting activities (generally sustaining in nature) are also listed. These supporting activities will probably relate primarily to U.S. headquarters, although they may be used to a lesser extent in the other segments as well.

Determine Cost Drivers. When the activities have been agreed on, then the cost drivers can be identified. Where an activity is performed in a country or branch with direct responsibility for business delivery, the drivers invariably are the volume, value, or quality of products and services undertaken. Inevitably, some costs are incurred for several business areas (joint costs). Assigning these activities and the associated costs to individual business activities may be difficult.

TABLE 8–5
ABC Bank—chart of accounts income definitions

Areas of business	Interest income	Foreign exchange	Fees and commissions	Other income
Branch networks	Interest income and interest expense relating to retail customer loans and deposits (including checking accounts).	Foreign exchange income relating to exchange of currency and purchase or sale of travelers' checks.	Fees and commissions received for services offered through branches and other retail account-related transactions.	Miscellaneous other income received through branches.
Card services		Foreign exchange income relating to use of credit and debit cards.	Fees and commissions payable by merchants and card holders for use of credit and debit card services.	
Insurance services	Interest income received on the insurance reserves.		Premiums paid in relation to insurance policies sold through branches, brokers, and other agents.	
Leasing				Income received on leases to retail customers.

(continued)

TABLE 8–5
(*continued*)

Areas of business	Interest income	Foreign exchange	Fees and commissions	Other income
Treasury	Interest income received through management of assets, liabilities, and cash on behalf of the bank.	Foreign exchange income received through currency management of the balance sheet.	Fees and commissions paid and payable in relation to management of the balance sheet.	Any other income received in relation to management of the balance sheet.
Capital markets	Interest margins received as a result of capital markets activity.	Foreign exchange income received as a result of capital markets activity	Fees and commissions received as a result of capital markets activity.	
Corporate banking	Interest income and interest expense relating to corporate and commercial customer loans and deposits (including checking accounts).	Foreign exchange income relating to exchange of currency in corporate banking centers and on behalf of corporate account holders.	Fees and commissions received for services offered through corporate banking centers and other commercial account-related transactions, including trade finance.	Miscellaneous other income received through corporate banking centers. *(continued)*

TABLE 8–5
(*continued*)

Areas of business	Interest income	Foreign exchange	Fees and commissions	Other income
Correspondent banking	Interest income and interest expense relating to balances held on behalf of correspondent banks.	Foreign exchange income relating to exchange transactions performed on behalf of correspondent banks.	Fees and commissions received for services performed on behalf of correspondent banks.	Miscellaneous other income received from correspondent banks.
International banking	Interest income and interest expense relating to international customer loans and deposits.	Foreign exchange income relating to exchange of currency on behalf of international account holders.	Fees and commissions received for services offered to international customers, including trade finance.	Miscellaneous other income received from international customers.
Corporate finance			Fees and commissions received in relation to corporate finance and merchant banking advisory services.	
Developing countries	Interest income and interest expense relating to transactions undertaken within developing countries.	Foreign exchange income relating to exchange of currency on behalf of developing countries.	Fees and commissions received for services offered to developing countries, including trade finance.	Miscellaneous other income received from developing countries.

(*continued*)

TABLE 8–5
(*concluded*)

Areas of business	Interest income	Foreign exchange	Fees and commissions	Other income
Private banking	Interest income and interest expense relating to private bank customer loans and deposits, including accounts.	Foreign exchange income relating to exchange of currency in private banking centers and on behalf of private bank account holders.	Fees and commissions received for services offered through private banking centers and other private bank account-related transactions.	Miscellaneous other income received from private banking centers.
Investment management		Foreign exchange relating to conversion of investment balances between currencies.	Fees and commissions received for investment management and related advisory services.	
Global custody			Fees and commissions received for custodian services.	
Offshore trust			Fees and commissions received in relation to offshore trust management.	

TABLE 8–6
ABC Bank—strategic activity list

Strategic activities
Branch banking
ATMs
Card services
Insurance
Leasing
Treasury
Capital markets
Corporate banking
Correspondent banking
International banking
Developing countries
Corporate finance
Private banking
Investment management
Global custody
Offshore trust
Banking operations
IT
Executive
Finance
Human resources
Premises/facilities
Regional management
Country management

Retail banking systems, for example, may be used by retail branches, corporate banking offices, and private banking. The costs associated with operations, maintenance, and development of enhancements may relate to any type of activity. At the strategic level it may be sufficient to identify any material costs that can be separately identifiable and to allocate the costs based on usage. Obviously, given the scale of the retail banking activity, such systems would not be curtailed or eliminated without affecting the retail banking business strategy.

Those activities defined as sustaining activities may have drivers that bear no relation to direct business-related activity (the drivers for ABC Bank are shown in Table 8–7).

Identify Customers and Customer Groups. Identification of customers and customer groups is not normally necessary in a strategic review of this type.

Commence Data Collection

It is important to begin data collection as soon as the data requirements have been defined. This way, the data can be accumulated and stored until it is required for analysis and reporting. The data required for this strategic review within ABC Bank may be obtained from a variety of sources, including:

- Transaction processing systems.
- Interviews with country managers.
- Financial systems.
- Other analysis (internal and external).

Develop an Activity-Based Costing System

The activity-based costing system for ABC Bank will be very straightforward, but the approach to its development will require the standard steps described in Chapter 3, "The Framework for Activity-Based Costing Implementation."

Develop Reporting Requirements and System Characteristics. The reporting requirements for ABC Bank are fairly simple. It wants strategic cost information that will enable it to analyze the profitability of the various activities it undertakes and identify the key cost drivers that would affect the strategic emphasis on the business activities and the components of the value chain.

The analysis will be run by a joint team from the finance department and the chief executive's department, and reports will be provided to the senior management on paper. Users will not be given access to the analysis and all data will be received and input to the analysis by the team.

TABLE 8–7
ABC Bank—strategic cost drivers

Services	Product development	Processing	Distribution	Risk management	Customer service	Marketing and sales
Branch banking	■		■			
ATMs			■			
Card services			■	■		
Insurance	■		■	■		
Leasing			■	■		
Treasury		■		■		
Capital markets	■			■	■	
Corporate banking		■		■	■	
Correspondent banking		■	■			
International banking		■	■	■	■	
Developing countries				■	■	
Corporate finance	■				■	
Private banking			■		■	
Investment management	■				■	■
Global custody		■			■	
Offshore trust	■		■			■
Banking operations	■	■		■	■	
IT	■	■		■		■
Executive	■				■	
Finance				■		
Human resources			■			
						(continued)

TABLE 8–7
(*concluded*)

Services	Product development	Processing	Distribution	Risk management	Customer service	Marketing and sales
Premises/ facilities			▓▓▓			
Regional management			▓▓▓			
Country management			▓▓▓			

The system's characteristics can be derived from these requirements as:

- A stand-alone system using a proprietary analysis package.
- Producing paper reports as required.
- Capable of being installed/maintained by financial analysts.
- With in-built security to ensure confidentially of data and reports.

Select and Install Software, Set System Parameters. Given the size of the organization, the volume of data required, the nature of the project, and the system's characteristics, ABC Bank decided to use a standard spreadsheet package.

To make sure the spreadsheet was designed and built in such a way that it could store and report the data efficiently, a data model was drawn that demonstrated how the base data would be used within the system. This enabled the analysts to develop the spreadsheet in an effective way.

Develop Automated Interfaces, Input Static Data. ABC Bank decided not to create automated interfaces, so it must ensure that data is provided in a standard format to be input directly into the system without needing to be transcribed onto input forms.

When the basic parameters have been set up on the system, it is possible to load the static data. Static data includes the standard linkages between activities and cost drivers and the relationships between countries and business activities to ensure consistent reporting and summarization. It also defines the report layouts and reporting hierarchies. For ABC Bank, identification of the linkages at business activity and country level will be relatively easy, but the links between the support functions of management, human resources, finance, and systems will be more difficult.

Load Data and Test Reporting Capability. Once the static data has been loaded and verified, the variable data can be input and the first reports produced.

Determine Costs and Revenues

ABC Bank identified the time taken on the activities performed within the bank by interviewing individual country managers and reviewing with them the statistical analysis that has been summarized. The analysis included:

- Number of accounts and customers, by type of customer.
- Income and balances by type of business activity.
- Number and grade of staff.

Calculate Costs. The analysts can immediately calculate the cost of the activities, identified as a percentage of departmental time, by taking the management accounts and using the departmental cost as a basis for the calculation. (The resulting cost analysis is shown in Table 8–8.)

Funding costs are driven by the average debit and credit balances used by the business activities and the cost of obtaining or utilizing the necessary funds. The rate applied to funds provided (cost of funds) or offered (earning credits) will be affected by the asset mix of the balance sheet and the funding policy of the institution.

Estimate Revenues. ABC Bank, as an international bank with a strong retail banking base, has access to a large base of customer deposits and can therefore match its book with relative ease. Individual business activities are treated separately and the treasury function assigns rates to areas of the business as business is accepted. The income figures shown in the trial balance (Table 8–4) are net of funding costs.

TABLE 8–8
ABC Bank—strategic activity list

Services	Direct Costs			Provisions		
	U.S.	Europe	Rest of World	U.S.	Europe	Rest of World
Branch network	$ 995	$270	$ 0	$ 788	$ 0	$ 0
ATMs	75	0	0	8	0	0
Card services	21	6	0	105	0	0
Insurance	62	27	0	77	59	0
Leasing	123	71	0	102	108	0
Treasury	3	0	0	0	0	0
Capital markets	3	6	23	0	0	0
Corporate banking	85	92	27	47	144	80
Correspondent Banking	16	8	21	0	0	0
International banking	38	32	21	6	6	3
Developing countries	53	0	0	945	0	0
Corporate finance	113	0	0	45	0	0
Private banking	6	92	0	18	20	0
Investment management	18	0	0	0	0	0
Global custody	8	3	0	0	0	0
Offshore trust	0	0	13	0	0	0
Banking operations	432	54	11	0	0	0
IT	218	24	8	0	0	0
Executive	18	0	0	0	0	0
Finance	32	5	5	0	0	0
Human resources	17	3	2	0	0	0
Premises/facilities	270	102	71	0	0	0
Regional management	0	6	2	0	0	0
Country management	0	9	4	0	0	0
Total	$2,606	$810	$208	$2,141	$337	$83

Review Results and Prioritize Recommendations

As with any activity-based costing exercise, producing the approach is only half the battle. Using the results in practice is more important.

Produce Output. The report for ABC Bank is shown in Table 8–8. The report shows the costs analyzed into direct costs (staff, premises, and systems-related) and the provisions (loan loss, insurance claims debt, and other loss provisions). The profitability report, shown in Table 8–9, presents the income received, direct costs, provisions, and profit before taxes.

Review Options.   Tables 8–8 and 8–9 demonstrate the profitability of the various business activities performed by ABC Bank. They analyze the income, cost, and provisions by business activity for each region of the world. This type of analysis can be used to focus attention on those activities that are highly profitable and could perhaps be extended and those that are unprofitable and could be reduced.

The insurance activity, for example, seems highly profitable in a very competitive market. This confirms the strategy agreed on five years ago, to invest in penetrating the retail insurance market in the United States and Spain. The investment in staff and marketing has been successful and senior management should now consider whether this performance could be repeated in other countries and how the positions in the existing markets can be consolidated.

Alternatively, international banking appears relatively unprofitable and senior management should consider whether this activity is necessary to provide a base from which to offer other services or how profitability could be improved by reviewing the drivers underlying the costs. As shown in Table 8–7, the strategic cost drivers that affect international banking activity include processing, distribution, risk management, and customer service. Processing speed is affected by the quality of the operating staff and the systems used to deliver the products and services to international customers. The bank is unlikely to invest in systems development for international banking. This activity is currently supported using the retail and corporate banking systems, and this is unlikely to change. ABC Bank should compare its customer service levels to those offered by its competitors and determine whether service levels could be reduced to reduce cost or whether improving the level of customer service could increase prices and/or customer numbers. This would permit better use of resources and improved profitability.

Recommend Action and Agree on Implementation Plans.   It is important for ABC Bank, then, to develop recommendations from the various options identified above, prioritize them, and agree on plans for their implementation.

TABLE 8–9
ABC Bank—strategic profitability analysis

Services / Profit	United States				Europe				Rest of world			
	Income	Cost	Provision	Pretax profit	Income	Cost	Provision	Pretax profit	Income	Cost	Provision	Pretax profit
Branch network	$2,520	$ (995)	$ (788)	$ 737	$ 720	$(270)	$ 0	$ 450	$ 0	$ 0	$ 0	$ 0
ATMs	0	(75)	(8)	(83)	0	0	0	0	0	0	0	0
Card services	233	(21)	(105)	107	68	(6)	0	62	0	0	0	0
Insurance	291	(62)	(77)	152	462	(27)	(59)	376	0	0	0	0
Leasing	180	(123)	(102)	(45)	270	(71)	(108)	91	0	0	0	0
Treasury	14	(3)	0	11	0	0	0	0	0	0	0	0
Capital markets	15	(3)	0	12	98	(6)	0	92	77	(23)	0	54
Corporate banking	179	(85)	(47)	47	330	(92)	(144)	94	168	(27)	(80)	61
Correspondent banking	66	(16)	0	50	18	(8)	0	10	45	(21)	0	24
International banking	17	(38)	(6)	(27)	52	(32)	(6)	14	8	(21)	(3)	(16)
Developing countries	420	(53)	(945)	(578)	0	0	0	0	0	0	0	0
Corporate finance	416	(113)	(45)	258	0	0	0	0	0	0	0	0
Private banking	0	(6)	(18)	(24)	552	(92)	(20)	440	0	0	0	0
Investment management	68	(18)	0	50	0	0	0	0	0	0	0	0
Global custody	41	(8)	0	33	20	(3)	0	17	0	0	0	0
Offshore trust	0	0	0	0	0	0	0	0	0	0	0	0
Banking operations	0	(432)	0	(432)	0	(54)	0	(54)	22	(13)	0	9
IT	0	(218)	0	(218)	0	(24)	0	(24)	0	(11)	0	(11)
Executive	0	(18)	0	(18)	0	0	0	0	0	(8)	0	(8)
Finance	0	(32)	0	(32)	0	(5)	0	(5)	0	(5)	0	(5)
Human resources	0	(17)	0	(17)	0	(3)	0	(3)	0	(2)	0	(2)
Premises/facilities	0	(270)	0	(270)	0	(102)	0	(102)	0	(71)	0	(71)
Regional management	0	0	0	0	0	(6)	0	(6)	0	(2)	0	(2)
Country management	0	0	0	0	0	(9)	0	(9)	0	(4)	0	(4)
Total	$4,460	$(2,606)	$(2,141)	$(287)	$2,590	$(810)	$(337)	$1,443	$320	$(208)	$(83)	$ 29

SUMMARY

The management team must understand the dynamics of the strategic cost and income profiles within the organization and ensure that the strategic goals concentrate on improving its value for the shareholders in both the short and longer term. This can be achieved only if corporate goals and strategic plans are based on an understanding of the factors that affect the profitability of the various areas of the business and the impact of changes on the market's perception of the institution's value.

Then the strategic cost drivers need to be considered in the development or review of the strategy. Activity-based costing can be used to assist in the review.

Chapter Nine

Using Activity-Based Costing for Product Costing

INTRODUCTION

Product costing is the most common use of activity-based costing and often forms the basis for product pricing and product profitability. This is of particular importance in the financial sector, where the increasingly competitive environment and the degree of product differentiation necessary to maintain or improve market share require effective information relating to the costs of developing and providing products and services.

Increasingly, competition is coming from other financial institutions throughout the world and from other types of organizations expanding out of traditional marketing into financial services. New entrants may focus on gaining market share and, therefore, may offer products and services at lower prices. They are likely to have new systems and procedures that provide effective, efficient processing. Customers are becoming increasingly aware of the differentiation in products and levels of service offered by the financial institutions. Institutions must therefore be aware of the impact on costs and quality of service and of the need to meet customer requirements at prices the market will bear.

Product costing and product profitability measurement use operational and financial information summarized into a form that aids the decision-making process. Product cost and profitability information can be used to analyze and monitor costs, revenues, and balances relating to defined products and services throughout the organization. The activities in each department that are performed to support particular products or services can be identified and their costs associated with each activity. The direct interest income, fee income, funding costs, and operating costs then form the basis of a product contribution toward support costs and provide information that can support pricing and marketing strategies.

Product costing can be based on activity-based costing and allows information to be made available by department, product, and cost driver. Reporting can be achieved at the lowest level, by the identification and monitoring of costs that are within the individual manager's control. It is, however, necessary to be able to attribute the costs associated with individual activities to products, product groups, or operations necessary to sustain the basic fabric of the business. This creates a multidimensional reporting system that ensures that all costs can be analyzed by organizational unit (cost center or profit center), activity, or product, as shown in Figure 9–1.

PRODUCT PROFITABILITY

Recent changes in the financial services sector have had a significant effect on profitability, forcing financial institutions to change their focus. Reduced interest rate spreads and balances and the increased risk of loss of lending have raised the importance of noninterest revenues, while competitive pressures have made price or volume increases more difficult to achieve. Managers must take responsibility for the profitability of products or groups of products and take control of the interest- and noninterest-related cost and income flows. Activity-based costing will help identify noninterest-related costs, but it will support analysis of income and interest costs only if products and the volume of activity are defined.

One of the most fundamental issues to be resolved is the identification and tracking of income by product. The types of revenue are discussed in detail in Chapter 6, "Calculating Costs." There will be wide variances in the capabilities of individual financial institutions to extract detailed income information from their transaction processing systems. If the amount and quality of information at the product level is limited, it may prove too expensive to enhance existing systems, and other options for tracking income will need to be identified.

In practice, most financial institutions can track fees and interest that are debited or credited to customer accounts, because they can be linked to products via the account number. However, income collected by means of check or cash (where an account number and hence a product cannot be clearly identified) will require either a change in procedures or manual tracking processes. It is not usually cost effective to try to track this income by product, as it usually represents no more than 1 percent of total income. This income should therefore be recorded as a

FIGURE 9–1
Multidimensional reporting

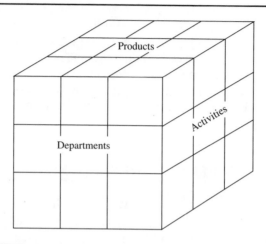

pool item, say, against a dummy product. The dummy product entries are essential to achieve a full reconciliation of total income to the total income figures in other profitability systems.

KEY ISSUES

The development of product costs is not always as simple as it sounds. Operating expenses are not usually associated with products in the financial accounting ledgers unless they relate to a department that is fully dedicated to one product or service. Definitions of products and services are frequently not established, and there may be many products for which no single manager has ultimate responsibility. Identification of interest cost by product may be difficult because of the need to identify and analyze the cost of funds utilized over a period of time and the availability of data relating to average balances and rates by product. Claims can normally be identified by product or policy type, but they may relate to products undertaken in previous accounting periods.

Associating Operation Expenses with Products

Operating expenses may not be associated with products in the financial accounting ledgers unless they relate to a department that is fully dedicated to one product or service. But by analyzing the activities performed within the department, activity-based costing can align individual activities to products more easily. Where an activity is performed to support more than one product, then the cost can be included in the total product cost of all products that use that particular activity in ratio to the usage.

Definitions of Products and Services

One of the most difficult questions for any financial institution to answer is what products does it sell. Each functional area is likely to have a different perspective on this issue. For example, the sales force may argue that the checking account and remittance/funds transfer services are one product, whereas the operational staff are likely to view the checking account and remittance/funds transfer business in terms of a number of different products requiring individual processing treatment. For reporting purposes, as we have seen, it is important to agree on product definitions that can be supported by the tracking of clearly identifiable income and cost but that also provide adequate sales and marketing information to the end users.

Another associated issue is the need to construct a product coding convention that supports the grouping of individual products into product "families" (for example, lending, deposits, investments, and advisory services) in order to satisfy product grouping reporting requirements.

Identification of Interest Cost by Product

The identification of interest cost by product may be difficult because of the need to identify and analyze the cost of funds utilized over a period of time and the availability of data relating to average balances and rates by product. For asset-type products, such as overdrafts and loans, financial institutions will need to calculate the cost of funding products and then to set this off against the interest paid. In essence, the objective is to calculate the *net* interest income position for each product. The net interest income figure, plus associated fees, represents the gross profit before deduction of product delivery and maintenance costs.

Similarly, for liability-type products, such as deposits and high-interest accounts, financial institutions will need to calculate the income to be derived from use of each type of deposit. In this way, the net interest income for each deposit product can be quantified.

Insurance-related products are generally supported by the investment fund, but in a bad cycle the value of claims paid may exceed the reserves available for a particular product type. In these circumstances, it is necessary to estimate the cost of funding the excess and to include this cost in the product cost calculation. In general, insurance funds must be allocated to products to match interest and investment income to the specific policy types in order to estimate product profitability.

To facilitate these calculations, construct periodic average balances (monthly or quarterly depending on individual reporting requirements) for each asset- and liability-based product and agree on what funds transfer pricing rates should be used for calculating both the cost and use of funds for each product. The finance staff of the organization should be consulted regarding this latter decision.

Specific and General Bad Debt Provisions

The majority of banks raise specific provisions at the individual customer level without allocating provision coverage against individual products. However, to analyze product profitability effectively, it is necessary to review profitability at three levels: gross profit, net profit after deduction of operating costs, and net profit after deduction of operating costs and specific bad debt provisions. It may therefore be necessary to modify provisioning procedures so specific provisions are established at the product as well as customer level. An associated issue is whether it is appropriate to designate general provisions to individual products (perhaps in relation to risk/asset weighting).

Claims

Claims can normally be identified by product or policy type, but they may relate to products undertaken in previous accounting periods. As profit margins are squeezed, actuaries begin to examine the underwriting assumptions on which their calculations are based. Many insurers have not conducted their business on a sufficiently conservative basis and are now having difficulty meeting continuing administrative costs and claims received.

Increased technological developments in medicine also increase the incidence of claims of life and health insurance because incidents can be traced back to insured risks (such as asbestosis). Policies that may generate claims relating to activities undertaken in past policy periods creating "long tail exposure" give rise to further uncertainty on profit margins, such as employer's liability claims relating to health hazards in the working environment, which may not be identified until years after the period of employment.

THE RELEVANCE OF PRODUCT COSTING

Product costing can relate to new product development or to the costing of the existing product range. Activity-based costing can be the basis of product costing in all types of financial institutions, although the importance of detailed analysis of operational costs by product may be less relevant to organizations where many costs are related not to activities but to interest cost or reinsurance cost. This former type of activity is more common in certain types of financial institutions, as shown below.

Retail Banking and Savings & Loans

The large volume of relatively small analogous transactions processed in the retail market is an ideal environment for product costing. The pricing of products tends to be market-led, and identifying loss leaders and unprofitable products can be a key to maintaining a competitive advantage.

Corporate and Wholesale Banking

Most corporate and wholesale banks offer a range of comparable products and services from each office. Product costing can therefore be performed either by office or by average costs calculated across a group of offices.

Private Banking

The services offered by private banks are generally tailored retail banking products but may be extended to provide more specialist services, such as tax and investment advice. They may calculate product costs for all standard products and provide a time-based unit charge for advisory services.

Capital Markets

Capital markets organizations generally offer tailored deals for each large corporate client. The major costs associated with these types of products involve the time value of money and the related interest and exchange rate risks. The operational costs associated with the delivery of these services are normally a small part of the overall cost equation. It may still be important, however, to manage the cost base, but not in relation to product costing.

Life Insurance

Life insurance product costs constitute the actuarial value of the expected claim, the cost of administration, and a projected profit contribution. Since the major component is the value of the expected claim, the importance of product costing may be brought into question. The margins on this type of product, however, are such that it may be important to understand the makeup and timing of the administration costs to ensure that the profitability of the portfolio reported can be justified.

A high proportion of administration costs are incurred at the application and acceptance stage of the policy and at its maturity, claim, or termination. The maintenance costs of receipt of installment payments and issuance of statements are minor in comparison.

Product longevity also creates pressures on profitability, particularly on long tail business, where products sold in the past must continue to be administered and managed even when no longer sold. Insurance products tend to have a shorter shelf life than most financial services products, but product changes in long-term business have a higher cost impact than in short-term insurance. Existing policies must continue to be administered and systems support provided until their maturity. Any new product cannot, therefore, simply replace existing products, but will create the need for additional administrative systems support.

Property and Casualty

Property and casualty products tend to be short-term products whose costs are incurred at inception and on claim. Product analysis has traditionally been limited to calculating premiums less underwriting profit and has concentrated on premium and claims management. It has often included reinsurance analysis but generally has placed less emphasis on allocation of support and indirect costs, for costing and pricing purposes. The costs are left to the individual administration managers to control. The differentiation between costs of new and renewed policies can be significant. Product costing is important in this market to monitor the value of claims paid and ensure that the premium rates remain sufficient to provide a profit contribution.

Reinsurance

Reinsurance activity relates to the sharing of risks associated with various types of insurance coverage. The costs, therefore, relate to the risk of claim and the administrative costs of managing the portfolio. The definition of products in this type of business can be difficult, as the coverage normally relates to either a batch of retail policies or a large individual policy. Product costing may be irrelevant because each transaction will be different. It may be more appropriate to identify the generic processing costs and apply them to each transaction and/or customer as appropriate.

Investment Management

The importance of product costing investment management depends on the type of clients and the service provided. Those investment management organizations that focus on large pension funds and investment trusts normally analyze the costs of the components of the services provided and estimate the costs of managing a fund by accumulating the components applicable to the particular characteristics of the portfolio and level of service required.

Those organizations that provide retail pension funds and unit trust services are more likely to calculate a composite product cost and use it to calculate the level of management fee that should be charged. In practice, however, the percentage management fee is generally defined by the market and the decision to be made may relate to the need to participate.

Resource Deployment

The applications of activity-based costing really go beyond product costing. As discussed earlier in Chapter 1, accurate product cost information obtained using ABC can improve the bottom line in two ways. First, accurate product/service costs will help management focus marketing effort/dollars on the right mix of products/services. This will lead to more revenue from the more profitable products/services, thereby improving profits. Second, nonvalue-added activites can be reduced or eliminated over time, leading to cost reductions and improvement in profits.

Sustaining Costs

There are some types of costs that are incurred to sustain operations and have no contribution towards the product/service production or delivery process. These costs should be separated from other cost categories and created seperately. Managers have to use judgment to determine if these costs ought to be allocated to arrive at the full cost of products/services.

PRODUCT COSTING IN PRACTICE

The use to which the product costs will be put may have a significant impact on the complexity of the exercise and the frequency, style, and content of the reporting required. Activities must be defined at a level that enables costs to be attributed and activity costs to be aligned to products or product groups. Or they must be identified as part of the structure required to sustain the overall operation of the organization. Costs of funds and the related earnings credits are prime cost components of all depository and lending products. These costs usually vary over time and may have a significant impact on the price and profitability of the product base, so the development of funds transfer pricing can be an exercise in its own right.

Where full absorption costing is required, the indirect costs must also be allocated to products. This can be a complex issue, as these costs could have a significant impact on the overall product costs and hence on the pricing and profitability of the individual products. There are many gray areas in cost allocation. These relate mainly to the definition of direct and indirect costs. Activity-based costing does assist in the area, as it attempts, by means of cost drivers, to align costs to products or product groups. Only those costs that exist to sustain the basic fabric of the business should remain to be allocated as part of fully absorbed product costs.

When the technical exercise has been completed and the product costs produced, the real work must start. It is very important that the information produced is used effectively. For new product development, direct costs provide an indication of the marginal costs of undertaking additional products or services. For product pricing and prioritization of marketing and sale initiatives, both direct cost and total costs should be shown. This assures management that the prices at least contribute to indirect costs in order to ensure overall profitability, and the product initiatives can be concentrated on the products that are profitable after indirect cost allocation.

Case Study II

XYZ Bank

XYZ Bank provides an opportunity to highlight some of the problems encountered in the data collection and analysis of information for product costing in a small bank servicing retail and small corporate customers. It is an example of a practical approach to the solution of some issues encountered, such as the use of productivity information in activity analysis, the identification and allocation of systems and other central costs, and the presentation and use of product cost information.

BACKGROUND

XYZ Bank is a small financial institution that has a head office and centralized processing environment handling transaction processing for 10 branches. Transaction types include trade finance, funds transfer, foreign exchange, lending, deposit taking, and checking accounts. The organization concentrates on servicing retail and small corporate customers.

The management accounts for the current period are shown in Table 9–1, and Table 9–2 shows the analysis of departmental costs in the

TABLE 9–1
XYZ Bank—management accounts ($ 000s)

	Current Month			Year to Date			
	Actual	*Budget*	*Variance*	*Actual*	*Budget*	*Variance*	*Full-Year Budget*
Interest income	$ 7,766	$ 7,500	$ 266	$ 70,662	$ 67,500	$ 3,162	$ 90,000
Interest expense	(5,151)	(4,950)	(201)	(45,842)	(44,550)	(1,292)	(59,400)
Net interest income before provisions	2,615	2,550	65	24,820	22,950	1,870	30,600
Provisions	(1,040)	(900)	(140)	(9,405)	(8,100)	(1,305)	(10,800)
Net interest income after provisions	1,575	1,650	(75)	15,415	14,850	565	19,800
Arrangement fees	81	113	(32)	740	1,013	(273)	1,350
Commissions	960	900	60	8,739	8,100	639	10,800
Total revenue	$ 2,616	$ 2,663	$(47)	$ 24,894	$ 23,963	$ 931	$ 31,950
Human resource costs	(1,109)	(1,050)	(59)	(10,083)	(9,450)	(633)	(12,600)
Premises costs	(309)	(300)	(9)	(2,813)	(2,700)	(113)	(3,600)
Equipment costs	(696)	(600)	(96)	(6,329)	(5,400)	(929)	(7,200)
Other costs	(173)	(225)	52	(1,569)	(2,025)	456	(2,700)
Total costs	$(2,287)	$(2,175)	$(112)	$(20,794)	$(19,575)	$(1,219)	$(26,100)
Contribution	$ 329	$ 488	$(159)	$ 4,100	$ 4,388	$ (288)	$ 5,850

TABLE 9–2
XYZ Bank—analysis of departmental costs ($ 000s)

Departmental Costs	Current Month			Year to Date			Full-Year Budget
	Actual	*Budget*	*Variance*	*Actual*	*Budget*	*Variance*	
Branches	$ (111)	$ (150)	$ 39	$ (986)	$(1,350)	$ 364	$ (1,800)
Documentary services	401	375	26	3,683	3,375	308	4,500
Foreign exchange	144	150	(6)	1,397	1,350	47	1,800
Payment transmission	135	150	(15)	1,419	1,350	69	1,800
Loan services	1,596	1,725	(129)	14,768	15,525	(757)	20,700
Contribution to fixed costs	2,165	2,250	(85)	20,281	20,250	31	27,000
Premises	(314)	(300)	(14)	(2,781)	(2,700)	(81)	(3,600)
Systems	(1,047)	(990)	(57)	(9,075)	(8,910)	(165)	(11,880)
Finance	(81)	(74)	(7)	(732)	(675)	(57)	(900)
Human resources	(54)	(53)	(1)	(489)	(472)	(17)	(630)
Management	(345)	(345)	0	(3,104)	(3,105)	1	(4,140)
Contribution	$ 324	$ 488	$(164)	$4,100	$ 4,388	$(288)	$ 5,850

central processing unit. The bank has a small production support unit within the management group that is responsible for production control and productivity improvement. It has now decided to develop product cost information from an activity-based costing analysis.

APPROACH

The approach to be undertaken is discussed in Chapter 3, "The Framework for Activity-Based Costing Implementation." Its practical application to XYZ Bank follows.

Review and Confirm Requirements

The first step in developing product costs is to interview key users and identify their information requirements, taking account of best market practice and experience. XYZ Bank wishes to have product cost information that will enable it to find those products and services that are profitable and should be accentuated and those that are unprofitable. It also wishes to differentiate the products and services that must be provided but contribute to the profitability of the bank from those that do not make a contribution and so can be curtailed.

Define Reporting Entities

XYZ Bank has identified its product types as being documentary services, payment transmission services, foreign exchange, safe keeping, lending, deposit taking, and checking accounts.

Define Products and Transactions.   It is now necessary to define the detailed products and services the bank offers its customers. The easiest way to determine the products and services provided is to consider the price list used in the branches. The standard price list for XYZ Bank is shown in Table 9–3. This differentiates the products and services performed for commercial customers and provides a basic list of the full range of products offered by the bank. It also identifies some products offered for which no standard price is quoted and those for which a minimum charge is quoted.

It may be necessary to define some products and services at a lower level than that quoted in the standard tariff, as the cost profile may vary significantly within some of the products. Checking accounts, for example, comprise account opening and issuance of a checkbook and may then include any number of payment and withdrawals within the branches, payments by check in other organizations, balance notifications, ATM usage, statement requests, standing instructions, direct payments, and so on. For any individual checking account, therefore, the *costs* may vary significantly, even if the *revenue* does not.

Agree on Activities. Activities should be defined at a low enough level to allow the operations within a department to be related to the various products and services agreed on and to enable significant differences in cost to be identified. In several circumstances, the activities necessary for product costing may be a standard product or service where that service is performed wholly within one department. Activities must also be defined for the support functions within the organization, as discussed in Chapter 4, "Agreeing on Activities." The activities to be used within XYZ Bank are shown in Table 9–4.

Determine Cost Drivers. When the products and activities have been agreed on, the cost drivers can be identified. Where an activity is performed in a branch or department with direct responsibility for product delivery, then the cost drivers invariably are the volume, value, or quality of products and services undertaken. Some costs will inevitably be costs incurred for several products (joint costs). Assigning these activities and the associated costs to individual products, or even product groups, may be difficult. Counter staff, for example, perform activities relating to deposits, loans, and current accounts, and the costs of cash deposits, withdrawals, standing instructions, and statements could relate to any type of product. It is important, therefore, that the account maintenance system be able to identify the type of account to which the deposit or withdrawal relates and the source of the transaction (branch, ATM, or other bank).

Those activities defined as sustaining activities may have cost drivers that bear no relation to direct, product-related activity (the nonactivity cost drivers for XYZ Bank are shown in Table 9–5).

Cost drivers have been assigned to each activity. Some of the activities, such as training and counseling, can be linked to products on the

TABLE 9–3
XYZ Bank—standard charges

Products and services	Standard charges	
Bills		
Inward documentary/clean collections	$30 minimum charge	$1.50 per $1000
Payment of collections	$30 minimum charge	$1.50 per $1000
Discount of bills	$30 standard charge	
Dollar advance against bill/ check purchased	$40 minimum charge	$1.50 per $1000
Dollar advance repaid	$30 standard charge	
Negotiation of exchange	$40 minimum charge	$3 per $1000
Currency loan against bill	$40 minimum charge	$3 per $1000
Outward documentary/ clean collection	$30 minimum charge	$1.50 per $1000
Collection proceeds paid away	$30 standard charge	
Credits—inward		
Confirmation of letter of credit	$60 minimum charge	$3 per $1000
Advising letter of credit without confirmation	$40 standard charge	
Amendment to letter of credit	$60 minimum charge	$3 per $1000
Pay/check documentation presented under letter of credit	$90 minimum charge	$3 per $1000
Payment of bills at maturity drawn on opening bank	$90 minimum charge	$3 per $1000
Credit bills negotiated (advances under acceptances)	Charge on application	
Clean reimbursements	$40 minimum charge	$1.50 per $1000
Credits—outward		
Opening/issuing letter of credit	$60 minimum charge	$3 per $1000
Amendment to letter of credit	Charge on application	
Check documentation presented under letter of credit	$60 minimum charge	$3 per $1000
Dispatch documentation presented under letter of credit	$40 standard charge	
Accept draft in respect of documents presented	$60 minimum charge	$3 per $1000
Payment of documents presented under letter of credit	$60 minimum charge	$3 per $1000
		(continued)

TABLE 9–3
(continued)

Products and services	Standard charges	
Commercial lending		
Fixed-rate dollar loan	Charge on application	
Fixed-rate currency loan	Charge on application	
Variable-rate dollar loan	Charge on application	
Variable-rate currency loan	Charge on application	
Overdraft facility	Charge on application	
Foreign exchange		
Wire transfer	$15 minimum charge	
Inward remittance	$25 minimum charge	
Mail transfer	$25 standard charge	
Journal entries (intercurrency account transfer)	$15 minimum charge	
Journal entries (single-currency account transfer)	No charge	
Issue of dollar/other currency bankers' payments/checks	$25 minimum charge	
Forward foreign exchange deal	$15 minimum charge	
Dollar transfers		
Effect payment by bankers' payment/check	$25 standard charge	
Effect payment by SWIFT	$25 standard charge	
Receive payment by SWIFT	$7.50 standard charge	
In-house funds transfer	No charge	
Receipt of payments over $10,000	$15 standard charge	
Effect cover payment, etc. by bankers' payment/check	$25 standard charge	
Wire transfer	$15 minimum charge	
Mail transfer	$22.50 standard charge	
Issue of draft	$22.50 minimum charge	
Effect payment by CHIPS	$22.50 standard charge	
Corporate banking		
Commercial checking account	$15 standard charge	
Business account	$15 standard charge	
21-day notice/other special accounts	$15 standard charge	
		(continued)

TABLE 9–3
(continued)

Products and services	Standard charges	
Safe keeping		
Issue of standard corporate checkbooks	$10 standard charge	
Issue of special corporate checkbooks	$15 standard charge	
Deposit of safe keeping items	$15 standard charge	
Withdrawal of safe keeping items	$15 standard charge	
Temporary withdrawal of safe keeping items	$10 standard charge	
Provision of lists of securities held	$15 minimum charge	$1.50 per item
Provision of valuations of holdings	$30 minimum charge	$7.50 per item
Registration of death/probates, etc.	$30 minimum charge	$7.50 per item
Auditors' certificates	$45 minimum charge	$7.50 per item
Rental charge (per month)	$5 minimum charge	$5.00 per item
Counter services		
Issue of personal checkbooks	$3 minimum charge	
Issue of check cards	$3 minimum charge	
Personal—dollar deposit	$0.45 minimum charge	
Personal—cash dispenser	$0.30 minimum charge	
Personal—dollar withdrawal	$1.50 minimum charge	
Personal—currency deposit	$7.50 minimum charge	$7.50 per $100
Personal—currency withdrawal	$7.50 minimum charge	$7.50 per $100
Commercial—dollar deposit	$1.50 minimum charge	
Commercial—dollar withdrawal	$3 minimum charge	
Commercial—currency deposit	$7.50 minimum charge	$15 per $1000
Commercial—currency withdrawal	$7.50 minimum charge	$15 per $1000
Personal foreign exchange		
Travelers' checks purchased	$5 minimum charge	$7.50 per $100
Travelers' checks sold	$3 minimum charge	$7.50 per $100
Checking/savings accounts		
Personal checking accounts	Charge on application	
Personal high-interest checking accounts	No charge	
Personal savings accounts	No charge	
Personal 21-day notice/other special accounts	No charge	
	(continued)	

TABLE 9–3
(concluded)

Products and services	Standard charges	
Personal lending		
Fixed-rate mortgage	Charge on application	
Variable-rate mortgage	Charge on application	
Personal loan—secured	Charge on application	
Personal loan—unsecured	Charge on application	
Authorized overdraft	Charge on application	
Unauthorized overdraft	$15 minimum charge	$3 per $100

TABLE 9–4
XYZ Bank—list of activities and cost drivers

Activities	Cost driver
Documentary services department	
Documentary/clean collections	Number of inward collections
Payment of collections	Number of inward collections paid
Discount of bills	Number of bills discounted
Dollar advance against bill/check purchased	Number of advances made
Dollar advance repaid	Number of advances repaid
Negotiation of exchange	Number of negotiations
Negotiation repayments	Number of negotiations repaid
Currency loan against bill	Number of currency loans made
Outward documentary/clean collection	Number of outward collections
Collection proceeds paid	Number of outward collections paid
Confirmation of letter of credit	Number of letters of credit confirmed
Advising letter of credit without confirmation	Number of letters of credit advised
Amendment to inward letter of credit	Number of inward letters of credit amended
Pay/check documentation presented under letter of credit	Number of letters of credit paid
Payment of bills at maturity drawn on opening bank	Number of bills paid
Credit bills negotiated (advances under acceptances)	Number of bills negotiated
Clean reimbursements	Number of clean reimbursements
Opening/issuing letter of credit	Number of letters of credit opened/issued
Amendment to outward letter of credit	Number of outward letters of credit amended

(continued)

TABLE 9–4

(*continued*)

Activities	Cost driver
Check documentation presented under letter of credit	Volume of documents checked
Dispatch documentation presented under letter of credit	Volume of documents dispatched
Accept draft in respect of documents presented	Number of drafts accepted
Payment of documents presented under letter of credit	Number of payments made
Foreign exchange department	
Travelers' checks purchased	Number of checks purchased
Travelers' checks sold	Number of checks sold
Wire transfer	Number of telegraphic transfers made
Inward remittance	Number of remittances received
Mail transfer	Number of mail transfers made
Journal entries (intercurrency account transfer)	Number of intercurrency account transfers made
Journal entries (single-currency account transfer)	Number of single-currency account transfers made
Issue of dollar/sterling bankers' payments/checks	Number of bankers' payments/checks issued
Set up forward deal	Number of foreign exchange deals
Set up spot deal	Number of spot foreign exchange deals
Payment services department	
Effect payment by bankers' payment/check	Number of payments by bankers' payment/check
Effect payment by SWIFT	Number of SWIFT payments made
Receive payment by SWIFT	Number of SWIFT payments received
In-house funds transfer	Number of single-currency account transfers made
Receipt of payments over $10,000	Number of $10,000+ payments received
Effect cover payment, etc. by bankers' payment/check	Number of cover payments made by bankers' payment/check
Telegraphic transfer	Number of telegraphic transfers made
Mail transfer	Number of mail transfers made
Issue of draft	Number of drafts issued
Effect payment by CHIPS	Number of CHIPS payments made
Loan services department	
Open account	Number of loan accounts opened
Set up direct debit	Number of direct debits initiated
	(*continued*)

TABLE 9–4
(*continued*)

Activities	Cost driver
Input loan application	Number of applications made
Obtain credit authorization	Number of applications made
Obtain/verify security	Volume of security requested
Review facility	Number of loan accounts held
Monitor repayments	Number of loan accounts held
Debit account for loan fees	Number of applications accepted
Close account	Number of loan accounts closed
Custodian services (branches)	
Issue of special corporate checkbooks	Number of special corporate checkbooks issued
Deposit of safe keeping items	Number of items deposited
Withdrawal of safe keeping items	Number of items withdrawn
Temporary withdrawal of safe keeping items	Number of temporary withdrawals
Provision of lists of securities held	Number of lists requested
Provision of valuations of holdings	Number of valuations requested
Registration of death/probates, etc.	Number of registrations made
Auditors' certificates	Number of certificates issued
Rental charge (per month)	Number of items held
Counter services	
Issue of personal checkbooks	Number of personal checkbooks issued
Issue of check cards	Number of cards issued
Interview customer	Number of interviews held
Personal—dollar deposits	Number of personal dollar deposits made
Personal—cash dispenser	Number of ATM transactions made
Personal—dollar withdrawal	Number of personal dollar withdrawals made
Personal—currency deposit	Number of personal currency deposits
Personal—currency withdrawal	Number of personal currency withdrawals made
Commercial—dollar deposit	Number of commercial dollar deposits made
Commercial—dollar withdrawal	Number of commercial dollar withdrawals
Commercial—currency deposit	Number of commercial FX deposits
Commercial—currency withdrawal	Number of commercial FX withdrawals
Management	
General management	Quality of management team
Membership of external committees	Number of external committees attended

(continued)

TABLE 9-4

(*continued*)

Activities	Cost driver
Strategic planning	Level of detail required/market volatility
Contingency planning	Level of detail required/degree of organizational change
Marketing	Level of marketing activity
Public relations	Level of PR activity
Product development	Frequency of new product development
Relationship management	Number of key commercial accounts
Legal	Complexity of legal environment
Security	Number of branches
Organization and methods	Number of branches
Human resources	
Recruitment	Number of applications/recruitments
Training	Number of employees
Industrial relations	Number of employees
Appraisals/counseling	Number of employees
Payroll	Number of employees
Pensions management	Number of employees
Employee relations	Number of employees
Finance	
Accounts payable	Number of invoices paid
Financial accounting	Number of accounts payable/general ledger transactions/cost centers
Statutory and regulatory reporting	Regulatory requirements
Consolidations	Number of units to consolidate
Tax management	Complexity of tax environment
Property management	Number of properties occupied
Management reporting	Level of detail required/degree of automation
Budgeting and forecasting	Level of detail required/degree of automation
Capital appraisals	Number of projects appraised
Internal audit	Level of control necessary
Credit management	Number of loan accounts/applications
Cash management	Number of correspondent banking relationships maintained
Asset and liability management	Complexity of balance sheet structure

(*continued*)

TABLE 9–4
(*concluded*)

Activities	Cost driver
Systems	
Systems planning	Level of detail required/degree of organizational change
General management	Quality of management
Contingency planning	Level of detail required/degree of organizational change
Capacity planning	Number of hardware platforms/systems applications maintained
Computer operations	Number of transactions/level of service
Systems maintenance	Number of systems applications maintained
Systems development	Volume of development
Communications management	Number/complexity of communication channels
Storage management	Amount of storage required
PC support	Number of PCs supported
Network support	Size and complexity of the network

basis of the percentage of overall staff time spent on the activities. Others, such as general management, must be allocated on an arbitrary basis. More specific activities, such as systems, credit management, and marketing, can be apportioned on the basis of usage, as discussed in Chapter 5, "Determining Cost Drivers."

Identify Customers and Customer Groups. Identification of customers and customer groups is not normally necessary in an analysis of product cost.

Commence Data Collection

It is important to begin data collection as soon as the data requirements have been defined. In this way, the data can be accumulated and stored until it is required for analysis and reporting. The data required within XYZ Bank may be obtained from a variety of sources, including:

- Loan processing system.
- Foreign exchange system.

TABLE 9–5
XYZ Bank—nonactivity costs and their cost drivers

Nonactivity costs	Cost drivers
Marketing expenditure	Number of campaigns/brands
Premises costs—maintenance	Number/age of offices/branches
Premises costs—depreciation	Value of premises owned
Premises costs—rental	Cost of leased premises occupied
Systems costs—maintenance	Number/age/complexity of systems
Systems costs—depreciation	Value of equipment purchased
Systems costs—rental	Cost of leased equipment

- Documentary services system.
- Account administration system.
- Manual counts.

The source of each cost driver is shown in Table 9–6.

Develop an Activity-Based Costing System

The system for XYZ Bank will be based on the reporting characteristics and functional requirements that follow.

Develop Reporting Requirements and System Characteristics. The reporting requirements for XYZ Bank are very straightforward. It wants to have product cost information that will enable it to determine those products and services that are profitable, those that make a contribution, and those that are unprofitable. It wants this information in the form of standard reports and rankings and wants to review the various components of cost that make up the product costs.

The bank also wants to review the profitability of each product, so it will need to consider not just the product cost, but also the associated income areas. It wants this information periodically (at least once each year) with the facility to amend and rerun the reporting as necessary.

The system will be run by a joint team from the finance department and the production support section and reports will be provided on paper. Users will not be given access to the system and all data feeds will be manual initially.

TABLE 9–6
XYZ Bank—sources of information

Cost drivers	Source of information
Number of inward collections	Documentary services system
Number of inward collections paid	Documentary services system
Number of bills discounted	Documentary services system
Number of advances made	Documentary services system
Number of advances repaid	Documentary services system
Number of negotiations	Documentary services system
Number of negotiations repaid	Documentary services system
Number of currency loans made	Loans system
Number of outward collections	Documentary services system
Number of outward collections paid	Documentary services system
Number of letters of credit confirmed	Documentary services system
Number of letters of credit advised	Documentary services system
Number of inward letters of credit amended	Documentary services system
Number of letters of credit paid	Documentary services system
Number of bills paid	Documentary services system
Number of bills negotiated	Documentary services system
Number of clean reimbursements	Documentary services system
Number of letters of credit opened/issued	Documentary services system
Number of outward letters of credit amended	Documentary services system
Volume of documents checked	Documentary services system
Volume of documents dispatched	Documentary services system
Number of drafts accepted	Documentary services system
Number of payments made	Documentary services system
Number of checks purchased	Payments system
Number of checks sold	Payments system
Number of wire transfers made	Payments system
Number of remittances received	Payments system
Number of mail transfers made	Payments system
Number of intercurrency account transfers made	Payments system
Number of single-currency account transfers made	Payments system
Number of bankers' payments/checks issued	Payments system
Number of forward foreign exchange deals	Foreign exchange system
Number of spot foreign exchange deals	Foreign exchange system
Number of payments by bankers' payment/check	Payments system

(continued)

TABLE 9–6
(*continued*)

Cost drivers	Source of information
Number of SWIFT payments made	Payments system
Number of SWIFT payments received	Payments system
Number of $10,000+ payments received	Payments system
Number of cover payments made by bankers' payment/check	Payments system
Number of drafts issued	Payments system
Number of CHIPS payments made	Payments system
Number of accounts opened	Account maintenance system
Number of statements issued	Account maintenance system
Number of accounts held	Account maintenance system
Number of standing instructions initiated	Account maintenance system
Number of direct debits initiated	Account maintenance system
Number of accounts closed	Account maintenance system
Number of standard corporate checkbooks issued	Manual count
Number of special corporate checkbooks issued	Manual count
Number of items deposited	Manual count
Number of items withdrawn	Manual count
Number of temporary withdrawals	Manual count
Number of lists requested	Manual count
Number of valuations requested	Manual count
Number of registrations made	Manual count
Number of certificates issued	Manual count
Number of items held	Manual count
Number of personal checkbooks issued	Manual count
Number of cards issued	Invoiced from supplier
Number of interviews held	Manual count
Number of personal dollar deposits made	Payments system
Number of ATM transactions made	Payments system
Number of personal dollar withdrawals	Payments system
Number of personal currency deposits	Payments system
Number of personal currency withdrawals	Payments system
Number of commercial dollar deposits made	Payments system
Number of commercial dollar withdrawals	Payments system
Number of commercial FX deposits	Payments system
Number of commercial FX withdrawals	Payments system
Number of loan accounts opened	Loan system

(*continued*)

TABLE 9–6
(*continued*)

Cost drivers	Source of information
Number of direct debits initiated	Account maintenance system
Number of applications made	Loan system
Volume of security requested	Manual count
Number of loan accounts held	Loan system
Number of applications accepted	Loan system
Number of loan accounts closed	Loan system
Quality of management team	Management audit
Number of external committees attended	Manual records
Level of detail required in strategic plans	Manual records
Market volatility	External statistics
Level of detail required in contingency plans	Manual records
Degree of organizational change	Manual count
Level of marketing activity	Manual count
Level of PR activity	Manual count
Frequency of new product development	Manual count
Number of key commercial accounts	Manual count
Complexity of legal environment	Manual records
Number of branches	Manual count
Number of applications/recruitments	Manual count
Number of staff	Payroll system
Number of invoices paid	Accounts payable system
Number of payments made/received	General ledger
Number of accounts payable/general ledger transactions	Systems management system
Number of cost centers	General ledger
Regulatory requirements	Manual records
Number of units to consolidate	General ledger
Complexity of tax environment	Manual records
Number of properties occupied	Manual records
Level of detail in management reporting	Manual records
Degree of automation in management reporting	Manual records
Level of detail in budgeting and forecasting	Manual records
Degree of automation in budgeting and forecasting	Manual records
Number of projects appraised	Manual records
Level of control required by internal audit	Manual records

(*continued*)

TABLE 9–6
(*concluded*)

Cost drivers	Source of information
Number of loan accounts/applications	Loan system
Number of correspondent banking relationships maintained	General ledger
Complexity of balance sheet	Manual records
Number of hardware platforms	Manual records
Number of systems applications maintained	Systems management system
Number of transactions and level of service	Systems management system
Number of systems applications maintained	Systems management system
Volume of development	Manual records
Number of communication channels	Manual records
Complexity of communication channels	Manual records
Amount of storage required	Systems management system
Number of PCs supported	Manual records
Size and complexity of the network	Manual records

The system's characteristics can be derived from these requirements as:

- A stand-alone system.
- Producing paper reports including
  - Profitability statement by product and product group.
  - Profitability ranking by product and product group.
  - Cost ranking by product and product group.
- Capable of calculating activity costs based on times and percentages.
- Capable of allocating support and sustaining costs to products.
- Capable of reporting at contribution and fully absorbed cost levels.
- Capable of handling a minimum of 99 products, 200 activities, 20 departments, and 20 cost types.
- Capable of being installed/maintained by financial and production personnel.

Select and Install Software, Set System Parameters. Given the size of the organization, the volume of data required, the frequency of reporting, and the system's characteristics, XYZ Bank decided to use a standard spreadsheet package to develop its reporting system in-house.

A data model was drawn that showed how the base data is used within the system. This enabled the data to be defined in systems terms and the spreadsheet to be designed to store and report the data efficiently.

Develop Automated Interfaces, Input Static Data. XYZ Bank has decided not to create automated interfaces, so data must be provided in a standard format that lets it input directly to the system without needing to be transcribed onto input forms.

Load Data and Test Reporting Capability. When the basic parameters have been set up on the system, it is possible to load the static data. (Static data includes the standard linkages between activities, products, and cost drivers. It relates the regular variable data to the base data to ensure consistent reporting and summarization and defines the report layouts and reporting hierarchies.)

The data will be finalized only when data collection has started and costs have been calculated, so that definitions can be finalized based on data availability. For XYZ Bank, this will involve agreement of the activity/product linkages for operating departments, branches, and support departments in order for product costs to be calculated at both the contribution and fully absorbed cost levels. Identification of the linkages at branch and operating department level will be relatively easy, but the links between the support functions in management, human resources, finances, and systems will be more difficult.

Once the static data has been loaded and verified and the cost and revenue calculations described below have been agreed on and input, the first period of variable data can be input and the first reports produced. The product cost reports for XYZ Bank are shown in Table 9–7. They show the costs broken down into direct cost (staff-, premises-, marketing-, and systems-related) and the supporting costs (management, human resources, and other costs). The profitability reports in Table 9–8 present the income received, direct costs, contribution to supporting costs, and net profitability before bad debt provisions and taxation.

TABLE 9-7
XYZ Bank—product costs report

Products	Direct unit cost	Premises/ facilities	Systems	Human resources	Other	Total unit cost
Documentary services						
Documentary/clean collections	$3.50	$1.32	$6.35	$0.35	$3.89	$15.41
Payment of collections	$4.29	$1.62	$6.35	$0.42	$4.76	$17.44
Discount of bills	$15.83	$5.96	$6.35	$1.55	$17.60	$47.29
Dollar advance against bill/check purchased	$7.38	$2.78	$14.76	$0.72	$8.21	$33.85
Dollar advance repaid	$3.20	$1.20	$6.35	$0.32	$3.56	$14.63
Negotiation exchange	$7.01	$2.64	$3.21	$0.69	$7.79	$21.34
Negotiation repayments	$0.87	$0.33	$6.35	$0.09	$0.98	$8.62
Currency loan against bill	$8.66	$3.26	$12.24	$0.84	$9.63	$34.63
Outward documentary/clean collection	$5.54	$2.09	$6.35	$0.54	$6.15	$20.67
Collection proceeds paid	$2.43	$0.92	$6.35	$0.24	$2.70	$12.64
Confirmation of letter of credit	$6.42	$2.42	$3.21	$0.63	$7.14	$19.82
Advising letter of credit without confirmation	$5.75	$2.16	$3.21	$0.56	$6.39	$18.07
Amendment to letter of credit	$3.69	$1.40	$3.21	$0.36	$4.10	$12.76
Pay/check documentation presented under letter of credit	$20.25	$7.62	$6.35	$1.98	$22.50	$58.70
Payment of bills at maturity drawn on opening bank	$17.36	$6.54	$6.35	$1.70	$19.29	$51.24
Credit bills negotiated (advances under acceptances)	$24.45	$9.21	$3.21	$2.39	$27.18	$66.44
Clean reimbursements	$5.13	$1.94	$6.35	$0.50	$5.70	$19.62
Opening/issuing letter of credit	$10.40	$3.92	$3.21	$1.02	$11.57	$30.12
Amendment to letter of credit	$5.40	$2.04	$3.21	$0.53	$6.00	$17.18

(continued)

TABLE 9–7
(continued)

Products	Direct unit cost	Premises/ facilities	Systems	Human resources	Other	Total unit cost
Check documentation presented under letter of credit	$8.31	$3.14	$3.21	$0.81	$9.24	$24.71
Dispatch documentation presented under letter of credit	$2.01	$0.77	$3.21	$0.20	$2.24	$8.43
Accept draft in respect of documents presented	$5.79	$2.18	$6.35	$0.57	$6.44	$21.33
Payment of documents presented under letter of credit	$8.99	$3.39	$6.35	$0.87	$9.99	$29.59
Foreign exchange						
Travelers' checks purchased	$4.43	$1.67	$6.95	$0.44	$4.92	$18.41
Travelers' checks sold	$5.87	$2.21	$6.95	$0.57	$6.53	$22.13
Wire transfer	$5.25	$1.98	$6.95	$0.51	$5.84	$20.53
Inward remittance	$3.56	$1.34	$6.95	$0.35	$3.95	$16.15
Mail transfer	$3.47	$1.31	$6.95	$0.35	$3.86	$15.94
Journal entries (intercurrency account transfer)	$2.19	$0.83	$9.60	$0.21	$2.43	$15.26
Journal entries (single-currency account transfer)	$2.19	$0.83	$5.78	$0.21	$2.43	$11.44
Issue of dollar/sterling bankers' payments/checks	$4.70	$1.77	$6.95	$0.47	$5.22	$19.11
Set up forward deal	$7.71	$2.91	$3.81	$0.75	$8.57	$23.75
Set up spot deal	$5.15	$1.94	$3.81	$0.50	$5.72	$17.12
Payment transmission services						
Effect payment by bankers' payment/check	$0.53	$0.20	$3.14	$0.05	$0.59	$4.51
Effect payment by SWIFT	$0.41	$0.15	$3.14	$0.05	$0.45	$4.20
Receive payment by SWIFT	$0.41	$0.15	$3.14	$0.05	$0.45	$4.20
In-house funds transfer	$0.39	$0.15	$5.78	$0.05	$0.44	$6.81

(continued)

TABLE 9-7
(*continued*)

Products	Direct unit cost	Premises/ facilities	Systems	Human resources	Other	Total unit cost
Receipt of payments over $10,000	$0.45	$0.17	$3.14	$0.05	$0.50	$4.31
Effect cover payment, etc., by bankers' payment/check	$1.35	$0.51	$3.14	$0.14	$1.50	$6.64
Wire transfer	$1.76	$0.66	$3.14	$0.17	$1.95	$7.68
Mail transfer	$1.64	$0.62	$3.14	$0.17	$1.82	$7.39
Issue of draft	$1.23	$0.47	$3.14	$0.12	$1.37	$6.33
Effect payment by CHIPS	$0.33	$0.12	$3.14	$0.03	$0.38	$4.00
Account administration						
Commercial checking accounts	$0.00	$0.00	$2.66	$0.00	$0.00	$2.66
Commercial fixed-interest accounts	$0.00	$0.00	$2.66	$0.00	$0.00	$2.66
21-day notice accounts/other accounts	$0.00	$0.00	$2.66	$0.00	$0.00	$2.66
Personal checking accounts	$0.00	$0.00	$2.66	$0.00	$0.00	$2.66
Personal high-interest checking accounts	$0.00	$0.00	$2.66	$0.00	$0.00	$2.66
Personal savings accounts	$0.00	$0.00	$2.66	$0.00	$0.00	$2.66
Personal 21-day notice accounts/other accounts	$0.00	$0.00	$0.00	$0.00	$0.00	$0.00
Open account	$0.81	$0.30	$0.00	$0.08	$0.90	$2.09
Issue statement	$0.99	$0.38	$0.00	$0.09	$1.10	$2.56
Monitor activity	$0.42	$0.17	$0.00	$0.05	$0.47	$1.11
Set up standing instructions	$1.22	$0.47	$0.00	$0.12	$1.35	$3.16
Set up direct debit	$1.22	$0.47	$0.00	$0.12	$1.35	$3.16
Close account	$1.43	$0.54	$0.00	$0.14	$1.58	$3.69
Safe keeping						
Issue of standard corporate checkbooks	$2.91	$1.10	$0.00	$0.29	$3.23	$7.53
Issue of special corporate checkbooks	$3.93	$1.49	$0.00	$0.39	$4.37	$10.18
Deposit of safe keeping items	$3.71	$1.40	$0.00	$0.36	$4.13	$9.60

(*continued*)

TABLE 9–7
(continued)

Products	Direct unit cost	Premises/ facilities	Systems	Human resources	Other	Total unit cost
Withdrawal of safe keeping items	$4.41	$1.67	$0.00	$0.43	$4.91	$11.42
Temporary withdrawal of safe keeping items	$5.73	$2.16	$0.00	$0.56	$6.38	$14.83
Provision of lists of securities held	$1.94	$0.72	$0.00	$0.20	$2.15	$5.01
Provision of valuations of holdings	$8.57	$3.23	$0.00	$0.84	$9.51	$22.15
Registration of death/probates, etc.	$7.04	$2.66	$0.00	$0.69	$7.82	$18.21
Auditors' certificates	$9.92	$3.74	$0.00	$0.96	$11.01	$25.63
Rental charge (per month)	$0.00	$0.00	$0.00	$0.00	$0.00	$0.00
Counter services						
Issue of personal checkbooks	$2.52	$0.95	$0.00	$0.24	$2.81	$6.52
Issue of check cards	$2.03	$0.77	$0.00	$0.20	$2.25	$5.25
Interview customer	$12.15	$4.58	$0.00	$1.19	$13.52	$31.44
Personal—dollar deposit	$0.60	$0.23	$3.14	$0.06	$0.66	$4.69
Personal—cash dispenser	$0.02	$0.00	$3.14	$0.00	$0.02	$3.18
Personal—dollar withdrawal	$0.95	$0.36	$3.14	$0.09	$1.05	$5.59
Personal—currency deposit	$1.19	$0.45	$6.95	$0.12	$1.32	$10.03
Personal—currency withdrawal	$1.91	$0.72	$6.95	$0.18	$2.12	$11.88
Commercial—dollar deposit	$1.43	$0.54	$3.14	$0.14	$1.59	$6.84
Commercial—dollar withdrawal	$2.28	$0.86	$3.14	$0.23	$2.54	$9.05
Commercial—currency deposit	$2.85	$1.08	$6.95	$0.29	$3.17	$14.34
Commercial—currency withdrawal	$4.56	$1.73	$6.95	$0.45	$5.07	$18.76
Loan services						
Fixed-rate mortgage	$0.00	$0.00	$0.00	$0.00	$0.00	$0.00
Variable-rate mortgage	$0.00	$0.00	$0.00	$0.00	$0.00	$0.00
Personal loan—secured	$0.00	$0.00	$0.00	$0.00	$0.00	$0.00

(continued)

TABLE 9–7
(*concluded*)

Products	Direct unit cost	Premises/ facilities	Systems	Human resources	Other	Total unit cost
Personal loan—unsecured	$0.00	$0.00	$0.00	$0.00	$0.00	$0.00
Authorized overdraft	$0.00	$0.00	$0.00	$0.00	$0.00	$0.00
Unauthorized overdraft	$0.00	$0.00	$0.00	$0.00	$0.00	$0.00
Fixed-rate dollar commercial loan	$0.00	$0.00	$0.00	$0.00	$0.00	$0.00
Fixed-rate currency commercial loan	$0.00	$0.00	$0.00	$0.00	$0.00	$0.00
Variable-rate dollar commercial loan	$0.00	$0.00	$0.00	$0.00	$0.00	$0.00
Variable-rate currency commercial loan	$0.00	$0.00	$0.00	$0.00	$0.00	$0.00
Commercial overdraft facility	$0.00	$0.00	$0.00	$0.00	$0.00	$0.00
Open account	$1.37	$0.51	$2.66	$0.14	$1.52	$6.20
Set up direct debit	$2.06	$0.78	$2.66	$0.20	$2.28	$7.98
Input loan application	$2.40	$0.90	$8.43	$0.24	$2.67	$14.64
Obtain credit authorization	$19.37	$7.29	$8.43	$1.89	$21.53	$58.51
Obtain/verify security	$8.85	$3.33	$0.00	$0.87	$9.84	$22.89
Review facility	$13.29	$5.01	$8.43	$1.29	$14.76	$42.78
Monitor repayments	$0.65	$0.24	$8.43	$0.06	$0.72	$10.10
Debit account for loan fees	$2.90	$1.10	$2.66	$0.29	$3.23	$10.18

TABLE 9-8
XYZ Bank—profitability report

Product income	Total volume	Income	Total unit cost	Total cost	Profit
Documentary services					
Documentary/clean collections	1,334	$54,027	$15.41	$20,557	$33,470
Payment of collections	1,313	49,238	17.44	22,899	26,339
Discount of bills	35	1,890	47.29	1,655	235
Dollar advance against bill/check purchased	15	1,058	33.85	508	550
Dollar advance repaid	31	930	14.63	454	476
Negotiation exchange	35	2,258	21.34	747	1,511
Negotiation repayments	30	900	8.62	259	641
Currency loan against bill	136	12,036	34.63	4,710	7,326
Outward documentary/clean collection	386	24,318	20.67	7,979	16,339
Collection proceeds paid	412	12,978	12.64	5,208	7,770
Confirmation of letter of credit	226	16,272	19.82	4,479	11,793
Advising letter of credit without confirmation	443	16,613	18.07	8,005	8,608
Amendment to letter of credit	550	19,800	12.76	7,018	12,782
Pay/check documentation presented under letter of credit	483	57,236	58.70	28,352	28,884
Payment of bills at maturity drawn on opening bank	120	12,060	51.24	6,149	5,911
Credit bills negotiated (advances under acceptances)	21	2,615	66.44	1,395	1,220
Clean reimbursements	430	21,930	19.62	8,437	13,493
Opening/issuing letter of credit	463	28,475	30.12	13,946	14,529
Amendment to letter of credit	0	0	17.18	0	0
Check documentation presented under letter of credit	368	25,392	24.71	9,093	16,299
Dispatch documentation presented under letter of credit	564	21,150	8.43	4,755	16,395
Accept draft in respect of documents presented	426	24,282	21.33	9,087	15,195
Payment of documents presented under letter of credit	675	48,600	29.59	19,973	28,627

(continued)

TABLE 9-8
(*continued*)

Product income	Total volume	Income	Total unit cost	Total cost	Profit
Foreign exchange					
Travelers' checks purchased	769	$ 2,885	$ 18.41	$ 14,157	$ (11,272)
Travelers' checks sold	934	2,102	22.13	20,669	(18,567)
Wire transfer	1,891	76,586	20.53	38,822	37,764
Inward remittance	1,246	28,035	16.15	20,123	7,912
Mail transfer	755	16,988	15.94	12,035	4,953
Journal entries (intercurrency account transfer)	1,899	34,182	15.26	28,979	5,203
Journal entries (single-currency account transfer)	390	0	11.44	4,462	(4,462)
Issue of dollar/sterling bankers' payments/checks	1,062	39,825	19.11	20,295	19,530
Set up forward deal	214	9,951	23.75	5,083	4,868
Set up spot deal	5,791	0	17.12	99,142	(99,142)
Payment transmission services					
Effect payment by bankers' payment/check	4,041	36,369	4.51	18,225	18,144
Effect payment by SWIFT	6,297	47,228	4.20	26,447	20,781
Receive payment by SWIFT	5,426	40,695	4.20	22,789	17,906
In-house funds transfer	30,446	0	6.81	207,337	(207,337)
Receipt of payments over $10,000	1,372	20,580	4.31	5,913	14,667
Effect cover payment, etc., by bankers' payment/check	370	0	6.64	2,457	(2,457)
Wire transfer	779	31,550	7.68	5,983	25,567
Mail transfer	0	0	7.39	0	0
Issue of draft	65	1,365	6.33	411	954
Effect payment by CHIPS	63,504	0	4.00	254,016	(254,016)

(*continued*)

TABLE 9-8
(*continued*)

Product income	Total volume	Income	Total unit cost	Total cost	Profit
Account administration					
Commercial checking accounts	11,210	$155,997	$ 2.66	$ 29,819	$126,178
Commercial fixed-interest accounts	8,052	240,191	2.66	21,418	218,773
21-day notice accounts/other accounts	1,422	39,047	2.66	3,783	35,264
Personal checking accounts	46,521	226,650	2.66	123,746	102,904
Personal high-interest checking accounts	8,279	148,892	2.66	22,022	126,870
Personal savings accounts	5,049	329,073	2.66	13,430	315,643
Personal 21-day notice accounts/other accounts	442	14,645	0.00	0	14,645
Open account	2,429	0	2.09	5,077	(5,077)
Issue statement	40,487	0	2.56	103,647	(103,647)
Monitor activity	80,975	0	1.11	89,882	(89,882)
Set up standing instructions	2,192	0	3.16	6,927	(6,927)
Set up direct debit	1,644	0	3.16	5,195	(5,195)
Close account	437	0	3.69	1,613	(1,613)
Safe keeping					
Issue of standard corporate checkbooks	135	1,013	7.53	1,017	(4)
Issue of special corporate checkbooks	9	68	10.18	92	(24)
Deposit of safe keeping items	1,190	17,850	9.60	11,424	6,426
Withdrawal of safe keeping items	1,099	16,485	11.42	12,551	3,934
Temporary withdrawal of safe keeping items	100	750	14.83	1,483	(733)
Provision of lists of securities held	22	825	5.01	110	715
Provision of valuations of holdings	1	71	22.15	22	49
Registrations of death/probates, etc.	14	735	18.21	255	480
Auditors' certificates	123	8,672	25.63	3,152	5,520
Rental charge (per month)	5,479	20,547	0.00	0	20,547

(*continued*)

TABLE 9-8
(continued)

Product income	Total volume	Income	Total unit cost	Total cost	Profit
Counter services					
Issue of personal checkbooks	19,089	$	$ 6.52	$124,460	$(124,460)
Issue of check cards	4,194	0	5.25	22,019	(22,019)
Interview customer	2,118	0	31.44	66,590	(66,590)
Personal—dollar deposit	13,956	0	4.69	64,454	(65,454)
Personal—cash dispenser	29,848	0	3.18	94,917	(94,917)
Personal—dollar withdrawal	15,230	0	5.59	85,136	(85,136)
Personal—currency deposit	1,568	11,760	10.03	15,727	(3,967)
Personal—currency withdrawal	3,991	29,933	11.88	47,413	(17,480)
Commercial—dollar deposit	9,234	0	6.84	63,161	(63,161)
Commercial—dollar withdrawal	214	0	9.05	1,937	(1,937)
Commercial—currency deposit	192	2,880	14.34	2,753	127
Commercial—currency withdrawal	426	6,390	18.76	7,992	(1,602)
Loan services					
Fixed-rate mortgage	728	44,511	0.00	0	44,511
Variable-rate mortgage	963	124,611	0.00	0	124,611
Personal loan—secured	672	36,875	0.00	0	36,875
Personal loan—unsecured	395	10,931	0.00	0	10,931
Authorized overdraft	829	7,152	0.00	0	7,152
Unauthorized overdraft	516	22,146	0.00	0	22,146
Fixed-rate dollar commercial loan	1,027	104,805	0.00	0	104,805
Fixed-rate currency commercial loan	102	9,776	0.00	0	9,776
Variable-rate dollar commercial loan	4,987	736,382	0.00	0	763,382
Variable-rate currency commercial loan	192	18,449	0.00	0	18,449

(continued)

TABLE 9–8
(concluded)

Product income	Total volume	Income	Total unit cost	Total cost	Profit
Commercial overdraft facility	6,923	$579,521	$ 0.00	$ 0	$579,521
Open account	75	61,875	6.20	465	61,410
Set up direct debit	75	0	7.98	599	(599)
Input loan application	75	0	14.64	1,098	(1,098)
Obtain credit authorization	75	0	58.51	4,388	(4,388)
Obtain/verify security	68	0	22.89	1,557	(1,557)
Review facility	3,856	0	42.78	164,960	(164,960)
Monitor repayments	9,066	0	10.10	91,567	(91,567)
Debit account for loan fees	75	0	10.18	764	(764)

Determine Costs and Revenues

As XYZ Bank requires product cost and profitability reports, it will need to gather costs and revenues. For simplification of this example, revenues consist of standard prices and exclude discounts or waivers offered.

Calculate Costs. XYZ Bank has identified the time taken on the activities performed within the bank in two ways:

- By using work measurement to estimate the minutes taken to perform an activity.
- By estimating the percentage of time spent within a department on the activity.

The costs of the activities, identified as a percentage of departmental time, can be calculated immediately from the management accounts, using the departmental cost as a basis.

The cost of the activities for which minute values have been identified can be calculated in two ways. First, you can estimate the value of a minute in the relevant department by taking the cost of the department divided by the total available staff time and thus calculating the value of the time taken to perform the activity. Or you can take the normal volume of activity within the department and calculate the number of productive minutes within the department before estimating the value of a minute on which to base the cost of each activity. (The advantages and disadvantages of each method are discussed in more detail in Chapter 6, "Calculating Costs.")

In this example, the latter method has been used and the costs estimated by calculating the cost of each productive minute within the relevant departments, as shown in Table 9–9. Activities within the support functions have been defined as shown in Table 9–4.

Many systems-related costs vary with the diversity of products offered, not with the volume of transactions. The system must have sufficient available capacity, however, to cope with the maximum number of deals that could be performed. It is not sufficient to apportion the activities within the systems department to the products, because many of the costs incurred are not related to activities but to other types of cost. The detailed expense report for the systems department in XYZ Bank

TABLE 9–9
XYZ Bank—activity costs

Activity list	Unit time (mins)	Total volume	Total time (mins)	Direct unit cost ($)
Documentary services				
Documentary/clean collections	2.9185	1,334	3,893	$ 3.50
Payment of collections	3.5765	1,313	4,696	4.29
Discount of bills	13.2137	35	462	15.83
Dollar advance against bill/check purchased	6.1609	15	92	7.38
Dollar advance repaid	2.6709	31	83	3.20
Negotiation exchange	5.8491	35	205	7.01
Negotiation repayments	0.7270	30	22	0.87
Currency loan against bill	7.2298	136	983	8.66
Outward documentary/clean collection	4.6192	386	1,783	5.54
Collection proceeds paid	2.0318	412	837	2.43
Confirmation of letter of credit	5.3647	226	1,212	6.42
Advising letter of credit without confirmation	4.8026	443	2,128	5.75
Amendment to letter of credit	3.0765	550	1,692	3.69
Pay/check documentation presented under letter of credit	16.9044	483	8,165	20.25
Payment of bills at maturity drawn on opening bank	14.4868	120	1,738	17.36
Credit bills negotiated (advances under acceptances)	20.4214	21	429	24.45
Clean reimbursements	4.2817	430	1,841	5.13
Opening/issuing letter of credit	8.6837	463	4,021	10.40
Amendment to letter of credit	4.5054	0	0	5.40
Check documentation presented under letter of credit	6.9438	368	2,555	8.31
Dispatch documentation presented under letter of credit	1.6834	564	949	2.01
Accept draft in respect of documents presented	4.8290	426	2,057	5.79
Payment of documents presented under letter of credit	7.5047	675	5,066	8.99

(continued)

TABLE 9–9
(continued)

Activitiy list	Unit time (mins)	Total volume	Total time (mins)	Direct unit cost ($)
Foreign exchange				
Travelers' checks purchased	2.9890	769	2,299	$ 4.43
Travelers' checks sold	3.9588	934	3,698	5.87
Wire transfer	3.5470	1,891	6,707	5.25
Inward remittance	2.3950	1,246	2,984	3.56
Mail transfer	2.3370	755	1,764	3.47
Journal entries (intercurrency account transfer)	1.4800	1,899	2,811	2.19
Journal entries (single-currency account transfer)	1.4800	390	577	2.19
Issue of dollar/sterling bankers' payments/checks	3.1670	1,062	3,363	4.70
Set up forward deal	5.2050	214	1,114	7.71
Set up spot deal	3.4700	5,791	20,095	5.15
Payment transmission services				
Effect payment by bankers' payment/check	0.7284	4,041	2,943	0.53
Effect payment by SWIFT	0.5593	6,297	3,522	0.41
Receive payment by SWIFT	0.5503	5426	2,986	0.41
In-house funds transfer	0.5450	30,446	16,593	0.39
Receipt of payments over $10,000	0.6125	1,372	840	0.45
Effect cover payment, etc.	1.8584	370	688	1.35
Wire transfer	2.4056	779	1,874	1.76
Mail transfer	2.2435	0	0	1.64
Issue of draft	1.6887	65	110	1.23
Effect payment by CHIPS	0.4560	63,504	28,958	0.33

(continued)

TABLE 9–9
(continued)

Activity list	Unit time (mins)	Total volume	Total time (mins)	Direct unit cost ($)
Account administration				
Commercial checking accounts	0	11,210	0	$ 0.00
Commercial fixed-interest accounts	0	8,052	0	0.00
21-day notice accounts/other accounts	0	1,422	0	0.00
Personal checking accounts	0	46,521	0	0.00
Personal high-interest checking accounts	0	8,279	0	0.00
Personal savings accounts	0	5,049	0	0.00
Personal 21-day notice accounts/other account	0	442	0	0.00
Open account	1.1240	2,429	2,730	0.81
Issue statement	1.3670	40,487	55,346	0.99
Monitor activity	0.5870	80,975	47,532	0.42
Set up standing instructions	1.6887	2,192	3,702	1.22
Set up direct debit	1.6887	1,644	2,776	1.22
Close account	1.9728	437	862	1.43
Safe keeping				
Issue of standard corporate checkbooks	2.5984	135	351	2.91
Issue of special corporate checkbooks	3.5078	9	32	3.93
Deposit of safe keeping items	3.3140	1,190	3,944	3.71
Withdrawal of safe keeping items	3.9452	1,099	4,336	4.41
Temporary withdrawal of safe keeping items	5.1288	100	513	5.73
Provision of lists of securities held	1.7263	22	38	1.94
Provisions of valuations of holdings	7.6536	1	8	8.57
Registrations of death/probates, etc.	6.2873	14	88	7.04
Auditors' certificates	18.8636	123	2,320	9.92
Rental charge (per month)	0	5,479	0	0.00

(continued)

TABLE 9–9
(continued)

Activity list	Unit time (mins)	Total volume	Total time (mins)	Direct unit cost ($)
Counter services				
Issue of personal checkbooks	3.1181	19,089	59,521	$ 2.52
Issue of check cards	2.4945	4,194	10,462	2.03
Interview customer	15.0000	2,118	31,770	12.15
Personal—dollar deposit	0.7328	13,956	10,227	0.60
Personal—cash dispenser	0.0192	29,848	573	0.02
Personal—dollar withdrawal	1.1725	15,230	17,857	0.95
Personal—currency deposit	1.4656	1,568	2,298	1.19
Personal—currency withdrawal	2.3450	3,991	9,359	1.91
Commercial—dollar deposit	1.7587	9,234	16,240	1.43
Commercial—dollar withdrawal	2.8140	2,144	6,033	2.28
Commercial—currency deposit	3.5175	192	675	2.85
Commercial—currency withdrawal	5.6280	426	2,398	4.56
Loan services				
Fixed-rate mortgage	0	728	0	0.00
Variable-rate mortgage	0	963	0	0.00
Personal loan—secured	0	672	0	0.00
Personal loan—unsecured	0	395	0	0.00
Authorized overdraft	0	829	0	0.00
Unauthorized overdraft	0	516	0	0.00
Fixed-rate dollar commercial loan	0	1,027	0	0.00
Fixed-rate currency commercial loan	0	102	0	0.00
Variable-rate dollar commercial loan	0	4,987	0	0.00
Variable-rate currency commercial loan	0	192	0	0.00

(continued)

TABLE 9-9
(continued)

Activity list	Unit time (mins)	Total volume	Total time (mins)	Direct unit cost ($)
Commercial overdraft facility	0	6,923	0	$ 0.00
Open account	1.1240	75	84	1.37
Set up direct payment	1.6887	75	127	2.06
Input loan application	1.9784	75	148	2.40
Obtain credit authorization	15.9286	75	1,195	19.37
Obtain/verify security	7.2831	68	495	8.85
Review facility	10.9284	3,856	42,140	13.29
Monitor repayments	0.5293	9,066	4,799	0.65
Debit account for loan fees	2.3820	75	179	2.90

Activity list	Percent of department time	Person-years	Direct unit cost ($)
Management			
General management	10.53	57.00	$ 24,636
Membership of external committees	1.75	6.00	4,106
Strategic planning	3.51	1.00	8,212
Contingency planning	1.75	2.00	4,106
Marketing	5.26	1.00	124,815*
Public relations	3.51	3.00	8,212
Product development	1.75	2.00	4,106
Relationship management	17.54	1.00	41,060
Legal	3.51	10.00	8,212
Security	42.12	24.00	98,544
Organization and methods	8.77	5.00	20,530

(continued)

*Includes $112,000 of advertising expense in addition to the allocated portion of expenses.

179

TABLE 9–9
(concluded)

Activity list	Percent of department time	Person-years	Direct unit cost ($)
Human resources			
Recruitment	6.25	8.00	$ 3,391
Training	25.00	0.50	13,564
Industrial relations	12.50	2.00	6,782
Appraisals/counseling	12.50	1.00	6,782
Payroll	25.00	2.00	13,564
Pensions management	6.25	0.50	3,391
Employee relations	12.50	1.00	6,782
Finance		12.00	
Accounts payable	4.00	0.48	3,256
Bank reconciliations	4.00	0.48	3,256
Financial accounting	15.00	1.80	12,210
Statutory and regulatory reporting	7.50	0.90	6,105
Consolidations	4.00	0.48	3,256
Tax management	2.00	0.24	1,628
Property management	5.00	0.60	4,070
Management reporting	10.50	1.26	8,547
Budgeting and forecasting	6.25	0.75	5,088
Capital appraisals	2.00	0.24	1,628
Internal audit	18.75	2.25	15,263
Credit management	10.00	1.20	8,140
Cash management	5.00	0.60	4,070
Asset and liability management	6.00	0.72	4,884

is shown in Table 9–10. This enables the costs to be analyzed by number of application systems; the management of storage, communications, and networks; and transaction volumes as shown in Table 9–11.

There are still costs within the systems department that may be classified as sustaining costs and will be apportioned on an arbitrary basis, as shown in Table 9–12.

Marketing costs within XYZ Bank can be identified at two levels: corporate marketing and product marketing. Corporate marketing may be treated as a sustaining cost and will be apportioned on an arbitrary basis, as shown in Table 9–12, while product marketing may be apportioned to product groups on the basis of actual expenditure and then to individual products as a percentage of revenue generated.

Funding costs are driven by the average debit and credit balances utilized by individual products and the cost of obtaining or using the necessary funds. Debit and credit products will, therefore, be treated differently in product costing.

XYZ Bank, as a small consumer bank, has access to a large base of customer deposits and can therefore match its book with relative ease. The bank aims to control risk by means of a pricing policy, so it uses a midpoint funding rate for funds transfer pricing.

The cost drivers shown in Table 9–4 relate only to costs driven by activities and exclude the marketing budgets, premises/facilities costs, capital expenditure, and the related depreciation and other systems costs. Cost drivers can also be assigned to these cost types, as shown in Table 9–5.

Estimate Revenues. As product charges are stated in the price list, no further analysis is necessary.

Review Results and Prioritize Recommendations

The reports in Tables 9–7 and 9–8 show the cost and profitability reports produced by the system.

Produce Output. The unit cost reports need to be compared with the standard charges to identify any products that do not contribute to sustaining costs and any that generate extraordinary profits. This analysis is shown in Table 9–13. Most of the products are profitable, and even those that are not profitable do contribute to sustaining

TABLE 9–10
XYZ Bank—expense report for systems department

Systems	Staff cost	Premises cost	Equipment cost	Systems cost	Other cost	Total costs
Computer operations	$ 81	$ 8	$153	$ 75	$ 9	$ 326
Systems maintenance	18	3	18	23	5	67
Storage management	21	12	162	50	2	247
Communications management	23	5	54	27	6	115
Network management	29	6	45	38	3	121
Support functions	113	20	17	9	12	171
Total system costs	$285	$54	$449	$222	$37	$1,047

TABLE 9–11
XYZ Bank—analysis of systems costs

Application systems	Computer operations	Systems maintenance	Storage management	Communications management	Network management	Support functions	Total costs
Documentary services system	$ 38	$ 9	$ 20	$ 8	$ 6		$ 81
Foreign exchange system	30	8	17	6	5		66
Payments system	65	17	34	14	11		141
Loan system	44	11	23	9	8		95
Account maintenance system	95	24	50	21	15		205
General ledger	21	6	11	5	3		46
Accounts payable	9	3	5	0	0		17
Systems development	92	22	50	0	0	$ 90	254
Subtotal	394	100	210	63	48	90	905
Other costs				23	18	101	142
Total	$394	$100	$210	$86	$66	$191	$1,047

TABLE 9–12
XYZ Bank—sustaining costs

Sustaining activities	Percent of department Time	Person-years
Management		57.00
General management	10.53	6.00
Membership of external committees	1.75·	1.00
Strategic planning	3.51	2.00
Contingency planning	1.75	1.00
Marketing	5.26	3.00
Public relations	3.51	2.00
Product development	1.75	1.00
Relationship management	17.54	10.00
Legal	3.51	2.00
Security	42.12	24.00
Organization and methods	8.77	5.00
Human resources		8.00
Recruitment	6.25	0.50
Training	25.00	2.00
Industrial relations	12.50	1.00
Appraisals/counseling	12.50	1.00
Payroll	25.00	2.00
Pensions management	6.25	0.50
Employee relations	12.50	1.00
Finance		12.00
Accounts payable	4.00	0.48
Bank reconciliations	4.00	0.48
Financial accounting	15.00	1.80
Statutory and regulatory reporting	7.50	0.90
Consolidations	4.00	0.48
Tax management	2.00	0.24
Property management	5.00	0.60
Management reporting	10.50	1.26
Budgeting and forecasting	6.25	0.75
Capital appraisals	2.00	0.24
Internal audit	18.75	2.25
Credit management	10.00	1.20
Cash management	5.00	0.60
Asset and liability management	6.00	0.72

TABLE 9–13
XYZ Bank—average profitability report

Products and services	Standard charges	Direct unit cost	Total unit cost	Average profit
Documentary/clean collections	$30 minimum charge	$ 3.50	$15.41	$14.59
Payment of collections	$30 minimum charge	4.29	17.44	12.56
Discount of bills	$30 standard charge	15.83	47.29	(17.29)
Dollar advance against bill/check purchased	$40 minimum charge	7.38	33.85	6.15
Dollar advance repaid	$30 standard charge	3.20	14.63	15.37
Negotiation of exchange	$40 minimum charge	7.01	21.34	18.66
Negotiation repayments		0.87	8.62	(8.62)
Currency loan against bill	$40 minimum charge	8.66	34.63	5.37
Outward documentary/clean collection	$30 minimum charge	5.54	20.67	9.33
Collection proceeds paid	$30 standard charge	2.43	12.64	17.36
Confirmation of letter of credit	$60 minimum charge	6.42	19.82	40.18
Advising letter of credit without confirmation	$40 standard charge	5.75	18.07	21.93
Amendment to letter of credit	$60 minimum charge	3.69	12.76	47.24
Pay/check documentation presented under letter of credit	$90 minimum charge	20.25	58.70	31.30
Payment of bills at maturity drawn on opening bank	$90 minimum charge	17.36	51.24	38.76
Credit bills negotiated (advances under acceptances)	Charge on application	24.45	66.44	(66.44)
Clean reimbursements	$40 minimum charge	5.13	19.62	20.38
Opening/issuing letter of credit	$60 minimum charge	10.40	30.12	29.88
Amendment to letter of credit	Charge on application	5.40	17.18	(17.18)
Check documentation presented under letter of credit	$60 minimum charge	8.31	24.71	35.29
Dispatch documentation presented under letter of credit	$40 standard charge	2.01	8.43	31.57
Accept draft in respect of documents presented	$60 minimum charge	5.79	21.33	38.67

(continued)

TABLE 9–13
(*continued*)

Products and services	Standard charges	Direct unit cost	Total unit cost	Average profit
Payment of documents presented under letter of credit	$60 minimum charge	$ 8.99	$ 29.59	$ 30.41
Travelers' checks purchased	$5 minimum charge	4.43	18.41	(13.41)
Travelers' checks sold	$3 minimum charge	5.87	22.13	(19.13)
Wire transfer	$15 minimum charge	5.25	20.53	(5.53)
Inward remittance	$25 minimum charge	3.56	16.15	8.85
Mail transfer	$25 standard charge	3.47	15.94	9.06
Journal entries (intercurrency account transfer)	$15 minimum charge	2.19	15.26	(0.26)
Journal entries (single-currency account transfer)	No charge	2.19	11.44	(11.44)
Issue of dollar/other currency bankers' payments/ checks	$25 minimum charge	4.70	19.11	5.89
Set up forward deal	$15 minimum charge	7.71	23.75	(8.75)
Set up spot deal	Charge on application	5.15	17.12	(17.12)
Effect payment by bankers' payment/check	$25 standard charge	0.53	4.51	20.49
Effect payment by SWIFT	$25 standard charge	0.41	4.20	20.80
Receive payment by SWIFT	$7.50 standard charge	0.41	4.20	3.30
In-house funds transfer	No charge	0.39	6.81	(6.81)
Receipt of payments over $10,000	$15 standard charge	0.45	4.31	10.69
Effect cover payment, etc., by bankers' payment/check	$25 standard charge	1.35	6.64	18.36
Wire transfer	$15 minimum charge	1.76	7.68	7.32
Mail transfer	$22.50 standard charge	1.64	7.39	15.11
Issue of draft	$22.50 standard charge	1.23	6.33	16.17
Effect payment by CHIPS	$22.50 standard charge	0.33	4.00	18.50
Commercial checking accounts	$15.00 standard charge	0.00	2.66	12.34
Commercial fixed-interest accounts	$15.00 standard charge	0.00	2.66	12.34

(*continued*)

TABLE 9–13
(*continued*)

Products and services	Standard charges	Direct unit cost	Total unit cost	Average profit
21-day notice/other special accounts	$15.00 standard charge	$ 0.00	$ 2.66	$ 12.34
Personal checking accounts	Charge on application	0.00	2.66	(2.66)
Personal high-interest checking accounts	No charge	0.00	2.66	(2.66)
Personal savings accounts	No charge	0.00	2.66	(2.66)
Personal 21-day notice/other special accounts	No charge	0.00	0.00	0.00
Open account	Charge on application	0.81	2.09	(2.09)
Issue statement	Charge on application	0.99	2.56	(2.56)
Monitor activity	Charge on application	0.42	1.11	(1.11)
Set up standing instructions	Charge on application	1.22	3.16	(3.16)
Set up direct debit	Charge on application	1.22	3.16	(3.16)
Close account	Charge on application	1.43	3.69	(3.69)
Issue of standard corporate checkbooks	$10.00 standard charge	2.91	7.53	2.47
Issue of special corporate checkbooks	$15.00 standard charge	3.93	10.18	4.82
Deposit of safe keeping items	$15.00 standard charge	3.71	9.60	5.40
Withdrawal of safe keeping items	$15.00 standard charge	4.41	11.42	3.58
Temporary withdrawal of safe keeping items	$10.00 standard charge	5.73	14.83	(4.83)
Provision of lists of securities held	$15.00 minimum charge	1.94	5.01	9.99
Provision of valuations of holdings	$30.00 minimum charge	8.57	22.15	7.85
Registration of death/probates, etc.	$30.00 minimum charge	7.04	18.21	11.79
Auditors' certificates	$45.00 minimum charge	9.92	25.63	19.37
Rental charge (per month)	$5.00 minimum charge	0.00	0.00	5.00
Issue of personal checkbooks	$3.00 minimum charge	2.52	6.52	(3.52)
Issue of check cards	$3.00 minimum charge	2.03	5.25	(2.25)
Interview customer	No charge	12.15	31.44	(31.44)

(*continued*)

TABLE 9–13
(concluded)

Products and services	Standard charges	Direct unit cost	Total unit cost	Average profit
Personal—dollar deposit	$0.45 minimum charge	-$ 0.60	$ 4.69	$ (4.24)
Personal—cash dispenser	$0.30 minimum charge	0.02	3.18	(2.88)
Personal—dollar withdrawal	$1.50 minimum charge	0.95	5.59	(4.09)
Personal—currency deposit	$7.50 minimum charge	1.19	10.03	(2.53)
Personal—currency withdrawal	$7.50 minimum charge	1.91	11.88	(4.38)
Commercial—dollar deposit	$1.50 minimum charge	1.43	6.84	(5.34)
Commercial—dollar withdrawal	$3.00 minimum charge	2.28	9.05	(6.05)
Commercial—currency deposit	$7.50 minimum charge	2.85	14.34	(6.84)
Commercial—currency withdrawal	$7.50 minimum charge	4.56	18.76	(11.26)
Fixed-rate mortgage	Charge on application	0.00	0.00	0.00
Variable-rate mortgage	Charge on application	0.00	0.00	0.00
Personal loan—secured	Charge on application	0.00	0.00	0.00
Personal loan—unsecured	Charge on application	0.00	0.00	0.00
Authorized overdraft	Charge on application	0.00	0.00	0.00
Unauthorized overdraft	$15 minimum charge	0.00	0.00	0.00
Fixed-rate dollar commercial loan	Charge on application	0.00	0.00	0.00
Fixed-rate currency commercial loan	Charge on application	0.00	0.00	0.00
Variable-rate dollar commercial loan	Charge on application	0.00	0.00	0.00
Variable-rate currency commercial loan	Charge on application	0.00	0.00	0.00
Commercial overdraft facility	Charge on application	0.00	0.00	0.00
Open account	Charge on application	1.37	6.20	(6.20)
Set up direct payment	Charge on application	2.06	7.98	(7.98)
Input loan application	Charge on application	2.40	14.64	(14.64)
Obtain credit authorization	Charge on application	19.37	58.51	(58.51)
Obtain/verify security	Charge on application	8.85	22.89	(22.89)
Review facility	Charge on application	13.29	42.78	(42.78)
Monitor repayments	Charge on application	0.65	10.10	(10.10)
Debit account for loan fees	Charge on application	2.90	10.18	(10.18)

costs. The checking accounts and lending facilities need further analysis, because the products for which standard prices are identified are not those for which costs can be estimated. The activities for which costs can be estimated must be accumulated in relation to the standard prices.

For any checking account, the costs of the following services can be combined in relation to usage over one year as shown below:

- Open account × 1.
- Set up direct debit × 3.
- Set up standing instructions × 4.
- Issue check books × 2.
- Issue check card × 1.
- Issue statements × 12.
- Monitor activities × 12.
- Close account × 1.

The mix of activities will vary with the customer or type of customer.

Review Options, Recommend Action, and Agree on Implementation Plans. It is important for XYZ Bank to review the reports in detail so it can identify and recommend actions. The actions can then be presented to the users in order of priority and plans agreed on for their implementation.

SUMMARY

Product costing is the most common use of activity-based costing and often forms the basis for product pricing and product profitability. This is of particular importance in the financial sector, where increasing competition from other financial institutions throughout the world and from other types of organizations expanding out of traditional marketing into financial services is squeezing profit margin. Customers are becoming increasingly aware of the differentiation in products and levels of service offered by the various financial institutions. Banks must therefore be aware of the impact on costs and quality of service of the need to meet customer requirements at prices the market will bear.

Product cost and profitability information monitors cost, revenues, and balances relating to defined products and services throughout the organization. It pinpoints the activities in each department that are performed to support particular products or services and measures the costs associated with each activity. The direct interest income, fee income, funding costs, and operating costs then form the basis of a product contribution toward support costs and provide information to support product pricing and marketing strategies.

Reduced interest rate spreads and balances and the increased risk of loss on lending have increased the importance of noninterest revenues, while competitive pressures have made price or volume increases more difficult to achieve. Activity-based costing will assist in the identification of noninterest-related costs only when products have been defined and the volume of activity is known.

The development of product costs may not always be as simple as it sounds. Operating expenses are not usually associated with products in the financial accounting statements unless they relate to a department that is fully dedicated to one product or service. Definitions of products and services are frequently not established, and there may be many products for which no single manager has ultimate responsibility. The identification of interest cost by product may also be difficult because of the need to identify and analyze the cost of funds utilized over a period of time and have available data relating to average balances and rates by product. Claims can normally be identified by product or policy type but may relate to products undertaken in previous accounting periods.

Activity-based costing will support the development of product profitability information, but it may require information to be gathered from a variety of sources and will need to be supplemented with income data that is collated by product.

Chapter Ten

Using Activity-Based Costing for Customer Profitability

INTRODUCTION

One of the major challenges facing all financial institutions is the identification of unprofitable relationships and products. The emphasis is moving away from volume-based sales targets toward profit objectives, so line managers are looking for guidance on where to concentrate their limited resources. The primary concern of business managers is to be able to analyze each component of the profit equation (income, costs, business volumes) in terms of customers, customer groups, products, and product groups in order to convert lossmakers into profit contributors.

Senior executives of the leading financial institutions have consistently promoted product and customer profitability information as a key strategic input into strategic marketing plans, as well as an operational tool that enables management to manage their service and product delivery costs.

The requirements for product and customer profitability information can most effectively be demonstrated by considering the needs of three levels of management: the account officer or client relationship manager, the product manager, and the unit manager (for example, the branch or divisional manager). Account officers can focus on the reasons for unprofitable customers (price, delivery costs, bad debts, number of products used) and the cross-selling of profitable products. Product managers can identify the relative profitability of products and concentrate marketing/sales resources on the most profitable product/customer combinations. Unit managers can use this information to identify profitable product mixes and motivate account managers to cross-sell.

Profitability measurement and reporting by product and customer are based on the multidimensional analysis of balances, revenues, and costs by activities performed in relation to the products and services provided to customers throughout the bank. They should break down departmental barriers and enable management to gain a greater understanding of customer relationships and markets.

Customer profitability reporting identifies and analyzes the costs and revenues by customer or customer group. Its applicability depends on the types of customers toward which the business is directed and the degree of emphasis on marketing and strategic planning in the organization.

Customer profitability reporting is generally the last component of profitability reporting to be considered by any organization because there has been so little emphasis on customer development in the past. As more and more attention has been directed toward managing the customer relationship, however, knowing the profitability of specific customer groups and individual customers has increased in importance.

Customer profitability analysis generally builds on product information by taking actual revenues and specific customer relationship-related costs and attaching direct product costs in relation to actual product usage by customer. This enables the analysis of the cross-product contribution and the impact of waived fees and negotiated commissions to be made by customer and customer type. It also means that international and interdepartmental customer relationships can be monitored and compared. It requires data to be collected relating to product usage, average balances, income, and costs by individual customer or group of customers.

The income associated with each customer is normally available, although there may be some types of fee or commission income that are not debited to a customer account. These fees or commission payments may be paid by cash or transfer from another financial institution and are therefore credited directly to "commissions paid accounts." In many financial institutions, no record is maintained of the amount paid by customer. This type of income can generally be identified only by product or service and applied to customer analysis as average fee rates. In these instances, the income per customer can only be estimated, based on the level of activity.

Many financial institutions find it difficult to justify the cost of developing and maintaining customer profitability information for individual customers, as this involves the capture and storage of large amounts of data from all automated and manual systems within the organization as well as the maintenance of up-to-date customer profiles. How valuable this information is perceived to be depends to a large extent on how it will be used, which generally relates to how important the individual customer relationship is to the institution.

Today, many organizations realize that customer profitability reports can yield valuable insights on how to deal differently with less profitable customers and customer groups. They can make unprofitable customers and customer groups profitable by systematically reviewing the process-related activities and taking actions that reduce activities and cost. With corporate customers, for example, this may involve responses such as fee discounts if certain document processing services are processed in large enough batches. Customer profitability analysis, therefore, does more than report on the profitability of different strata of customers. It provides activity information that can suggest directions for re-engineering the time, frequency, and volume of customer interactions and on occasion convert an unprofitable customer/customer group into a profitable one.

DEFINING CUSTOMERS AND CUSTOMER GROUPS

Customers are defined as users of products and services who generate costs and revenues. Customers include external individuals and organizations as well as individuals and functions in other parts of the company. The type and mix of customer will vary by type of activity and market perception of the organization.

The types of customers could include individuals, commercial organizations, other financial institutions, government, other regulatory bodies, and other internal responsibility centers. Which of these customer types exist within the company will depend, in part, on the types of financial services provided. In organizations with large numbers of customers, analysis of each customer may not be necessary or practical, especially in the retail market. Analysis of customers grouped by common demand patterns instead may be sufficient. How they are grouped will vary by financial institution but should facilitate the recognition of common buying and risk patterns. The following generic customer groups may provide sufficient analysis to enable strategic activity to be directed at particular market sectors:

- Other financial institutions.
- Government agencies.
- Multinational corporations.
- Large corporate customers.
- Middle-market customers.
- Small corporate customers.
- High-net-worth individuals.
- Ordinary individuals.
  - Age groups.
  - Socio-economic groups.
  - Geographic groups.

Alternatively, an analysis of a specific group of customers, measured by activity, value, or profitability potential, may satisfy the information needs that have been identified. The analysis of certain types of customers such as "global" customer relationships, may have particular relevance for large companies. These are defined as those customers, or related customers (corporate or family groups), who may be serviced by one or more responsibility centers within the institution. These relationships may be important to the organization as a whole, so their profitability should be monitored. Sometimes a relationship that is unprofitable in one unit is profitable in total, but this is not always the case. Some form of customer profitability analysis is important for all financial institutions, although the level of detail applied will vary by institutional type.

Retail banks and all similar companies with a large number of homogeneous customers are unlikely to be able to justify individual customer profitability, although it may become more common as the level of competition and customer sophistication increase. They may, however, require profitability analysis by customer group, defined as any identifiable segment of the customer base. Segments may be based on any combination of socio-economic groupings, occupations, geographic locations, or any other common classification. They may vary by organization.

The customer base of a private bank is normally small enough to justify the development of individual customer profitability. Fees charged to individual customers should be based on the level of activity necessary to maintain the client relationship, so the activity-based cost analysis can provide the volume and cost information needed to derive the appropriate fee rates.

Corporate and wholesale banks are much more likely to require profitability by individual customer because of the higher value of each customer relationship, although this may depend on the number and scale of the customer base. A middle-market bank, for example, with a large number of similar small corporate customers may prefer to group the customers by industry and asset base rather than to analyze each individual customer. An international wholesale bank may, however, have a smaller number of international corporate customers serviced by many offices in different locations. In these circumstances, it may be necessary to analyze customer profitability across the global customer relationship for each individual customer to balance lossmaking activities in one office with profitable business in another.

Individual customer profitability is generally irrelevant to retail life insurance companies, although those companies that offer group or corporate life policies (where the policy is held by a corporation and relates to a large group of employees) will be interested in the claims history and inherent profitability of the corporate account relationship. Retail life insurance organizations tend to be more interested in segments of the customer base and normally relate the segment profitability to the actuarial forecasts.

The importance of customer profitability in property and casualty insurance, as with life insurance, relates to the types of customer. Retail insurers are interested only in the profitability of segments of the customer base and tend to classify customers by a combination of geographic location and economic grouping. Corporate and specialist insurers, however, may be interested in the profitability of particular accounts.

Customer profitability in reinsurance activity is important in analysis of the incidence of claims and hence the risk associated with the insurer. Activity-based costing assists in the profitability analysis by enabling the cost associated with administration of the claim to be estimated and separated by its cost driver. That is, costs relating to administering the claim are separated from those relating to management of the relationship. It will not, however, provide additional analysis of the claims themselves.

The importance of product costing and customer profitability in investment management depends on the types of clients and the service provided. Those investment management organizations that focus on the large pension funds and investment trusts normally analyze the costs of the components of the services provided and estimate the costs of managing a fund by accumulating the components applicable to the particular characteristics of the portfolio and level of service required. This information will then assist in fee negotiations with individual clients.

Capital markets institutions tend to be one of two types—those organizations that handle individual deals on a discrete basis and are therefore unlikely to require customer profitability, which would normally relate to a number of products or services, and those organizations that provide a relationship-based service (often part of a larger financial institution offering a wider financial relationship) and who are interested in full customer profitability and must be able to analyze customers across the range of services offered.

Customers can be classified in many ways to facilitate target marketing and provide a focus for product differentiation. Types of customer segments for which profitability information can be summarized are shown in Table 10–1. These segments are not mutually exclusive and may be combined to fit the reporting needs of any organization.

In large institutions, it is common for information to be analyzed in several ways (by customer within geographic areas, by product type, and by global customer relationship). In smaller ones with relatively small numbers of customers, the types of classification may be more specialized and relate to the types of customers and relationships within that particular organization alone.

THE IMPORTANCE OF INTERRELATIONSHIPS

The importance of interrelationships between customers may vary significantly between organizations but should not be ignored. A dissatisfied customer will complain to all of his or her friends and associates about the fault, and a satisfied customer may recommend the level of services to some friends. One organization, for example, analyzes its customers by employer and by grade, because it offers personal financial services to high-net-worth individuals in key corporate clients and targets new customer development on individuals who are promoted to managerial positions in particular industries. Another institution analyzes individual customers by family connection to maximize cross-selling opportunities and minimize competition within the customer groups.

Interrelationships between customers may be less important in commercial financial services, but maintaining personal contact and ensuring that customers know who to turn to with a problem will affect the

TABLE 10–1
Types of customer segments

Classification Type	Examples	
1. Customer type	High-net-worth individuals Ordinary individuals Multinational corporations Large businesses Medium-sized businesses Small businesses Associations	Unions Government organizations Partnerships Pension funds Agents/producers
2. Socio-economic grouping	A, B, C1, C2, D, E	
3. Profession	Accountant Banker Government employee Doctor	Real estate developer Lawyer Journalist Professor
4. Sex	Male Female	
5. Age	0–18 19–25 26–35	36–50 51–65 66+
6. Marital status	Single Married	Divorced Widowed
7. Salary	$0–20,000 $20–35,000 $35–50,000 $50–100,000	$100,000+
8. Industrial (standard industry code)	Shipping Oil and gas Chemical Retail Manufacturing Engineering	Telecommunications Leisure industry Food manufacture Banking and finance Government
9. Geographic	County Region	State Town/city
10. Size of business	Asset base Number of employees Turnover	Profitability Sales

(continued)

TABLE 10–1
(*concluded*)

Classification Type	Examples
11. Products provided	Asset-based products Liability-based products Documentary services Foreign exchange services Capital markets products Investment management services Advisory services Life insurance products Property and casualty insurance products Health insurance products
12. Responsibility center	Customers by responsibility area within the organizations (may be product, location, or customer type)
13. Account manager	Customers by account manager

level of customer service and the way the customer perceives the company. Financial services to commercial customers may be differentiated from the competition by level of service and price, but at the very least they require some knowledge of the products and services undertaken for the client and the current status of the account relationship.

CUSTOMER PROFITABILITY IN PRACTICE

In practice, customer profitability analysis can generally be built more efficiently on an activity-based costing system designed to analyze activities by product or service offered by the financial institution. As discussed earlier, the costs associated with individual activities may be consolidated by customer where the definition of a generic product is not relevant. This applies particularly to private banking and investment management where activities are combined to provide tailored services by customer or portfolio.

Most operating costs within a financial institution can be attributed to a specific product or service. However, some costs may be driven by the service offered to a particular customer or customer group. These costs must be isolated for customer profitability and the appropriate cost driver identified (see Chapter 5, "Determining Cost Drivers"). In order to calculate customer profitability, it is important to be able to measure product usage, income, cost, and the associated balances by customer. Product costs can generally be assumed to be standard for a range of customers and can, therefore, be used as the basis of customer cost analysis when related to actual product usage by customer. Income and balances, however, vary significantly by customer and should be identified separately. Income in financial institutions can arise in five ways— interest income, fee or commission income, premiums, trading, and investment income. The following paragraphs summarize the types of income and the availability of information by customer. More detail is given in Chapter 6, "Calculating Costs."

Interest Income

Interest is the charge made by the lender to the borrower for the use of the lender's funds over time. Interest is normally shown as two separate items—interest revenue and interest expense. Net interest income is the difference between interest revenue and interest expense and is the spread of contribution to profits and operating costs made by the asset- and liability-related products.

Where products and services need to be identified separately for customer profitability reporting, interest revenue should usually be adjusted for the cost of funds (see Chapter 6). In summary, lending products have gross interest revenue, calculated as the interest received from the customer on the loan, but because the funds had to be obtained from a depositor before they could be lent, interest expense had to be paid to the depositor for those funds.

Interest income is calculated in relation to the balance on the account. Since the balance is likely to vary during the reporting period, the interest should reflect the actual balances as they change. In practice, most financial institutions calculate interest on the transaction processing systems daily, but they may not keep records on the daily balances or calculate the internal funding cost at the same time. Balances are generally stored in financial accounting systems as actual balances at the end of the period. To calculate a more accurate interest margin, calculate the average balance. Accumulate daily balances and calculate a daily average debit or credit balance to the end of the reporting period. Some institutions still use an average of the current and prior period end, but because this ignores any fluctuation between reporting dates, it may misrepresent the margins reported as return on assets. This generally provides more favorable margins, as many customers try to reduce their borrowing at the period end for reporting purposes. The interest paid by the customer may, therefore, reflect higher balances during the period but be reported against the lower actual balance at the period end.

Checking accounts can be more difficult to analyze, as they may fluctuate between debit and credit balances. To calculate the interest payable and receivable and the associated cost of funds, maintain and report both average debit and credit balances for any account that may fluctuate and calculate the interest payable and receivable on both balances.

Fee- or Commission-Based Income

Fee- or commission-based income is revenue generated by means of charges levied for products or services provided. These services include most credit advisory, foreign exchange and transmission, documentary, advisory, and brokering services. The increase or decrease in revenue is generally related to the volume of services provided and can be analyzed in detail by means of product and customer reporting.

Fees or commissions are also payable by customers for the initiation and management of most funded products in the form of loan, new issue underwriting, and arrangement fees. This revenue could be identified separately and reported in conjunction with the spread or yield made on the product.

Fee- or commission-based revenue is usually related to the institution's agreed-on fee structure and is predetermined. Exceptions arise when fees are waived or discounted for particular customers. Profitability reporting must take account of the reduced fees for those customers, and the sources of data capture must identify the transactions to which they relate.

Premium Income

Insurance premiums are generally stated gross and net of reinsurance and may represent single premiums (to create an annuity, for example) or recurring annual premiums that may be paid weekly, monthly, quarterly, or annually. Policies are generally stored by policy holder on the administration systems, although no attempt may be made to combine the different policy types held by any customer. Premiums and any related claims should then be available for profitability reporting, the only problem will be the need to accumulate the profitability of all policy types with the range of other services used by the customer.

Trading Income

Trading income is that revenue made by speculative trading in the money markets and exchanges on behalf of the company. Speculative trading can take place in any negotiable instruments, including foreign exchange, certificates of deposit, Eurocurrency, futures, options, stocks, bonds, and other securities. Trading income rarely relates to external customers and is performed on behalf of the internal organization. Trading performed for an external customer generates fee income as discussed above.

Investment Income

Investment income is the revenue made by holding any negotiable instrument with the intention of gaining financial advantage in the longer term. The principal source of profit for a life insurance office is the earnings obtained directly or indirectly from investment income. Investment income can be generated for a customer through investment management and trusts. It can also be generated as part of the profitability of an insurance policy. It is necessary to review not just the premium income net of claims and administrative costs but also the investment income gained on the premiums held in relation to the policy. Insurance premiums are not normally invested by policy holder but are generally identifiable by policy type. To calculate customer profitability, apportion the income generated among the individual customers or policyholders.

In mutual insurance companies, the policy holders benefit directly from the investment performance and the life office normally receives a management fee defined as a percentage of the fund. The management fee is the principal source of profit on these contracts, though the office will receive jobbing profits if a bid/offer spread is built into the unit price.

Profitability Recognition

Customer profitability can be recognized at several points in the financial analysis, depending on the definition of sustaining or overhead costs. As shown in the following case study, income is normally recognizable by customer or customer group and costs may be attributed to customers directly via product utilization or allocated as a proportion of sustaining or overhead expenses. Hence, contribution to sustaining cost by customer may be an important measure. Indeed, it is the one used in the case study here.

Case Study III
_____

Private Bank "A"

This case study considers a small segment of a private bank and was developed as a prototype for a larger, longer-term profitability measurement and reporting system. It uses a sample of customer relationships utilizing a range of lending, depository, investment, advisory, and custodial services.

APPROACH
_____

The exercise is discussed in relation to the six phases of development of an activity-based costing system detailed in Chapter 3, "The Framework for Activity-Based Costing Implementation."

Review and Confirm Requirements

Private Bank "A" prefers to analyze its customers by individual customer, account officer, profession, age, and geographic area. The customers in this sample fall within the responsibility of four account officers or customer relationship managers and within four geographic areas.

The customer names, account numbers, and interrelational information are shown in Table 10–2 and are totally fictional. Any similarities to real circumstances are purely accidental.

TABLE 10–2
Private Bank "A"—customer information

Customer		Account officer		Customer relationships		
Name	Number	Name	Number	Profession	Geographic area	Age group
Lee	20486	Vine	120	431	SW	1
James	57620	Vine	120	286	SW	1
Price	10928	Vine	120	309	NE	3
Hall	28541	Vine	120	286	SW	4
Nunn	29856	Vine	120	312	SE	4
Good	69875	Vine	120	257	NE	2
Day	56930	Vine	120	257	SE	3
Lunn	24566	Vine	120	312	NE	3
Page	28943	Vine	120	286	SW	4
White	12394	Vine	120	309	NE	5
Gray	39853	Trout	197	303	NE	2
Jones	94547	Trout	197	183	NW	5
Smith	92847	Trout	197	431	NW	4
Black	75783	Trout	197	312	NE	3
Cray	56749	Trout	197	195	NW	2
Bush	87593	Trout	197	286	NW	1
Noon	97573	Trout	197	303	SE	3
Davis	29745	Trout	197	312	SE	3
Allen	89563	Trout	197	257	SE	2
Johnson	38536	Sage	236	183	SE	1
Freeman	60928	Sage	236	257	NE	3
Cook	97534	Sage	236	195	SW	1
Taylor	39856	Sage	236	303	SE	4
King	38754	Sage	236	257	NE	3
Baker	82583	Sage	236	243	NW	5
Brown	69654	Sage	236	431	SW	4
Crown	65368	Sage	236	243	SW	5
Rose	48486	Sage	236	257	NE	3
Astor	75375	Sage	236	414	SW	5
Howe	57301	Ford	105	303	NE	2
Evans	20597	Ford	105	414	SW	5
Thomas	32984	Ford	105	309	NE	2
Simms	97825	Ford	105	414	SE	4
Rush	10938	Ford	105	309	NW	5

(continued)

TABLE 10–2
(*concluded*)

Customer		Account officer			Customer relationships	
Name	*Number*	*Name*	*Number*	*Profession*	*Geographic area*	*Age group*
Green	37545	Ford	105	183	NE	1
Turner	29384	Ford	105	312	SE	1
Ellis	47364	Ford	105	243	SE	3

Key

Profession		Age
183 = Scientist	303 = Accountant	1 = 0–20
195 = Academic	309 = Lawyer	2 = 21–35
243 = Government employee	312 = Senior executive	3 = 36–50
257 = Real estate developer	414 = Artist	4 = 51–65
286 = Doctor	431 = Actor	5 = 66+

The organization chart in Figure 10–1 shows the matrix management structure, where the operating areas of the bank are managed by product managers and the client account management activities remain the responsibility of the client service division. The ultimate objective of the financial information strategy is to have full internal transfer pricing between the product management and the client services staff so that product development and service levels can be focused on client needs and driven by client relationship initiatives.

Define Reporting Entities

When activity-based costing is used for customer profitability, products, activities, and cost drivers must all be defined in the same way as shown in Chapter 9, "Using Activity-Based Costing for Product Costing."

Define Products and Transactions.   The sample of Private Bank "A" customers uses a range of lending, depository, investment, advisory, and custodial services, which are defined at a high level for this prototype of the eventual customer profitability system.

FIGURE 10–1
Private Bank "A"—organization/product structure

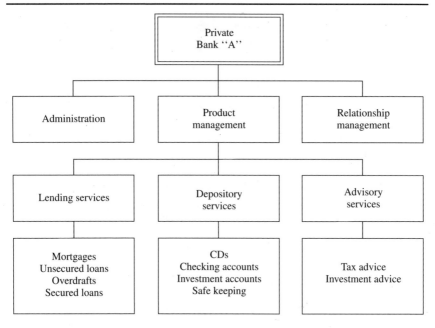

The products include:
- Variable-rate loans.
- High-interest deposits.
- Interest-bearing checking accounts.
- Investment accounts.
- Financial advisory services.
- Safe keeping.

Agree on Activities. For this exercise, activities are defined at a similar level to that used in Chapter 9. They can then be classified as operational or sustaining, as discussed in Chapter 4. In Private Bank "A," the classification has been further refined as shown in Table 10–3. Operational costs have been subclassified as:
- Direct.
- Premises.
- IT.
- Marketing.
- Customer-specific.

TABLE 10–3
Private Bank "A"—product- and customer-related costs

Costs	Loans	Deposits	Checking accounts	Investment accounts	Financial advice	Safe keeping	Total
Operational activities	$1,056	$194	$ 8,602	$11,330	$1,170	$245	$22,597
Premises costs	333	61	3,872	3,532	370	84	8,252
IT costs	521	103	4,836	3,259	397	37	9,153
Marketing costs	215	45		1,435			1,695
Total product costs	$2,125	$403	$17,310	$19,556	$1,937	$366	$41,697
Customer-specific costs							$ 7,457
Total operating costs							49,154
Sustaining costs at 40 percent							19,662
Total costs attributable to customer sample							$68,816

Determine Cost Drivers. Cost drivers are defined as shown in Chapter 9, but care must be taken in any customer profitability analysis to ensure that customer-specific activities have cost drivers related to the individual customers or types of customers.

Identify Customers and Customer Groups. Customers are defined as individual customers analyzed by profession, age group, geographic location, and account officer. Reports will be needed that demonstrate this analysis. This will enable Private Bank "A" to focus its marketing activity on particular customer groups and to measure the performance of individual account officers in terms of customer type, customers, and product profitability.

Commence Data Collection

As this exercise is a prototype, it is important not just to concentrate on the data required for the cross-section of customers and products within the sample. Data sources were identified for all products and customers, incorporating transaction volumes, average balances, and the related costs and income.

Develop an Activity-Based Costing System

In this case, the system required is for full customer profitability information, rather than just activity-based costing. Figure 10–2 shows the data structure diagram for the customer profitability prototype on which this case study is based. It highlights the static data stored by customer so reporting can be achieved by individual customer, account officer, profession, age, or geographic area. It also identifies the variable information that must be collected and input to the calculation model for each reporting period. This data includes the balance and income data relating to each customer as well as the product volume information by customer.

Determine Costs and Revenues

Customer profitability is derived using activity-based costing to calculate the operating costs of the products and services provided to the individual customers, as shown in Chapter 9. These costs are then linked with interest costs and income by customer to develop customer profitability reports.

FIGURE 10–2
Prviate Bank "A"—data structure

Input data

Customer	Product	Average balance	Interest income	Interest expense	Fees and commissions	Product volumes

Static data

Customer	Account officer	Customer relationships	Product	Operating cost

Calculated data

Contribution margin by:	Account officer	Product	Customer	Customer relationship
Account officer				
Product				
Customer				
Customer relationship				

Calculate Costs. Costs are analyzed at three levels: product-related operating costs driven by product volume, transaction mix, and average balances; customer-related costs driven by client relationship management activities; and sustaining costs that cannot be assigned to customer relationships or products and services but form part of the basic infrastructure of the organization.

In this case study, product- and customer-related operating costs include the cost classifications shown in Table 10–3. This includes premises, IT, and marketing costs because the activities are undertaken within a product-driven organization where responsibility for management costs is firmly within the control of the product manager.

Estimate Revenues. Lending and depository services are analyzed by average balance (calculated on the basis of average daily spot balances), against which interest income and interest expense must be calculated, together with the associated loan fees where appropriate.

Private Bank "A" pays interest on checking account balances and charges interest on overdraft balances, so these interest figures should also be calculated. To keep the example simple, it is assumed that checking accounts remain in credit or debit throughout the period being analyzed and therefore an average checking account balance can be used to estimate interest payable or receivable. Transaction charges are payable on overdraft accounts. A fee is also charged for the use of an overdraft facility, as shown in the analysis. The fee relates only to facilities of less than $5,000, as the interest charges on large facilities are assumed to cover costs.

Investment services offered by Private Bank "A" are fee-based products. Fee scales currently relate to the value of the portfolio under management at the reporting date. Private Bank "A" is, however, considering a change in its fee rates to take account of the variations in cost in managing portfolios with differing mixes of local and international equities and government stocks. Advisory services are also fee-based; fees are charged based on the time the advisor spends with the customer. Safe keeping fees are based on the number of items held and the degree of access required.

Income used in the analysis in Table 10–4 assumes that account officers charge customers according to the standard price list. Any waived fees or discounted interest rates must therefore be recorded by the relationship manager and will be assigned to the customer as part of the customer profitability calculation. Any additional expenditure or time spent by the account manager over the norm spent on each customer should also be recorded so the additional cost can be included in the customer profitability estimate.

TABLE 10–4
Private Bank "A"—product- and customer-related income

Name	Number	Interest income Loans	Deposits	Checking accounts	Interest expense Loans	Deposits	Checking accounts	Fee income Loans	Checking accounts	Investment fees	Advisory	Safe keeping
Ellis	47364	$12,375	$ 0	$ 414	$(10,500)	$ 0	$ (322)	$500	$87	$ 0	$ 0	$ 0
Evans	20597	0	(90)	72	0	126	(56)	0	66	100	630	0
Green	37545	0	0	0	0	0	0	0	0	1,875	126	0
Howe	57301	48,050	0	(10)	0	0	35	500	0	2,900	252	0
Rush	10938	0	(2,500)	0	0	3,500	0	0	0	160	0	0
Simms	97825	0	0	0	0	0	0	0	0	5,000	0	0
Thomas	32984	22,400	0	(540)	0	0	1,260	500	0	0	0	0
Turner	29384	16,500	0	(38)	(14,000)	0	133	500	0	0	567	0
Astor	75375	0	0	0	0	0	0	0	0	1,260	0	31
Baker	82583	0	0	(180)	0	0	420	0	0	500	0	0
Brown	69654	0	0	(2,950)	0	0	4,130	0	0	600	315	0
Cook	97534	0	0	(1,240)	0	0	2,170	0	0	0	0	21
Crown	65368	0	(500)	(38)	0	700	133	0	0	0	252	0
Freeman	60928	5,775	(14,625)	(26)	(4,900)	16,380	91	500	0	0	126	42
Johnson	38536	0	(2,500)	2,700	0	3,500	(2,100)	0	30	0	0	0
King	38754	15,180	0	1,206	(12,880)	0	(938)	500	81	0	252	0
Rose	48486	38,750	0	(2,550)	(35,000)	0	3,570	500	0	1,900	0	76

(continued)

TABLE 10–4
(concluded)

Name	Number	Loans	Deposits	Checking accounts	Loans	Deposits	Checking accounts	Loans	Checking accounts	Investment fees	Advisory	Safe keeping
		Interest income			Interest expense			Fee income				
Taylor	39856	$ 3,298	$ 0	$3,060	$ (2,716)	$ 0	$(2,380)	$388	$ 31	$ 0	$ 0	$ 0
Allen	89563	0	0	(4)	0	21,420	14	0	0	0	0	20
Black	75783	13,530	0	(960)	(11,480)	0	1,680	500	0	0	0	55
Bush	87593	63,525	0	144	(5,390)	0	(112)	500	120	0	441	0
Cray	56749	0	(1,000)	252	0	1,400	882	0	0	0	378	0
Davis	29745	10,230	(500)	9	(8,680)	700	(7)	500	73	0	126	0
Gray	39853	20,000	0	(414)	(17,500)	0	1,449	500	0	0	0	0
Jones	94547	0	(500)	0	0	700	0	0	0	1,740	126	0
Noon	97573	14,850	0	(2)	(12,600)	0	7	500	0	0	0	105
Smith	92847	0	0	0	0	0	0	0	0	1,500	189	0
Day	56930	14,025	0	1,062	(11,900)	0	(826)	500	95	0	0	0
Good	69875	50,325	(11,500)	225	(4,270)	14,000	(175)	500	105	1,500	0	0
Hall	28541	0	0	0	0	0	0	0	0	1,000	0	0
James	57620	0	(1,500)	45	0	2,100	(35)	0	96	0	0	0
Lee	20486	0	0	540	0	0	(420)	0	66	0	567	0
Lunn	24566	5,016	0	(210)	(4,256)	21,000	490	500	0	0	0	0
Nunn	29856	5,115	0	2,700	(4,340)	0	(2,100)	500	23	0	0	0
Page	28943	0	0	(30)	0	0	105	0	0	0	378	0
Price	10928	0	(11,500)	216	0	14,000	(168)	0	58	0	0	61
White	12394	0	0	(378)	0	0	882	0	0	4,500	0	0

Table 10–5 summarizes the contribution to sustaining costs, and hence to profitability, by customer, showing the contribution by product for each customer as well as any customer-specific costs. Customer-specific costs have been recorded against only 11 customers. These relate to either waived fees or additional time and expense on the part of the account relationship manager. They represent a significant portion of the overall cost base assigned to this customer sample, adding 18 percent to the direct product-related costs.

Review Results and Prioritize Recommendations

Table 10–6 analyzes the customer contribution by customer and account officer (customer relationship manager), ranking customers by profitability who are the responsibility of each account manager. This report highlights the account officers' performance and any unprofitable relationships. It also identifies circumstances where fees have been waived or additional expenditure incurred for customers, enabling management to review the impact of this practice on overall profitability.

In Table 10–7, the customer contribution by product within age group is analyzed, highlighting the profitability of customers in age groups 2 (21–35 years old) and 3 (36–50 years old) within this particular sample of customers. Product utilization also varies by age in this case study. Loan services and depository services tend to be used more heavily by groups 2 and 3, while investment services seem to be used mainly by the older customers. Advisory service usage seems to be concentrated at the two ends of the age groups.

If this sample is representative of the customer base within Private Bank "A," then marketing activity should be targeting lending and depository products at the middle age groups and some action should be taken to improve the profitability of the investment and advisory products and services used by older customers.

Table 10–8 analyzes the customer contribution by geographic location and highlights those geographic areas that appear to attract more profitable customers. Customers in the northeastern and southeastern areas seem to generate higher profits than those in the northwestern and southwestern ones. This may be because of the products and services utilized—these profitable customers tend to use the lending and savings account services, which are inherently profitable. Many of the customers in the northwestern area in this sample also seem to use savings account services; this may be a market that could be extended.

TABLE 10-5
Private Bank "A"—product and customer profitability contribution calculation

	Customer		Net contribution to customer-specific and sustaining costs						Product contribution	Customer-specific costs	Total operating contribution
Name	*Number*	*Account officer*	*Loans*	*Deposits*	*Checking accounts*	*Investment accounts*	*Advisory services*	*Safe keeping*			
Howe	57301	Ford	$5,021	$ 0	$(545)	$ 666	$149	$ 0	$5,291	$ (888)	$4,403
White	12394	Vine	0	0	293	3,370	0	0	3,663	0	3,663
Thomas	32984	Ford	3,186	0	345	0	0	0	3,531	0	3,531
Lunn	24566	Vine	1,151	2,219	(28)	0	0	0	3,342	0	3,342
Rose	48486	Sage	4,126	0	521	867	0	8	5,522	(2,476)	3,046
King	38754	Sage	2,682	0	(206)	0	149	0	2,625	0	2,625
Good	69875	Vine	1,127	2,469	(711)	229	0	0	3,114	(500)	2,614
Gray	39853	Trout	2,883	0	(327)	0	0	0	2,556	0	2,556
Freeman	60928	Sage	1,244	1,724	(534)	0	74	5	2,513	(167)	2,346
Price	10928	Vine	0	2,469	(171)	0	0	7	2,305	0	2,305
Black	75783	Trout	2,410	0	2	0	0	6	2,418	(137)	2,281
Turner	29384	Ford	2,888	0	(252)	0	335	0	2,971	(1,067)	1,904
Day	56930	Vine	2,496	0	(618)	0	0	0	1,878	0	1,878
Ellis	47364	Ford	2,252	0	(462)	0	0	0	1,790	0	1,790
Noon	97573	Trout	2,597	0	(887)	0	0	12	1,722	0	1,722
Allen	89563	Trout	0	2,264	(818)	0	0	2	1,448	0	1,448
Nunn	29856	Vine	1,163	0	157	0	0	0	1,320	0	1,320
Davis	29745	Trout	1,938	0	(390)	0	74	0	1,791	(699)	1,092
Johnson	38536	Sage	0	169	77	0	0	0	1,046	0	1,046
Taylor	39856	Sage	852	969	145	0	0	0	997	0	997
Green	37545	Ford	0	0	0	833	74	0	907	0	907
Jones	94547	Trout	0	169	0	345	74	0	588	0	588
Rush	10938	Ford	0	969	0	(421)	0	0	548	0	548

(continued)

TABLE 10–5
(concluded)

Customer			Net contribution to customer-specific and sustaining costs						Product contribution	Customer-specific costs	Total operating contribution
Name	Number	Account officer	Loans	Deposits	Checking accounts	Investment accounts	Advisory services	Safe keeping			
Hall	28541	Vine	$ 0	$ 0	$ 0	$ 285	$ 0	$0	$ 285	$ 0	$285
Astor	75375	Sage	0	0	0	213	0	3	216	0	216
Brown	69654	Sage	0	0	511	(181)	186	0	516	(315)	201
Lee	20486	Vine	0	0	(186)	0	335	0	149	0	149
Smith	92847	Trout	0	0	0	(1)	112	0	111	0	111
Cray	56749	Trout	0	369	(502)	0	223	0	90	0	90
Cook	97534	Sage	0	0	38	0	0	2	40	(78)	(38)
Page	28943	Vine	0	0	(268)	0	223	0	(45)	0	(45)
James	57620	Vine	0	569	(638)	0	0	0	(69)	0	(69)
Crown	65368	Sage	0	169	(539)	0	149	0	(221)	0	(221)
Bush	87593	Trout	1,316	0	(891)	0	260	0	685	(1,061)	(376)
Simms	97825	Ford	0	0	0	(464)	0	0	(464)	0	(464)
Evans	20597	Ford	0	5	(291)	(483)	372	0	(397)	(69)	(466)
Baker	82583	Sage	0	0	(532)	(279)	0	0	(811)	0	(811)

Total operating contribution $53,971 $(7,457) $46,514
Less sustaining costs allocated at 40 percent of operating costs   (19,662)
Total profit before tax $26,852

TABLE 10–6
Private Bank "A"—customer contribution by account officer

Account officer	Customer Name	Customer Number	Product contribution by customer	Waived fees	Direct costs	Total operating contribution	
Ford	Howe	57301	$5,291	$ 752	$136	$4,403	$12,153
	Thomas	32984	3,531			3,531	
	Turner	29384	2,971	1,067		1,904	
	Ellis	47364	1,790			1,790	
	Green	37545	907			907	
	Rush	10938	548			548	
	Simms	97825	(464)			(464)	
	Evans	20597	(397)		69	(466)	
Sage	Rose	48486	$5,522	2,476		3,046	9,407
	King	38754	2,625			2,625	
	Freeman	60928	2,513		167	2,346	
	Johnson	38536	1,046			1,046	
	Taylor	39856	997			997	
	Astor	75375	216			216	
	Brown	69654	516	315		201	
	Cook	97534	40		78	(38)	
	Crown	65368	(221)			(221)	
	Baker	82583	(811)			(811)	
Trout	Gray	39853	$2,556			2,556	9,512
	Black	75783	2,418		137	2,281	
	Noon	97573	1,722			1,722	
	Allen	89563	1,448			1,448	
	Davis	29745	1,791	699		1,092	
	Jones	94547	588			588	
	Smith	92847	111			111	
	Cray	56749	90			90	
	Bush	87593	685	1,061		(376)	
Vine	White	12394	$3,663			3,663	15,442
	Lunn	24566	3,342			3,342	
	Good	69875	3,114	500		2,614	
	Price	10928	2,305			2,305	
						(continued)	

TABLE 10–6
(*concluded*)

Account officer	Customer Name	Number	Product contribution by customer	Customer-specific costs Waived fees	Direct costs	Total operating contribution	
	Day	56930	$ 1,878			$ 1,878	
	Nunn	29856	1,320			1,320	
	Hall	28541	285			285	
	Lee	20486	149			149	
	Page	28943	(45)			(45)	
	James	57620	(69)			(69)	
Total operating contribution			$53,971	$6,870	$587	$46,514	$46,514
Less sustaining costs allocated at 40 percent of operating costs							(19,662)
Total profit before tax							$26,852

Table 10–9 analyzes the customer contribution by profession and highlights those professions that appear more profitable from this sample of customers. It also identifies the product distribution by profession by showing the net contribution by product group.

If this sample is representative, scientists and academics appear not to borrow money, although real estate developers, accountants, and senior executives borrow heavily. Real estate developers and lawyers also tend to hold savings accounts, while investment accounts may be held by any profession. Scientists, actors, and doctors may pay for advisory services. Profitability seems to be generated by real estate developers, accountants, lawyers, and senior executives—possibly those professions who are prepared to pay for private banking services.

TABLE 10–7
Private Bank "A"—customer contribution analysis by age group

Customer			Net contribution to customer-specific and sustaining costs								
Name	Number	Age group	Loans	Deposits	Checking accounts	Investment accounts	Advisory services	Safe keeping	Product contribution	Customer-specific costs	Total operating contribution
Turner	29384	1	$2,888	$ 0	$(252)	$ 0	$335	$ 0	$2,971	$(1,067)	$1,904
Johnson	38536	1	0	969	77	0	0	0	1,046	0	1,046
Green	37545	1	0	0	0	833	74	0	907	0	907
Lee	20486	1	0	0	(186)	0	335	0	149	0	149
Cook	97534	1	0	0	38	0	0	2	40	(78)	(38)
James	57620	1	0	569	(638)	0	0	0	(69)	0	(69)
Bush	87593	1	1,316	0	(891)	666	260	0	685	(1,061)	(376)
Howe	57301	2	5,021	0	(545)	0	149	0	5,291	(888)	4,403
Thomas	32984	2	3,186	0	345	0	0	0	3,531	0	3,531
Good	69875	2	1,127	2,469	(711)	229	0	0	3,114	(500)	2,614
Gray	39853	2	2,883	0	(327)	0	0	0	2,556	0	2,556
Allen	89563	2	0	2,264	(818)	0	0	2	1,448	0	1,448
Cray	56749	2	0	369	(502)	0	223	0	90	0	90
Lunn	24566	3	0	2,219	(28)	0	0	0	3,342	0	3,342
Rose	48486	3	1,151	0	521	867	0	8	5,522	(2,476)	3,046
King	38754	3	4,126	0	(206)	0	149	0	2,625	0	2,625
Freeman	60928	3	2,682	1,724	(534)	0	74	5	2,513	(167)	2,346
Price	10928	3	1,244	2,469	(171)	0	0	7	2,305	0	2,305
Black	75783	3	0	0	2	0	0	6	2,418	(137)	2,281
Day	56930	3	2,410	0	(618)	0	0	0	1,878	0	1,878
Ellis	47364	3	2,496	0	(462)	0	0	0	1,790	0	1,790
Noon	97573	3	2,597	0	(887)	0	0	12	1,722	0	1,722

(continued)

TABLE 10-7
(concluded)

| Customer | | | Net contribution to customer-specific and sustaining costs | | | | | | | | |
Name	Number	Age group	Loans	Deposits	Checking accounts	Investment accounts	Advisory services	Safe keeping	Product contribution	Customer-specific costs	Total operating contribution
Davis	29745	3	$1,938	$169	$(390)	$ 0	$ 74	$0	$1,791	$(699)	$1,092
Nunn	29856	4	1,163	0	157	0	0	0	1,320	0	1,320
Taylor	39856	4	852	0	145	0	0	0	997	0	997
Hall	28541	4	0	0	0	285	0	0	285	0	285
Brown	69654	4	0	0	511	(181)	186	0	516	(315)	201
Smith	92847	4	0	0	0	(1)	112	0	111	0	111
Page	28943	4	0	0	(268)	0	223	0	(45)	0	(45)
Simms	97825	4	0	0	0	(464)	0	0	(464)	0	(464)
White	12394	5	0	0	293	3,370	0	0	3,663	0	3,663
Jones	94547	5	0	169	0	345	74	0	588	0	588
Rush	10938	5	0	969	0	(421)	0	0	548	0	548
Astor	75375	5	0	0	0	213	0	3	216	0	216
Crown	65368	5	0	169	(539)	0	149	0	(221)	0	(221)
Evans	20597	5	0	5	(291)	(483)	372	0	(397)	(69)	(466)
Baker	82583	5	0	0	(532)	(279)	0	0	(811)	0	(811)

TABLE 10-8
Private Bank "A"—customer contribution analysis by geographic area

	Customer		Net contribution to customer-specific and sustaining costs							Customer-specific costs	Total operating contribution
Name	Number	Geographic area	Loans	Deposits	Checking accounts	Investment accounts	Advisory services	Safe keeping	Product contribution		
Howe	57301	NE	$5,021	$ 0	$(545)	$ 666	$149	$0	$5,291	$ (888)	$4,403
White	12394	NE	0	0	293	3,370	0	0	3,663	0	3,663
Thomas	32984	NE	3,186	0	345	0	0	0	3,531	0	3,531
Lunn	24566	NE	1,151	2,219	(28)	0	0	0	3,342	0	3,342
Rose	48486	NE	4,126	0	521	867	0	8	5,522	(2,476)	3,046
King	38754	NE	2,682	0	(206)	0	149	0	2,625	0	2,625
Good	69875	NE	1,127	2,469	(711)	229	0	0	3,114	(500)	2,614
Gray	39853	NE	2,883	0	(327)	0	0	0	2,556	0	2,556
Freeman	60928	NE	1,244	1,724	(534)	0	74	5	2,513	(167)	2,346
Price	10928	NE	0	2,469	(171)	0	0	7	2,305	0	2,305
Black	75783	NE	2,410	0	2	0	0	6	2,418	(137)	2,281
Green	37545	NE	0	0	0	833	74	0	907	0	907
Jones	94547	NW	0	169	0	345	74	0	588	0	588
Rush	10938	NW	0	969	0	(421)	0	0	548	0	548
Smith	92847	NW	0	0	0	(1)	112	0	111	0	111
Cray	56749	NW	0	369	(502)	0	223	0	90	0	90
Bush	87593	NW	1,316	0	(891)	0	260	0	685	(1,061)	(376)
Baker	82583	NW	0	0	(532)	(279)	0	0	(811)	0	(811)
Turner	29384	SE	2,888	0	(252)	0	335	0	2,971	(1,067)	1,904
Day	56930	SE	2,496	0	(618)	0	0	0	1,878	0	1,878

(continued)

TABLE 10–8
(concluded)

	Customer		Net contribution to customer-specific and sustaining costs								
Name	Number	Geographic area	Loans	Deposits	Checking accounts	Investment accounts	Advisory services	Safe keeping	Product contribution	Customer-specific costs	Total operating contribution
Ellis	47364	SE	$2,252	$ 0	$(462)	$ 0	$ 0	$ 0	$1,790	$ 0	$1,790
Noon	97573	SE	2,597	0	(887)	0	0	12	1,722	0	1,722
Allen	89563	SE	0	2,264	(818)	0	0	2	1,448	0	1,448
Nunn	29856	SE	1,163	0	157	0	0	0	1,320	0	1,320
Davis	29745	SE	1,938	169	(390)	0	74	0	1,791	(699)	1,092
Johnson	38536	SE	0	969	77	0	0	0	1,046	0	1,046
Taylor	39856	SE	852	0	145	0	0	0	997	0	997
Simms	97825	SE	0	0	0	(464)	0	0	(464)	0	(464)
Hall	28541	SW	0	0	0	285	0	0	285	0	285
Astor	75375	SW	0	0	0	213	0	3	216	0	216
Brown	69654	SW	0	0	511	(181)	186	0	516	(315)	201
Lee	20486	SW	0	0	(186)	0	335	0	149	0	149
Cook	97534	SW	0	0	38	0	0	2	40	(78)	(38)
Page	28943	SW	0	0	(268)	0	223	0	(45)	0	(45)
James	57620	SW	0	569	(638)	0	0	0	(69)	0	(69)
Crown	65368	SW	0	169	(539)	0	149	0	(221)	0	(221)
Evans	20597	SW	0	5	(291)	(483)	372	0	(397)	(69)	(466)

TABLE 10–9
Private Bank "A"—customer contribution by profession

Customer			Net contribution to customer-specific and sustaining costs							Customer-specific costs	Total operating contribution
Name	Number	Profession	Loans	Deposits	Checking accounts	Investment accounts	Advisory services	Safe keeping	Product contribution		
Johnson	38536	183	$ 0	$ 969	$ 77	$ 0	$ 0	$0	$1,046	$ 0	$1,046
Green	37545	183	0	0	0	833	74	0	907	0	907
Jones	94547	183	0	169	0	345	74	0	588	0	588
Cray	56749	195	0	369	(502)	0	223	0	90	0	90
Cook	97534	195	0	0	38	0	0	2	40	(78)	(38)
Ellis	47364	243	2,252	0	(462)	0	0	0	1,790	0	1,790
Crown	65368	243	0	169	(539)	0	149	0	(221)	0	(221)
Baker	82583	243	0	0	(532)	(279)	0	0	(811)	0	(811)
Rose	48486	257	4,126	0	521	867	0	8	5,522	(2,476)	3,046
King	38754	257	2,682	0	(206)	0	149	0	2,625	0	2,625
Good	69875	257	1,127	2,469	(711)	229	0	0	3,114	(500)	2,614
Freeman	60928	257	1,244	1,724	(534)	0	74	5	2,513	(167)	2,346
Day	56930	257	2,496	0	(618)	0	0	0	1,878	0	1,878
Allen	89563	257	0	2,264	(818)	0	0	2	1,448	0	1,448
Hall	28541	286	0	0	0	285	0	0	285	0	285
Page	28943	286	0	0	(268)	0	223	0	(45)	0	(45)
James	57620	286	0	569	(638)	0	0	0	(69)	0	(69)
Bush	87593	286	1,316	0	(891)	0	260	0	685	(1,061)	(376)

(continued)

TABLE 10-9
(concluded)

| Customer | | | Net contribution to customer-specific and sustaining costs | | | | | | | | | |
Name	Number	Profession	Loans	Deposits	Checking accounts	Investment accounts	Advisory services	Safe keeping	Product contribution	Customer-specific costs	Total operating contribution
Howe	57301	303	$5,021	$ 0	$(545)	$ 666	$149	$ 0	$5,291	$ (888)	$4,403
Gray	39853	303	2,883	0	(327)	0	0	0	2,556	0	2,556
Noon	97573	303	2,597	0	(887)	0	0	12	1,722	0	1,722
Taylor	39856	303	852	0	145	0	0	0	997	0	997
White	12394	309	0	0	293	3,370	0	0	3,663	0	3,663
Thomas	32984	309	3,186	0	345	0	0	0	3,531	0	3,531
Price	10928	309	0	2,469	(171)	0	0	7	2,305	0	2,305
Rush	10938	309	0	969	0	(421)	0	0	548	0	548
Lunn	24566	312	1,151	2,219	(28)	0	0	0	3,342	0	3,342
Black	75783	312	2,410	0	2	0	0	6	2,418	(137)	2,281
Turner	29384	312	2,888	0	(252)	0	335	0	2,971	(1,067)	1,904
Nunn	29856	312	1,163	0	157	0	0	0	1,320	0	1,320
Davis	29745	312	1,938	169	(390)	0	74	0	1,791	(699)	1,092
Astor	75375	414	0	0	0	213	0	3	216	0	216
Simms	97825	414	0	0	0	(464)	0	0	(464)	0	(464)
Evans	20597	414	0	5	(291)	(483)	372	0	(397)	(69)	(466)
Brown	69654	431	0	0	511	(181)	186	0	516	(315)	201
Lee	20486	431	0	0	(186)	0	335	0	149	0	149
Smith	92847	431	0	0	0	(1)	112	0	111	0	111

SUMMARY

Profitability measurement and reporting by products and customer are based on the multidimensional analysis of balances, revenues, and costs by activities performed in relation to the products and services provided to customers throughout the bank. The applicability of profitability measurement depends on the types of customers to which the business is directed and the institution's emphasis on marketing and strategic planning.

The cost of providing the mix of products and services to a customer or type of customer is usually based on product cost information, but it may be enhanced to reflect those costs that can be attributed directly to individual customers or customer groups.

Customers are defined as the users of the products and services who generate costs and revenues. Customers include external individuals and organizations as well as individuals and functions in other parts of the institution. The type and mix of customer vary by type of activity and market perception of the organization.

Types of customers might include individuals, commercial organizations, other financial institutions, government, other regulatory bodies, and other internal responsibility centers.

In organizations with many customers, analysis by every customer may not be necessary or practical, especially in the retail market. Analysis of customers grouped by common demand patterns may be sufficient. The most useful types of groups will vary by financial institution, but they should facilitate the recognition of common buying and risk patterns. In large organizations, it is common for information to be analyzed in several ways (say, by customer within geographic areas, by product type, and by global customer relationship). In smaller institutions with relatively few customers, the types of classification may be more specialized and relate to the types of customers and relationships within the organization.

For customer profitability analysis, the activity-based costing system should be designed to analyze activities by product or service offered by the financial institution. Most operating costs within a financial institution can be attributed to a specific product or service. However, some costs may be driven by the service offered to a particular customer or customer group. These costs must be isolated and the appropriate cost drivers identified.

To calculate customer profitability, it is important to be able to measure product usage, income, cost, and the associated balances by customer. Product costs are fairly standard for a range of customers, so they can be used as the basis of customer cost analysis when related to actual product usage by customer. Income and balances, however, vary significantly by customer and should be identified separately. Income in financial institutions can arise in five ways: interest income, fee or commission income, premiums, trading, and investment income.

Chapter Eleven

Using Activity-Based Costing for Operational Cost Management

INTRODUCTION

Any organization must aim to maximize its profitability in either the short or the longer term. In order to achieve this, it must be able to manage its cost base. The cost base can be managed in a variety of ways. Traditionally the organization was divided into cost centers and the costs were controlled within each cost center through the regular reporting of actual expenditure. Many reports would compare expenditure for the period against the same period for the previous year, the previous period, or some form of budget or expected expense. Reports would be produced at least once each year and probably quarterly or monthly, although some organizations do produce reports on a weekly basis.

As markets become increasingly competitive and profit margins are squeezed, the need to control and reduce costs focuses attention on the means of cost management within the organization. Today, virtually all financial institutions are undertaking some form of cost reduction exercise. In most instances, cost reduction initiatives consist of a directive from the chief executive stating that costs will be held at last year's levels (a cost reduction in line with inflation) or will be reduced by a fixed percentage. Those cost center managers who have seen these kinds of initiatives in the past will have built slack into their budgets to ensure reductions can be achieved without damaging the infrastructure of their departments. Other managers, who have managed their costs down already, will suffer potentially damaging reductions in service levels that may affect the delivery capability of the organization as a whole.

Managing the cost base by activity, using activity-based costing as the basis of analysis and control, provides a means of looking at the expenditures from a new direction. The focus on activities instead of

225

cost centers reduces the emphasis on cost centers and hence on the domains of cost center managers. It can form the basis of cost/benefit analysis, which facilitates decision making based on the value placed on an activity within the organization and the costs that it incurs. The following sections look at activity-based costing as the basis of activity-based management, activity-based budgeting, performance management, and cost reduction and include a practical example of cost reduction in an insurance company.

USES OF THE INFORMATION

Activity-based costing information can be used in financial institutions as the basis for a variety of tools that will assist senior managers in the management of the cost base. It can be used as the basis of a regular means of managing the cost base by activity throughout the organization. It may include the need to set targets or budgets for activities and costs, but it tends to focus on longer-term improvements in the delivery of activities that enable the institution to move toward its corporate goals by monitoring productivity, capacity utilization, efficiency, and effectiveness. It may therefore be used as the basis of an activity-based budgeting system but can also be used simply as the basis of a one-time cost reduction exercise.

Activity-Based Management

Cost reduction is only one element within the wider framework of cost management. Traditionally cost reduction tends to be a short, sharp initiative that may only have a short-term effect because it does not address the underlying causes of the problems. An activity-based cost reduction exercise should provide the basis for better ongoing cost management and improvement, but it will not replace existing methods of cost management. Ways of managing the cost base depend on ongoing planning and control of all aspects of the business. Costs are an integral part of the business infrastructure, and any decision made by management will inevitably involve expenditure in either the long or the short term. Implementing a new cost management system may have far-reaching effects, changing the way in which performance is measured within the organization as a whole. Activity-based management may include activity value analysis, which identifies nonvalue-added activities and provides priorities for their reduction and subsequent elimination.

The objective of activity-based cost management is to determine the importance and costs of activities within the value chain, giving management the opportunity to focus resources strategically to realize maximum value and improve the effectiveness of costs continuously. Activity-based cost management uses activity-based costing as the basic component of financial management information. This information assists in the operational control of the business by focusing attention on the key cost drivers and the factors that influence the day-to-day dynamics of the cost base.

Activity-Based Budgeting

Activity-based budgeting differs from traditional budgeting in that it concentrates on the factors that drive the costs, not just historical expenditure. The volume of activity, for example, is a key driver of the costs within any operations function, and the quality of customer service has a significant effect on the costs associated with customer liaison. Figure 11–1 demonstrates the linkage between activity-based costing (the baseline) and the development of an activity-based budget.

The strategic objectives can drive the budgetary targets and determine the volume of activities to be performed. The budgets are then derived from the activities using estimated cost rates.

Activity-based budgeting is often compared to zero-based budgeting and, in some ways, is based on similar concepts. Zero-based budgeting requires that expenditure above a zero base be justified and that costs be estimated for differing levels of output and service. Activity-based budgeting, however, assumes an ongoing operation, justifying expenditure on the basis of activities performed in relation to the predetermined drivers, and places responsibility for cost control on the manager responsible for control of the driver. Activity-based budgeting separates the analysis of cost/benefit and value of activities from the more mechanistic budgeting exercise, reducing the complexity of the budgetary process and concentrating attention on the management of the business, not simply on the costs incurred.

Performance Management

Performance management combines objective setting, cost control, and responsibility by setting people-related targets or key performance indicators and monitoring activity against the indicators on a regular

FIGURE 11–1
Developing an activity-based budget

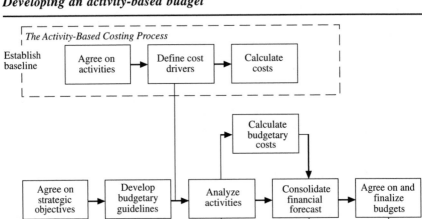

basis. Management can influence performance using these key performance indicators as the basis of regular reporting, identifying those areas where individual managers can control or influence behavior toward the achievement of corporate objectives. The control of cost is a key component of any performance measurement system, and activity-based analysis can focus attention on the areas of cost over which the individual has responsibility.

Activity-based management allows companies to move away from traditional financial performance measures and use nonfinancial measures instead. In fact, activities identified and costed can individually and/or collectively give rise to activity-based performance metrics. This allows a more efficient and pro-active performance appraisal process, usually conducted by tracking key activity measures over regular intervals.

Performance can be measured in relation to both long-term and short-term goals. For example, a manager may have responsibility for the development of a new market (which may take years to become profitable), and may also have short-term profit targets relating to existing business. Key performance indicators based on activity analysis enable both types of performance to be measured by focusing attention on the factors that influence the behavior. In this example, the key performance indicators may relate to the amount of time and investment made in the new market as well as the volume, quality, and profitability of existing business.

Cost Reduction Initiatives

Using activity-based costing as the basis of a one-time cost reduction exercise provides a means by which management can identify duplicate or extraneous activities and evaluate their benefit to the organization. Analysis by activity also allows a fundamental rethinking of the way the institution is organized and how it operates and may result in radical reorganization.

The primary benefit of using activity-based costs is that it focuses on activities, not responsibilities, and so is seen as less threatening to the managers of the various functions under review. It depersonalizes the cost review and enables management to value the activities undertaken in relation to the level and/or quality of service provided and factors that cause costs to be incurred.

As discussed in Chapters 1 and 2, activities identified through an ABC project can become candidates for quality improvement projects. The activity-based information can be leveraged to develop process improvement priorities with maximum cost-saving potential.

Implementing cost reduction in practice requires strong commitment from senior management. Without it, the initiative is likely to flounder when politically complex decisions must be taken relating to reorganization and redundancy.

ACTIVITY-BASED MANAGEMENT

The objective of activity-based cost management is to determine the importance and costs of activities within the value chain, giving management the opportunity to focus resources strategically to realize maximum value and continuously improve the effectiveness of costs. Activity-based cost management combines the cost analysis described above with the product and customer analysis described in Chapters 9 and 10.

Activity-based management may include activity-based budgeting or may simply include activity targets that monitor productivity, efficiency, and effectiveness on an ongoing basis. Costs may be monitored and controlled both through the existing budgetary systems (to monitor costs by department in the traditional way) and through the cost per unit of activity (to focus on efficiency and effectiveness). Productivity is monitored in volume and quality terms in parallel to cost analysis based on consistent definitions of activities.

Activity-based analysis, therefore, forms the basis of activity-based management. Key concepts in activity-based management include all those discussed in Chapter 3, "The Framework for Activity-Based Costing Implementation," and expanded in Chapters 4 through 7. In particular, attention must focus on the definition of products, activities, and customers; the classification of activities; and the calculation of both cost and contribution.

Defining Products and Services

Definitions of products and services are frequently not established unless some form of product costing or profitability analysis has already been performed. Each functional area of the organization is likely to have a different perspective on the issue of product definition. For reporting purposes, it is important to agree on product definitions that can be supported by the tracking of clearly identifiable income and costs but that also provide adequate sales and marketing information to the end users. An associated issue is the need to construct a product coding convention that supports the grouping of individual products into product families (such as deposits, investments, and advisory services) to satisfy product grouping reporting requirements.

Defining Activities

The process of defining activities for activity-based cost management involves pinpointing the principal activities throughout the organization and defining them on a consistent basis, then defining subactivities that can be assigned to products and customers. It is important that common activities are defined and the definitions agreed on before any analysis is undertaken, to avoid confusion and facilitate comparisons. Definition should be undertaken at two levels—first, the principal activities that are performed in the department (normally no more than 12 in each department) and second, the detailed subactivities that form the components of the principal activities and either relate to different products or are affected by different cost drivers. The emphasis of the activity analysis for activity-based cost management normally rests on the examination of subactivities at the product and customer level throughout the organization and summarizes it to identify any opportunities there may be to reduce, eliminate, or improve the individual activities performed. Those activities that are identified in this process enable the detailed analysis of operational activities, such as transaction processing and customer relationship management, and a reduced emphasis on the sustaining activities except for cost reduction purposes.

Defining Customers and Customer Groups

Customers are the users of the products and services that generate costs and revenues. Customers include external individuals and organizations as well as individuals and functions in other parts of the company. The type and mix of customer will vary depending on the types of activities the organization carries out and how it is perceived in the market. In organizations with large numbers of customers, analysis by every customer may not be necessary or practical, especially in the retail market. Analysis of customers grouped by common demand patterns may be sufficient. The groups will, of course, vary by financial institution, but common buying and risk patterns can be recognized. The generic customer groups given in Chapter 10, "Using Activity-Based Costing for Customer Profitability," may provide sufficient information to pinpoint market sectors that are worth developing.

Alternatively, an analysis of a specific group of customers, measured by activity, value, or profitability potential, may be sufficient where the information need is known. The analysis of certain types of customer may have particular relevance in large institutions, but some degree of customer profitability analysis is important to all financial institutions.

Classifying Activities

The classifications are explained in detail in Chapter 4, "Agreeing on Activities," but briefly, all principal activities in any department should be identifiable as fundamental or discretionary and as operational or sustaining. A fundamental activity is one that *must* be done, either to fulfill a legal requirement or because the business will cease to function if the activity is not performed. Discretionary activities are those that are not fundamental and may not vary with the level of business undertaken.

Within the basic categories of fundamental and discretionary, activities should be further classified as sustaining or related to the provision of products or services. Sustaining activities are those nonproduct-related activities that are performed to stay in business (such as financial accounting). These activities are generally fundamental in nature but can include such discretionary activities as corporate advertising, which is not related to a product or product group but undertaken to maintain the corporate image in the marketplace.

Operational activities can be either fundamental or discretionary. How they are classified will determine, to some extent, how the analysis can be used. Classification of the activities will facilitate the search for ways to reduce costs or improve efficiency. When operational activities are classified as fundamental in a cost reduction initiative, they are eliminated from the cost/benefit analysis, and any cost reductions that may be identified are limited to what might be achieved by means of the efficiency improvements identified during the opportunity search. If operational activities are classified as discretionary, they may be reviewed in value terms as part of the cost/benefit exercise but will make the exercise more complex and time consuming. In general, those core activities that are unlikely to change may be considered fundamental and the operational activities to which changes and enhancements could be made may be considered discretionary.

Calculating Costs

The costs of activities will be calculated as discussed in Chapter 6, "Calculating Costs." The type of costs used as the basis of the calculations will depend on the scope of the activity-based management. It is likely to be actual costs to enable cost efficiency to be monitored on a regular basis. This requires a strong degree of structure and discipline to be built into the analysis to ensure that actual costs can be recalculated regularly on a consistent basis without allocation of indirect or sustaining costs as part of the ongoing cost management system. Budgets may be calculated on the basis of activity-based budgeting, but this is not essential if the existing budgeting system is understood and accepted by the management team.

Calculating Contribution

Cost analysis by activity is sufficient for working through cost reduction and cost/benefit initiatives, but for product and customer reporting it is necessary to analyze the sources and types of revenue streams as well as the cost base. (Income analysis is reviewed in detail in Chapters 6 and 9.) Activity-based costing assists in the identification of noninterest-related costs but can be used to support the analysis of income and interest costs only if the products have been defined and the volume of activity ascertained.

The identification and tracking of income by product is one of the most fundamental issues to be resolved in activity-based management. If the amount of information at the product level is limited, other options of tracking income will need to be identified.

In practice, most financial institutions will be able to track premiums, fees, and interest that are debited or credited to customer accounts, since they can be linked to products via account number. However, income collected by means of check or cash (where an account number and hence a product cannot be clearly identified) requires either a change in procedures or the implementation of manual tracking processes. The entries for this product are essential to achieve a full reconciliation of total income to the total income figures in other profitability systems.

Costs of funds and the related earnings credits are prime cost components of all depository and lending products. These costs usually vary over time and may have a significant impact on the prices and profitability of the product base. Implementing a funds transfer pricing system, therefore, can be a major task in itself.

The combination of income analysis and activity-based costing provides a powerful management tool for the appraisal of product and customer profitability. Its amalgamation with activity-based budgeting gives management effective control of the organization and provides a management tool that mirrors organizational restructuring easily by linking activities to responsibility only at the reporting level.

Over the past few years, it has become common practice to allocate all sustaining costs back to operating functions on sophisticated bases. This practice has a tendency to focus attention on the allocation process instead of the management of the underlying costs.

Activity-based costing, however, concentrates the mind on the analysis of activities and reviews sustaining costs by means of direct cost management without the need to allocate costs to operating functions. Where full absorption costs are required for certain types of product analysis, then sustaining costs may be apportioned. This does not, however, enable them to be managed any more effectively and should be avoided whenever possible. It is much better to define a target return that includes the contribution to sustaining costs and a relevant profit margin, which can then be used by product and customer management as the basis for pricing and fee negotiation.

ACTIVITY-BASED BUDGETING

As the concept of activity-based management becomes more common, the need to extend activity-based costing to the budgeting process becomes obvious, linking resources to cost drivers at the planning stage. Business unit goals can be linked directly to corporate objectives so that managers become accountable for managing their costs. As shown in Figure 11–1 earlier, the strategic objectives can drive the budgetary objectives and determine the volume of activities that need to be performed. The budgets are then derived from the activities using estimated cost rates. The steps involved are as follows.

Establish a Baseline

In any activity-based budgeting system, the activity-based cost baseline must be established first. This uses the standard activity-based costing approach described in Chapter 3 and defines the linkages among activities, cost drivers, and basic resource utilization. It can then be used as the basis of an activity-based budgeting system.

Whether the baseline is an established activity-based costing system or an isolated exercise, it will form the foundation of the initial budgetary process, ensuring consistency with actual data.

Develop Budgetary Guidelines

The budgetary guidelines will be based on the strategic goals of the organization and should link the objectives to the value chain and the associated cost drivers in order to determine the volume of products and services, the quality and service standards, and operational emphasis within the budgetary period.

Analyze Activities

The budgetary guidelines will provide the quantitative and qualitative cost drivers that will enable the volume of activities to be estimated for the period. This will be achieved using the activity-based costing baseline as a point of reference with which to link the cost drivers back to the underlying activities.

Calculate Budgetary Costs

Costs can then be calculated based on the activity levels estimated above, and the cost rates identified in the activity-based cost baseline can be adjusted to take account of any known changes (such as inflation or any planned efficiency improvements).

Determine Budgetary Revenue

In parallel to the cost calculations, when the budgetary guidelines have been agreed on, the revenue budgets can be determined, based on the estimated product and service volumes and the anticipated prices and margins.

Consolidate the Financial Forecast

The whole process of calculating costs and revenue and establishing budgetary guidelines may be iterative as the need to forecast adequate profits becomes paramount. The balance between cost and revenue will depend on the degree to which short-term volume drivers are balanced by the longer-term qualitative investments.

Agree on and Finalize the Budgets

When the values of the cost and revenue drivers have been balanced in such a way that adequate returns can be generated, the budgets can be agreed on and finalized by activity within responsibility. Since the budgets are derived by cost driver, they will be defined by the factors that cause the costs to be incurred and should be controllable within the areas of responsibility.

Use the Budgets for Reporting

When the budgets have been finalized, they can be used as the basis for monthly reporting. Management performance can be measured based on actual expenditure in relation to the cost drivers and can be related to volume, value, and quality of delivery. Activity-based budgeting can, therefore, form the basis of the type of cost management defined above.

PERFORMANCE MANAGEMENT

The objectives of activity-based performance management usually include motivating management to focus on the improvement of productivity and cost management by means of improvements in efficiency and effectiveness and prioritization of activities that drive the organization toward its corporate goals. The basis of any performance management system should be the key performance indicators, quantifiable measures of activities the manager must do well. Indicators generally relate to activities and should incorporate measures that focus on financial performance, staff management, risk management, quality, and customer service. The essence of a good performance management system is an effective activity analysis and the identification of drivers that enable quantifiable measures to be agreed on; there will thus be a strong connection between drivers and key performance indicators.

The agreement of key performance indicators is not normally part of an activity-based costing exercise, but it is linked to activity-based analysis in that the agreed on indicators will be related to cost drivers (such as volumes, values, quality, time, and level of service) and must be measurable to enable performance to be monitored. The regular reporting will therefore require a strong activity-based costing system that is capable of generating the volume and value data necessary to support the performance management.

COST REDUCTION INITIATIVES

Since activity-based cost reduction initiatives analyze cost by activity, not department, they are seen as less threatening than traditional cost reduction techniques by the managers. For activity-based cost reduction initiatives, all of the phases shown in Chapter 3 and repeated in Figure 11–2 need to be performed. The following paragraphs discuss the practicalities in more detail.

Review and Confirm Requirements

The requirements for a cost reduction initiative will focus on the sponsorship of senior management, the commitment of management at all levels, and the scope of the exercise.

Define Reporting Entities

The process involves noting the principal activities throughout the organization and defining them on a consistent basis. It is important that common activities are defined and the definitions agreed on before any analysis is undertaken to avoid confusion and enable true comparisons to be made. The emphasis of the cost reduction initiative normally rests on analyzing common activities throughout the organization and finding opportunities to reduce, eliminate, or improve the individual activities performed. The process of identifying activities enables more detailed and fruitful analysis of common activities such as training, secretarial support, and management reporting and reduces the usual emphasis on operational activities.

The activities can then be used as the core of the analysis. Each activity must be classified, as explained in detail in Chapter 4. In brief, all principal activities of any department should be identifiable as fundamental or discretionary. The classification is subjective and is used only to aid the search for opportunities for reducing costs or improving efficiency. The classification of an activity is an art, not a science, and may vary for different companies. For example, staff training may be viewed as absolutely fundamental in one organization but discretionary in another.

A fundamental activity is one that must be done, either because it is a legal requirement (such as meeting regulatory reporting requirements) or because the business will cease to function if the activity

FIGURE 11–2
The activity-based costing process

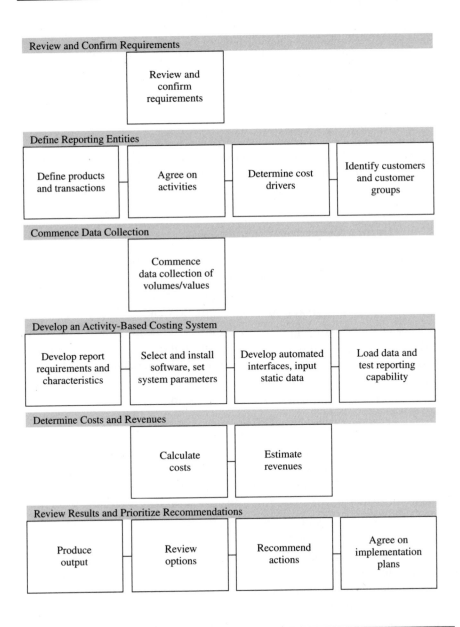

is not performed (such as maintenance on transaction processing systems). Fundamental activities must be performed at some level, and management must decide what level of effort and associated expenditure are necessary.

Discretionary activities are those activities that are not fundamental and may not vary with the level of business undertaken. They can be eliminated without affecting the basic fabric of the organization.

Commence Data Collection

After the common definitions of activities throughout the organization are agreed on, it is then necessary to identify the time spent on the various activities in each department. Some activities will be specific to individual departments; others may occur in a number of departments. For cost reduction initiatives, it is not normally necessary to go into more detail than principal activities, and time allocation is normally limited to units of one-tenth of a person-year.

Develop an Activity-Based Costing System

In any cost reduction initiative, there is inevitably a large volume of data to be analyzed. Activities must be measured and costs estimated, consistency applied, and data integrity maintained. There are several proprietary software packages used by consultants who specialize in this type of work and some packages on the market can be used without external consultants. They do, however, call for skills and experience if they are to be used effectively.

Determine Costs and Revenues

Costing, as we have seen, is the process of identifying, measuring, assigning, and analyzing the expenses associated with items that are to be costed. Costs within a financial institution can be of several basic types, including interest costs, claims, commissions paid, operating costs, and overhead or support costs. Interest costs, for example, are usually those within financial institutions that can be attributed directly to a fundamental activity related to a product or group of products. Claims costs can also be attributed to a fundamental activity that is related to a particular policy type or group of policies. Commissions may include insurance commissions paid to agents and brokers, trading commissions to securities or foreign exchange traders or brokers, payments commissions to members of the clearing organizations, commissions to credit agencies, and commissions or fees to research organizations that specialize in economic or industrial research. In general, all commissions paid can be assigned to fundamental activities.

Operating costs within a financial institution normally include all direct costs relating to the provision of products and services to customers or other parts of the organization. These costs may be identifiable by organizational unit and can be assigned to the activities performed within the operational area. Overhead or support costs may include all costs that are not directly attributable to fundamental activities and are therefore classified as sustaining activities that traditional cost accounting would apportion to products and services according to some standard allocation practice.

Costs can be based on a variety of timeframes. Historical, actual, budgeted, forecast, and long-term expenditure projections of cost are all cost bases that may be used in cost reduction initiatives. Any cost analysis should include all the costs of doing business in order to maintain integrity of the cost base. It is important, however, not to cloud the analysis by arbitrarily allocating costs just to ensure reconciliation to the financial accounts. The balance between the need to include all costs and the information needed for decision making can be achieved by means of reconciling statements and subtotals that highlight the key results.

Review Results and Prioritize Recommendations

In parallel to the costing exercise, the value of each discretionary activity to the organization can be determined. This involves obtaining consensus as to the value to be placed on each activity in relation to the strategic goals of the organization. Activities should be ranked in relation to each other. For example, does the organization value market research more than management accounting? Is training more important than staff counseling?

The values given to the discretionary activities can be used to develop a cost/benefit matrix that enables management to focus attention in different ways on the activities that fall under its various headings. (Figure 11–3 is an example of a cost/benefit matrix.)

FIGURE 11-3
Insurance Company "B"—cost/benefit analysis

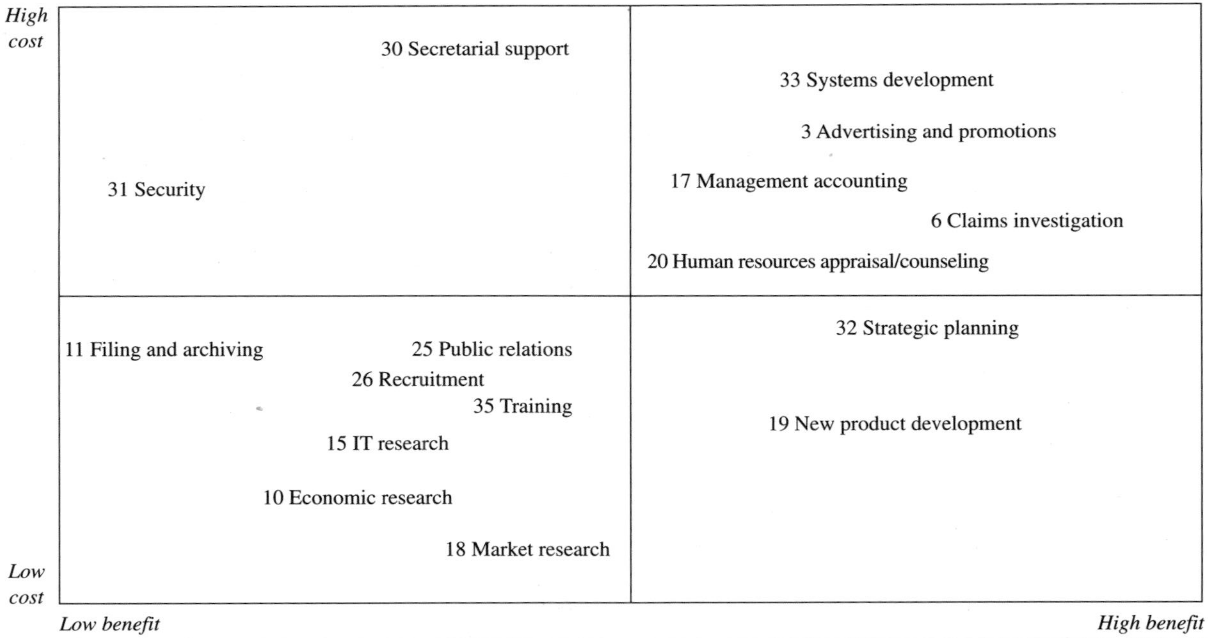

High cost

High benefit

33 Systems development

3 Advertising and promotions

6 Claims investigation

17 Management accounting

20 Human resources appraisal/counseling

32 Strategic planning

19 New product development

30 Secretarial support

25 Public relations

35 Training

26 Recruitment

15 IT research

18 Market research

10 Economic research

31 Security

11 Filing and archiving

Low cost

Low benefit

Management should initially focus on those high-cost, low-value activities that could be eliminated, reduced, improved, or automated to reduce the cost and increase the value placed on the activity. High-cost, high-benefit activities should also be reviewed to identify any ways costs can be reduced or improvements made in the efficiency and effectiveness of the activities.

Management should also consider the low-cost, high-benefit activities that could be promoted, increased, or enhanced to increase their value to the organization at minimal cost. Finally, management may review the low-cost, low-benefit activities to determine whether they should be performed at all or whether the value of these activities can be improved.

The process of reviewing the activities identified on the cost/benefit matrix and finding opportunities for reducing costs, improving efficiency, automating, eliminating, promoting, and enhancing is one of the most important steps in a cost reduction initiative. Involving the management and staff in identifying opportunities to change both the fundamental and discretionary activities performed within their environment helps ensure their commitment to implementing the recommendations.

This opportunity search can be performed in two ways—by interviews with those involved in actually performing the activities and by discussions between groups of senior or middle management within the organization. The manager responsible for the delivery of the activity or group of activities should discuss with his or her peers or users the value of the activity and the benefits derived. The group may decide that the level of service provided is too high and should be reduced, resulting in reduced costs. Or it may decide that the activity can be undertaken more efficiently in another manner. Ask the individuals undertaking the activities to suggest ways in which efficiency or effectiveness could be improved. They are closer to the tasks and often have good ideas that have never been voiced.

The opportunity search may also identify ways the organization should be reorganized or restructured to optimize the work flow and eliminate the duplication of activities performed in different departments.

When all the opportunities have been identified, they should be classified by cost/benefit and priority to enable an implementation plan to be produced. It is easy to develop the opportunities in theory, but it is important that the exercise be completed and the benefits achieved. The implementation plan must, therefore, be agreed on and the implementation monitored against the plan on a regular basis.

Insurance Company "B"

Insurance Company "B" is a small insurance company that undertook a cost reduction exercise last year to reduce costs by 10 percent across the company. This exercise was relatively successful: budgeted costs were reduced by 8 percent and, at the end of the year, the average overrun was only 2 percent. A net reduction of approximately 6 percent across the company was achieved. Unfortunately, last year there were a high number of claims, with the subsidence claims from a series of dry summers exceeding expectations by 300 percent. Management must now reduce costs in line with income and would like to aim for a reduction of 15 percent.

As discussed earlier, further savings are realized when the resources are redeployed or eliminated. Elimination or reduction of activities helps identify slack in resources, and these, when aggressively redeployed or eliminated, give rise to additional cost savings. These methods cause permanent cost reductions, as opposed to across-the-board cost cuts that invariably result in costs creeping back to original levels.

Some organizations that have already tried to reduce costs by traditional means have found that reductions in costs using activity-based costing of between 10 and 20 percent are achievable; even better savings are possible with an experienced team.

The CEO of Insurance Company "B" recently attended a seminar where a speaker was talking about activity-based costing and he thinks this may be the way to solve the problem.

THE PROCESS

The steps involved in the project are shown in Figure 11–2 earlier in this chapter.

Review and Confirm Requirements

The CEO is prepared to sponsor the project and the board of directors thinks this approach may work better than the traditional approach to cost reduction undertaken last year. The project will be organized by the v.p. of finance and a steering committee consisting of a senior manager from each of the key business areas (underwriting, actuarial services, administration, sales and marketing, and investment management). An organization chart of Insurance Company "B" is shown in Figure 11–4. The project will include all activities within Insurance Company "B" and no costs will be excluded from the analysis.

Defining Reporting Entities

The first step in the process involves the definition of and agreement on common activities throughout the company. After some discussion, the steering committee agreed on a list of 37 principal activities (to be subdivided if necessary in the key business areas). The list is Table 11–1.

The steering committee then completed an activity analysis for their key business areas, detailing the activities performed in each area and the person-hours spent on each activity. The human resources manager was made responsible for ensuring that the total time allocation equaled the establishment figures. The analysis is summarized in Table 11–2.

Commence Data Collection

The identified activities can then be used as the core of the analysis. Each activity must be costed and classified. The classifications for cost reduction initiatives are limited to fundamental or discretionary. Table 11–3 shows the classification finally agreed on by the steering committee.

Develop an Activity-Based Costing System

As in any cost reduction initiative, there will inevitably be a great deal of data to be analyzed. Activities must be measured and costs estimated, consistency applied, and data integrity maintained. Insurance Company "B" decided not to purchase one of the proprietary software packages, but rather to develop its own in-house database. This required a significant amount of time to design and develop. It does, however, link into the existing accounting system to obtain cost data directly.

FIGURE 11–4
Insurance Company "B"—organization chart

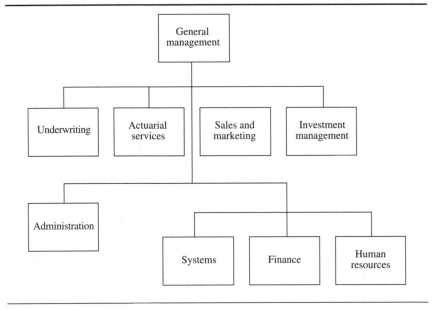

Determine Costs and Revenues

In parallel to the classification exercise, the finance director was given the task of estimating the costs of each activity identified. This had to include all costs within the company. Claims costs are costs that can be attributed to fundamental activities related to claims investigation activity. Commissions may include insurance commissions paid to agents and brokers and are included in the cost of sales. Commissions or fees paid to research organizations that specialize in economic or industrial research are charged to economic or market research as appropriate. Operating costs may be identifiable by organization unit and can be assigned to the activities performed within the operational area. Sustaining costs may include all costs in the management function.

Review Results and Prioritize Recommendations

As with any activity-based costing exercise, the most important part of the project is the final phase, in which the results are reviewed and action taken.

TABLE 11–1
Insurance Company "B"—list of activities

Activities	Activities
1 Accounts payable	20 Human resources appraisal/
2 Actuarial services	counseling
3 Advertising and promotions	21 Policy administration
4 Audit	22 Policy inception
5 Claims administration	23 Premium accounting
6 Claims investigation	24 Property management
7 Compliance	25 Public relations
8 Computer operation	26 Recruitment
9 Data maintenance	27 Regulatory reporting
10 Economic research	28 Reinsurance
11 Filing and archiving	29 Sales
12 Financial accounting	30 Secretarial support
13 General management	31 Security
14 Investment management	32 Strategic planning
15 IT research	33 Systems development
16 Litigation	34 Tax services
17 Management accounting	35 Training
18 Market research	36 Treasury management
19 New product development	37 Underwriting/risk assessment

Produce Output.   The cost analysis for Insurance Company "B" is shown in Table 11–4. It details the costs calculated for each activity with each key business area and the total expenditure on the activity in the organization as a whole.

Review Options.   When the activities had been classified (in parallel to the estimation of costs and revenues), the value of each discretionary activity to the organizaion could be determined. This involved obtaining consensus as to the value placed on each activity in relation to the strategic goals of the organization. The strategies of Insurance Company "B" are:

- Provide returns to the stockholders that match any in the industry.

TABLE 11-2

Insurance Company "B"—activity analysis for key business areas

Activities	Underwriting	Sales/ marketing	Actuarial	Administration	Investment management	Management	Total person- hours
1 Accounts payable				4.5		3.2	7.7
2 Actuarial services			15.0	2.0		3.0	20.0
3 Advertising and promotions		2.6					2.6
4 Audit						0.7	0.7
5 Claims administration			1.9	8.9		0.7	11.5
6 Claims investigation			7.4				7.4
7 Compliance	0.3					2.3	2.6
8 Computer operation		0.5		3.1		9.3	12.9
9 Data maintenance				2.5		4.8	7.3
10 Economic research	0.3	0.5	0.8			0.5	2.1
11 Filing and archiving	1.1	3.3	0.9	1.4	0.8	0.3	7.8
12 Financial accounting						1.5	1.5
13 General management	5.4	3.1	2.0	1.0	2.0	3.0	16.5
14 Investment management					18.4		18.4
15 IT research		0.4	0.5			1.7	2.1
16 Litigation			1.3			2.0	2.5
17 Management accounting	0.8	0.6		0.8	1.8	4.2	9.5
18 Market research	1.3						1.3
19 New product development	3.6	1.9					5.5

(continued)

TABLE 11–2
(concluded)

Activities	Underwriting	Sales/ marketing	Actuarial	Administration	Investment management	Management	Total person-hours
20 Human resources appraisal/ counseling	1.2	2.9	1.8	0.9	1.1	0.5	8.4
21 Policy administration	3.8		3.8	14.3			21.9
22 Policy inception	4.2	8.4	2.7	6.2		0.3	21.8
23 Premium accounting			4.7	5.2		3.1	13.0
24 Property management					5.6		5.6
25 Public relations		1.6	1.8		1.4	0.8	5.6
26 Recruitment	0.7	1.6	0.4	0.7	0.3	1.8	5.5
27 Regulatory reporting						2.5	2.5
28 Reinsurance	6.4						6.4
29 Sales		65.0	4.2			4.9	74.1
30 Secretarial support	7.6	3.3	8.5	3.6	6.8	12.4	42.2
31 Security		0.3				8.5	8.8
32 Strategic planning	0.4	0.2	1.6		0.2	3.6	6.0
33 Systems development	0.8	1.9		2.1		12.8	17.6
34 Tax services						1.3	1.3
35 Training	0.5	2.4	0.7	1.8	0.5	0.3	6.2
36 Treasury management					2.1	3.5	5.6
37 Underwriting/risk assessment	5.6						5.6
Total	44.0	100.5	60.0	59.0	41.0	93.5	398.0

TABLE 11–3
Insurance Company "B"—activity classification

Activities	Fundamental	Discretionary
1 Accounts payable	★	
2 Actuarial services	★	
3 Advertising and promotions		★
4 Audit	★	
5 Claims administration	★	
6 Claims investigation		★
7 Compliance	★	
8 Computer operation	★	
9 Data maintenance	★	
10 Economic research		★
11 Filing and archiving		★
12 Financial accounting	★	
13 General management		★
14 Investment management	★	
15 IT research		★
16 Litigation	★	
17 Management accounting		★
18 Market research		★
19 New product development		★
20 Human resources appraisal/ counseling		★
21 Policy administration	★	
22 Policy inception	★	
23 Premium accounting	★	
24 Property management	★	
25 Public relations		★
26 Recruitment		★
27 Regulatory reporting	★	
28 Reinsurance	★	
29 Sales	★	
30 Secretarial support		★
31 Security		★
32 Strategic planning		★
33 Systems development		★
34 Tax services	★	
35 Training		★
36 Treasury management	★	
37 Underwriting/risk assessment	★	

TABLE 11–4
Insurance Company "B"—cost analysis

Activities	Underwriting	Sales/marketing	Actuarial	Administration	Investment	Management	Total
1 Accounts payable	$ 0	$ 0	$ 0	$ 149	$ 0	$ 231	$ 380
2 Actuarial services	0	0	945	66	0	216	1,227
3 Advertising and promotions	0	98	0	0	0	750	848
4 Audit	0	0	0	0	0	51	51
5 Claims administration	0	0	120	294	0	51	465
6 Claims investigation	0	0	467	0	0	0	467
7 Compliance	17	0	0	0	0	165	182
8 Computer operation	0	20	0	102	0	669	791
9 Data maintenance	0	0	0	83	0	345	428
10 Economic research	17	20	17	0	0	36	90
11 Filing and archiving	62	125	57	47	41	21	353
12 Financial accounting	0	0	0	0	0	108	108
13 General management	300	117	126	33	102	216	894
14 Investment management	0	0	0	0	939	0	939
15 IT research	0	15	0	0	0	123	138
16 Litigation	0	0	32	0	0	144	176
17 Management accounting	45	23	82	27	92	303	572
18 Market research	72	0	0	0	0	0	72
19 New product development	200	72	0	0	0	0	272
20 Human resources appraisal/counseling	66	110	114	30	56	36	412

(continued)

TABLE 11-2
(*concluded*)

Activities	Underwriting	Sales/marketing	Actuarial	Administration	Investment	Management	Total
21 Policy administration	$ 212	$ 0	$ 240	$ 473	$ 0	$ 0	$ 925
22 Policy inception	233	315	170	204	0	224	1,146
23 Premium accounting	0	0	296	171	0	224	691
24 Property management	0	0	0	0	285	0	285
25 Public relations	0	60	114	0	72	57	303
26 Recruitment	39	60	26	23	15	129	292
27 Regulatory reporting	0	0	0	0	0	180	180
28 Reinsurance	356	0	0	0	0	0	356
29 Sales	0	2,438	264	0	0	353	3,055
30 Secretarial support	422	125	535	119	347	893	2,441
31 Security	0	12	0	0	0	612	624
32 Strategic planning	23	8	101	0	11	259	402
33 Systems development	45	72	0	69	0	921	1,107
34 Tax services	0	0	0	0	0	93	93
35 Training	29	90	44	60	26	21	270
36 Treasury management	0	0	0	0	107	252	359
37 Underwriting/risk assessment	311	0	0	0	0	0	311
Total	$2,449	$3,780	$3,750	$1,950	$2,093	$7,683	$21,705

- Maintain or improve market share without reductions in quality or profitability.
- Be a high-quality producer of premium policies.
- Recruit and retain high-quality, motivated staff.
- Maintain the social and environmental status of the company.

The management group and the steering committee ranked the activities within the company, as shown in Table 11–5.

The value of the discretionary activities was then used to develop the cost/benefit matrix shown in Figure 11–3. The process of reviewing the activities identified on the cost/benefit matrix and identifying opportunities for reducing costs, improving efficiency, automating, eliminating, promoting, and enhancing is one of the most important steps in the cost reduction initiative. The whole management team got involved in the identification of opportunities to change both the fundamental and discretionary activities performed within their environment. (The opportunities they found are shown in Table 11–6.)

Recommend Actions. When all the opportunities had been identified, they were classified by cost/benefit and priority so recommendations could be proposed to the management.

Agree on Implementation Plans. Finally, when the recommendations had been accepted, an implementation plan was agreed on in which the opportunities for cost reduction and improvements in efficiency could be achieved. A regular monitoring mechanism was built into the activity-based costing system so changes in actual costs could be monitored during the implementation.

SUMMARY

Any organization must aim to maximize its profitability in either the short or longer term. In order to achieve this, it must be able to manage its cost base. As markets become increasingly competitive and profit margins are squeezed, the need to control and reduce costs focuses attention on the means of cost management within the organization. Most financial institutions have undertaken some form of cost reduction exercise. Using activity-based costing as the basis of analysis and control provides a means of looking at the level of expenditures

TABLE 11–5
Insurance Company "B"—ranking of discretionary activities by value

Discretionary Activity Ranking		
Activities	Discretionary	Ranking
6 Claims investigation	★	1
32 Strategic planning	★	2
3 Advertising and promotions	★	3
33 Systems development	★	4
19 New product development	★	5
17 Management accounting	★	6
20 Human resources appraisal/ counseling	★	7
35 Training	★	8
18 Market research	★	9
25 Public relations	★	10
30 Secretarial support	★	11
26 Recruitment	★	12
15 IT research	★	13
10 Economic research	★	14
31 Security	★	15
11 Filing and archiving	★	16

from a new direction. The focus on activities instead of cost centers reduces the emphasis on the domains of cost center managers. It can form the basis of cost/benefit analysis, which facilitates decision making based on the value placed on an activity within the organization and the costs that it incurs. Activity-based costing allows intelligent cost management through elimination of activities and the redeployment of resources. Activities identified in the process can be used to develop performance metrics.

Activity-based costing analyses can be used in financial institutions as the basis for a variety of information tools that will assist senior managers in the management of the cost base. They can be used as the basis for managing the cost base by activity, including or excluding

TABLE 11-6
Insurance Company "B"— opportunities for change

Opportunities for Change
1 Review the cost of secretarial support to either improve the effectiveness or reduce the cost of the service provided.
2 Review the cost of providing security services (compare the costs of external/internal services).
3 Investigate the cost of systems development. Although the benefits are perceived to be high, the costs should be reduced if at all possible.
4 Reduce the cost of advertising and promotions; consider ways to make the investment in marketing more effective.
5 Consider ways to reduce the cost of management accounting by reducing the number of reports required or further automation.
6 Consider the cost/benefit of market research. It may be worth increasing the investment if the benefit can be increased at the current cost level.

activity-based budgeting. It can be used simply as a replacement budgeting system. It can also be used as a core component of a performance management system or as the basis of an isolated cost reduction initiative.

Cost reduction is only one element within the wider framework of cost management. An activity-based cost reduction exercise should provide the springboard for better ongoing cost management and improvements, but it will not replace existing methods of cost management. Ways of managing the cost base depend on ongoing planning and control of all aspects of the business. Costs are an integral part of the business infrastructure, and any decision made by management will inevitably involve expenditure in either the long or the short term. Implementing a new cost management system may have far-reaching effects, changing the way in which performance is measured within the organization as a whole.

Index